Lisa

Britt

MID-CENTURY DRAMA

by the same author
DRAMA IN THE SIXTIES

MID-CENTURY DRAMA

*

LAURENCE KITCHIN

FABER AND FABER

24 Russell Square

London

First published in 1960
by Faber and Faber Limited
*24 Russell Square London WC*1
Second edition (revised) 1962
Reprinted 1969
Printed in Great Britain by
Latimer Trend and Company Limited,
Whitstable
All rights reserved

SBN 571 09077 X
(*paper covered edition*)

SBN 571 05241 X
(*cloth edition*)

To
the memory
of my Father and Mother
*
JAMES TYSON KITCHIN 1866–1936
and
ELIZA AMELIA KITCHIN 1871–1947

'Did you see the new bridge they're building? It's a rum ole thing, isn't it . . . Not like the ones they built when I was a boy.'

Roots, Act I

' . . . a shock of delighted recognition struck the audience like a tidal wave.'

The Fervent Years

'Man cannot live by television receivers alone.'

The Times. 7/10/59

CONTENTS

*

ILLUSTRATIONS
after page 64

---★---

PREFACE

---------------------- * ----------------------

What Tolstoy wrote, about the outcome of a battle depending sometimes on the state of a corporal's digestion, applies also to the drama. War and the drama are both popular arts, conceived in ambition and pursued with fanatical discipline amid chaos. Both have their punctual, sketchy bulletins, their propaganda and compilations of statistics; and the essence of both tends to elude customary methods of assessment. This book, based on three years of intensive theatre-going, enquiry into managerial problems and discussion with interpretative artists, aspires to something like the function of a searchlight. That is to say, it ranges over the battlefield of drama in a confused phase of transition, missing a great deal, but always in search of significant action, the revealing silhouette which may show what course events are taking.

It happens that during the three years concerned English drama first assumed a demonstrable mid-century pattern. A period which began with protests at the destruction of old theatres ended in the opening of new ones—the Belgrade, the Mermaid—designed to be more comfortable and efficient, and in the planning of yet another, for Nottingham, by a distinguished architect. The historic Royal Court, opened again with a policy slanted in favour of new writers, gained for them the double success of serious critical notice and of commercial recognition by West End transfer, sale of film rights and mass publication in paperback editions. Joined to successes by Theatre Workshop, whose policy had a different emphasis but surprisingly similar results, this now constitutes a movement which gives every sign of striking roots in the West End. Bearing in mind that for some seventy years the West End has been predominantly a home for theatrical opportunism, apathy and conformism, its drastic penetration by work explicitly subversive of middle-class values, as first established by the Kendals, was not to be so soon expected.

The emergence of a new kind of theatre building and a new kind of play was accompanied by much reappraisal of the drama's place in national life. Was it obsolescent, its function increasingly taken over by professional sport, or by television, for which it would remain useful as a training ground of performers? Or was the drama a symbol of prestige, like the Rolls Royce and Chekhov, both exported by their countries of origin with the care and skill due to high quality? Again the Royal Court, financed by tycoons and an Arts Council grant, pointed to a solution. After a trickle of industrial patronage had culminated in the raising of a professional theatre, the first for two hundred and fifty years, in the City itself, demands for a National Theatre on the site assigned for one grew confident and insistent in the spring and summer of 1959. Coupled with the advocacy of the actor knights and dames, the advice of the Arts Council and the good impression made by subsidized companies from abroad, it seemed probable that the prestige lent to drama in general by industrial patronage, however meagre, would at last force Parliament into releasing the National Theatre grant earmarked a decade before.

Once that happened, we would be under an obligation to stage revivals of the best plays in the English language as well as we could, under fire from vested interests opposed to subsidy and from the Puritanism constant in the national character ever since civil war closed the theatres. Therefore the condition of classical acting became of crucial importance at a time when there was danger of a crippling break in its tradition. After the great seasons at the New and the Haymarket there had been a dispersal of the best exponents into management, the mass media and pioneering abroad, always for the most public-spirited of reasons. Undoubtedly this dispersal was also brought about by the prejudice of English managements against continental repertory, the only system under which exacting parts can be regularly alternated, instead of run to exhaustion by stultifying repetition. There grew up a generation of young actors and directors with little chance to study in live performance the models who had inspired them while still at school. One result of this deprivation was a decline in the standard of verse-speaking so drastic that the Marlowe Society and the Youth Theatre repeatedly excelled what was done at the Old Vic and the Shakespeare Memorial Theatre.

New buildings and a hope of new status for the drama, a style of writing found and a style of acting lost—such are the outlines into which all the flux has already hardened. This book attempts to convey the flavour of the process from two main points of view. First, there are the interviews, horse's-mouth statements from behind the scenes, the authority of which is implicit in the names of the people concerned. Second, as I have rejected what I regard as the lazy method of writing expanded commentaries on the authorities and calling it criticism, there are my own assessments as a member of the audience. They are based on the assumption that theatre critics can never master all the issues involved. Let them therefore admit the complexity of drama, respond to it wholeheartedly and drop any pretence of omniscience.

Drama lacks the convenient fixity of paint, bronze, stone, musical notation and print. By definition a thing done, it can only be meaningfully studied in performance and by discussion centred on performance. Hence the authority of Hazlitt, Shaw, MacCarthy and Tynan, who report from the thick of the conflict. Theirs is the fallible immediacy of the war correspondent, as compared with the tidiness of the academic historian, but they bring more of the essence of the subject through. On the other hand, stacked libraries of work based on reading the script—that plan never adhered to in action twice, if at all—remind me of Machiavelli's attempt to drill soldiers. The story goes that he made a mess of it until the field commander restored order at once by a blast on his whistle.

I take it, then, as axiomatic that the theatre critic's work should be done at first hand; for reading a play is like trying to visualize a statue by measuring the gap left in the quarry. Next he must chance his arm on value judgments, ransacking tradition and his own experience in the process. If he prefers Margaret Rawlings to Feuillère as Phèdre, or walked out of *Brand* when the mother agreed to part with her dead child's clothes, he may be on the defensive, but he has a case. Let him respond totally, with eyes, ears, memory and feelings, as well as his analytical powers. A joke from Castiglione, about words freezing in the air, turns up unexpectedly in the film *Pork Chop Hill*. At Sadler's Wells the stick with which Varya will attack Lopakhin falls to the ground during festivities. Yasha notices this and finds the right moment to replace it. A small mishap has linked the most obscure repertory company with the Moscow Art Theatre. Something, at the highest level of attainment, can go wrong in live performance.

A third duty of the critic, not often recognized, is towards the central mystery of dramatic art. More than two thousand years of Western civilization have produced only three writers, Aristotle, Coquelin the Elder and Stanislavsky, with anything crucial to say about it. We still do not know the exact nature of the communication which takes place, although it can scarcely be more complex than the poetic imagination, about which we know a great deal. Actors, in particular, have been let off far too lightly. Of course they are intuitive creatures, badgered by scandalmongers, who cherish any privacy they get. But there is no reason why Kean and Forbes-Robertson should not have left data about the conscious aspect of their work. Did nobody ask?

Therefore, when the searchlight caught Kedrov, Paxinou, Callas and Gielgud I was very much on the alert, and I have followed this survey with statements from practitioners in the certainty that they have scarcity value, and are often more to the point than chapters of exposition. Much can be learned from the practitioner enticed into discussion. He can also be subjected to detailed scrutiny in performance, though this rarely occurs. In the case of the influential Moscow Art Theatre I have resorted to a few passages of close visual analysis, contrary to the spirit of theatre-going, but also contrary to the usual ill-informed vaporizing about Stanislavsky. If only for a few minutes, here is what the M.A.T. actually did in *The Three Sisters*. It was Chekhov who said: 'Don't paint pictures you have not seen.'

Two chapters, Nos. II and IV, of the present survey require some explanation as to their place in the scheme. The first of them takes notice of Shakespearian acting as far back as the nineteentwenties, not as an excuse for reminiscence, but because even the most elementary chain of impressions may be of some use in bridging the gap in tradition between our raucous mid-century style and aspects of the classics which do not yield to it. True enough, an emphasis on agitation, colour, texture and the feel of things generally, is typical of contemporary sensibility. Revivals are bound to reflect it, but they have a duty to the originals, too, and to the psychological working of drama. Little as is known about that, there is a lot of evidence within everyone's experience to favour the view that the most exciting events in a theatre are not necessarily the noisiest or the most elaborate. I do not emphasize the intellectual element in acting from a preference for it, on

the contrary. When it is neglected beyond a certain point, however, there follows a lack of cohesion which ends in the actors
resembling circus animals. Even my favourite Shakespearian
character, Fortinbras, compared with whom Horatio is a self-
lacerating introvert, is human in his way. The court he intrudes
on, though rotten, is not a clip-joint.

A similar impulse towards inchoate activity can be found in
American drama, now impressive only in the work of Jerome
Robbins, the exception to prove the rule, for his creations do not
speak. Whether Arthur Miller will again act as a corrective is in
doubt, but he is today's master playwright in the English language
and a major influence on the young English writers not wholly
committed to expressionism. By a strange quirk of social history
the society analysed in Miller's best work is being widely repro-
duced in England a decade later, so that there are abundant
reasons, apart from his intrinsic merit, for what might otherwise
be an intrusive chapter (No. IV) on American plays. Since it was
written, there has been a chance to see Arnold Wesker's *The
Kitchen*, which reveals a distinct late O'Neill influence.

The Kitchen, as it happens, though written before the work by
the same author discussed in Chapter VII, is a fully-fledged
masterpiece which crystallizes the three trends—American, expressionist and native vernacular—isolated in that chapter. It
achieves the extraordinary marriage of lively surface texture,
throbbing with backchat and documentary zip from start to finish,
and an unforced symbolism which can use a mob of chefs and
kitchen porters as mouthpieces for the final, unanswerable questions we ask about life. Comparison with *Serjeant Musgrave's
Dance* reveals that John Arden, little older than Wesker, is less
mature as a playwright though more in the fashionable groove.
He, too, recalls late O'Neill in so far as Musgrave is a mixed-up
revivalist with a suspect message, but for all Arden's ingratiating
use of expressionist ferment I am more conscious in performance
of the play's director than of what the author is getting at*. It is a
characteristic of literary playwrights, Wilder for example, to con-
fuse one with too conscious a display of theatrical technique.
What confusion there is in *The Kitchen* applies to one character:
Peter, the German chef. Idealistic, romantic, hysterical and violent,
he is an authentic product of Theatre in the Raw, who bears much,

* *Cf.* Chapter VIII pp. 118-19.

but not too much, of the dramatic weight. He is not the volcano itself, so much as the vulnerable area lava breaks through. Being limited and defined by other characters and other versions of his conflict, Peter's eruption is dramatic. It does not merely fray the nerves.

No survey of drama carried out now can ignore the influence of television. I share the general gratitude to the B.B.C., and, with greater reservations, to the commercial channels, for masterpieces transferred to the screen. This, however, is not a book about moving pictures or drama by remote control. I have tried in Chapter I to define the limitations of television as a substitute for live theatre, but the dismissive attitude adopted towards the new medium is realistically based on its present social misuse. Although we are always being told how exciting and potentially enlightening television is, a glance at any day's output reveals an emphasis on tawdry conformism side by side with low-grade excitement. Since the viewer's relationship to performance resembles that of a hypnotic subject rather than a theatre-goer, there can be little encouragement of the kind of response, often quite strenuous, demanded by the arts. For the individual the rule holds good: no effort, no growth.

Finally, it should be pointed out that the consumer society referred to so often in the following pages is not a sociologist's fantasy. Many have ascribed the Labour Party's defeat in the 1959 election to the fact that the British working class was on the whole more interested in cars and washing-machines than in Socialism. There was the case of a man drawing National Assistance who took a fortnight's holiday on the Côte-d'Azur and drove a £565 car on hire purchase. In America, the Van Doren case revealed the intelligentsia in a mid-century conflict of values, an unusually clear-cut opposition, at work in one man's conscience, of commercial success and professional ethics, of money and the mind. It is a measure of the new English drama's vitality that a recluse withdrawn from all other communication with his fellow men would be able to form an accurate picture of our society today, simply by going to the theatre. If the young and articulate have little to say in favour of subtopian conformism, perhaps that is all to the good. Nothing we know of other societies leads one to suppose that regimentation, either by force or persuasion, is a way to liberty and the pursuit of happiness.

In general the aim of this study, which makes no claim to be comprehensive, is to find some shape in recent theatrical events. The amount of help I have been given is great. This is the time to thank W. A. J. Lawrence for his inexhaustible patience, encouragement and wit; my wife, Hilary, for many enlightening discussions; Charles Monteith, for timely advice; Michael Brazil, Edward Mallett and Doris Stow, for help in overcoming various obstacles; Marjorie Burcher and Martin Davies for invaluable secretarial work; and Desmond King-Hele, for reading the MS. and criticizing it as precisely as he tracks missiles on the move in outer space.

To the *New Statesman* my thanks are due for leave to include the excerpt from a notice by their Dramatic Critic, A. Alvarez, and to *Encounter* for the use of an article, here reprinted as Chapter IX. All the interviews in this book were carried out for *The Times* and first appeared on the Arts Page of that newspaper. I am most grateful to The Times Publishing Company for permission to reproduce them.

LAURENCE KITCHIN

London 1960

PREFACE
TO THE SECOND EDITION

———————————*———————————

Little or no dissent has been made from my estimates of classical acting in the first edition of *Mid-Century Drama*. As was to be expected, the sections dealing with what has since come to be called New Wave writing drew mixed reactions, like the work itself. Apart from the special case of John Arden, nothing has since made me revise my original estimates. Indeed they have been confirmed by the receptions given to *The Hostage* at the Odéon Théâtre-Français (1962), *A Taste of Honey* on Broadway and *The Kitchen* (revived 1961). I'm now very glad to have adequate space for Pinter (Chapter VIII) and more data on Brecht in performance for the chapter on cosmopolitans; only a preference for studying dramatic writing in action, coupled with publisher's deadline, prevented this from being done in the first edition.

Now in its sixth year, the New Wave is up against economic facts, favourable to the careerist but not to the creative playwright's need for artistic security. The alternatives seem to be assimilation to show business, always eager to cash in on yesterday's rebel, or else the time-consuming drudgery of creating new institutions to embody new artistic forms. Between real estate speculators, fixated on inter-war boulevard drama, and the disciples of O'Neill and Brecht there are fewer points of contact every day. I have no doubt that the future lies with a constellation of civic and suburban theatres, heavily subsidized and bright as new pins. One job for the National Theatre will be to serve as a model for them.

The future inheritors of a context fit for the English drama are scattered over television, films, university groups, theatre-in-the-round and amateur fringe ventures. When they take over in proper buildings the results will be exciting. I have included interviews reflecting their tastes, along with one or two correctives. My thanks are due to The Times Publishing Company for leave to reproduce this new material from the Arts Page.

Other acknowledgements are to Miss Mary Clarke and the British Theatre Museum Association for unearthing the photograph of Olivier's Old Vic Henry V; to Miss Sasha Trone for her help in preparing the edition for the press; and to my wife, for sharing the stress of this kind of work and meeting all drama with a warm, alert response.

LAURENCE KITCHIN

London 1962

Chapter I

THE CONTEMPORARY
BACKGROUND

*

On April 2nd, 1956, the English Stage Company gave its first performance at the Royal Court, and on July 7th, 1959, Olivier played Coriolanus at Stratford-on-Avon. Of these two events, the first was to tap new sources of creative energy; the second brought together a great heroic actor and a director still in search of heroic style. They share an idiom and a sensibility which arouse the kind of responses we reserve for something new and vital. Live drama depends on new writing and on worthy interpretation of the classics. During these three years a number of young playwrights emerged one after another, until it was possible to recognize in them enough common factors to constitute a style. This outburst of talent, more encouraging than any comparable impulse since the Restoration and widely spread, was accompanied by a decline in classical acting, generally agreed to have achieved by 1945 the highest standard within living memory.

Such, in fact, are the two main themes of this book: classical drama in the English language and new writing with the promise of growth, the achieved and the potential. It leaves room for the possibility that the drama's centre of gravity may shift decisively to the ballet, the opera, even to professional sport, but it assumes that durable art, with intellect and emotion held in the high tension reached by Shakespeare, Jonson and Synge, is the ultimate standard. The rest is entertainment, and the critic's great difficulty is to find where one leaves off and the other begins. He must be ready to discard old forms in responding to new work, like *The Hostage*, which conforms to none of them. The tone of *The Hostage* is frivolous, its construction by naturalistic standards faulty, its diction colloquial. Yet through all this there is com-

23

municated pathos and wisdom, emotion and a mind. Anybody who can digest the horrors of Cyprus and Dublin in the personage of an accurately observed Cockney private has my respect. So has Marcello Moretti of the Piccolo Teatro di Milano from his acrobatic waiting on two tables at once; and Sacha Guitry once had me in fits with forks and spoons. But Behan in *The Hostage*, however clumsily, is in touch with drama at a more significant level.

One day it should be plain enough where the new work is coherent, where it is just a rag-bag of stale expressionism, gutter exoticism and drab routines evicted from the music halls. At its worst it is drama withering away into its constituent elements; at its best it offers meaningful conflict, the backbone of creative theatre. In any case the classics will remain a necessity and a challenge. What happened to them, during the years emphasized in this survey? Some idea can be gained from the relevant interviews which follow it. In one of them Michael Benthall points out that fifty per cent of the Old Vic Company has to be replaced every year. Peter Hall gives his opinion in another that it takes twenty years to make a mature Shakespearian actor. Taken together these statements mean only one thing: that we are reviving our classics under conditions of shoddy improvisation which no other country in Western Europe, not to mention the munificent Soviet bloc, would tolerate.

As we live under the same conditions of economic opportunism as condemned Forbes-Robertson to slave labour in *The Passing of the Third Floor Back* in order to pay for his Hamlet, it may seem quixotic to protest. It is now obvious, however, that our approach to our own classics is amateurish. Visits by the Comédie Française, the Moscow Art Theatre, the Berliner Ensemble and the Classical Theatre of China have proved it. Not that we lack the artistic resources. Simply they are misused to such an extent that we have Gielgud giving one-man shows and envying the conditions of continental repertory, Wolfit doing extracts from Shakespeare, Olivier deprived of resources to film *Macbeth*, Richardson tied up in long runs of naturalistic drama of the second and third grade, Scofield impersonating a Tin Pan Alley shark and a suburban seducer.

It is wastage prodigal enough to end in a fatal break of tradition, for classical style is transmitted in performance. Already there are directors of the younger generation whose memories of the great

New Theatre and Haymarket seasons of the mid-forties are growing dim. To most young people Olivier is a recorded voice or a
presence on the screen, Richardson a feckless white-collar worker,
home at seven; Wolfit is Joe Lampton's father-in-law, and Evans
Jimmy Porter's aunt. At times it has seemed easier to find an
authentic Giorgione than to catch any of these great actors at
work on a live audience in the parts which draw out their powers
to the full. If all they want is a National Theatre, they must be
given it at once. As Wolfit remarked: 'We are growing old.'

Into the vacuum created by this iniquitous dispersal have come
son et lumière. People who spent their childhood in wartime
blackout are not to be contented by miniature conflicts aflicker
on a domestic screen. They leave that to infants and sedate adults.
It is not their fault if they have had few opportunities to hear
Shakespeare expressively spoken and so accept shaggy production
based on Porterism or misapplications of the Method. These, since
they rightly reject the fag-end of Pinero Aunt Edna favours, are as
near as they can get to a conception of theatrical style. I will try to
define that style in the proper place. Clearly, however, it involves
a very limited use of the spoken word's resources, which go far
beyond the strident sector of 'telegrams and anger'. With the great
interpreters dispersed, music, from jazz to Verdi, has encroached
on poetry as a technique of theatrical communication. Mozart and
Congreve remain minority tastes. So much for *son*.

Light, which Wolfit calls 'the new magician', and colour, an
aspect of light, seem to have played a subordinate role in the
greatest theatrical art. Before the curtain was invented light was
sometimes used to blind the audience during a change of scene.
It was indispensable to Baroque illusionism and gives pleasure in
pantomime transformation scenes or a child's peep-show. Oddly
enough it is often the very people most fond of using the term
peep-show abusively who now make the greatest fetish of light.
From John Christie's sensitive levers at Glyndebourne to the
orthodox American console unit, the equipment is a technological
triumph. Deplorable amateur productions are often well lit.
Higher up, Carl Ebert will ask for a particular note to be echoed
in the lighting, and sometimes the tonality of Rembrandt's 'Night
Watch' is given to *Hamlet*. Mid-century audiences expect this
kind of thing. How far it is a concession to a public visually educated and verbally corrupted, how far it is relevant to the purposes

of drama, are questions related to the chapter on décor and directors. There is always the example of Irving's Lyceum productions to be kept in mind. They appear to have been loaded with spectacle to the detriment of the text.

Sound and colour, then, tend to dominate mid-century revivals of the classics, with the director, the designer and their stage machinery addressing a public inexperienced in sustained listening other than to music. While *The Playboy of the Western World* is put on as a musical and *Pygmalion* is a smash hit as *My Fair Lady*, a strong production of *Major Barbara* is dismantled after a few weeks' run at the Royal Court. *Caste*, *Rape upon Rape*, *Candide* and even *The Importance of Being Earnest* are set to music. None of this would matter, were it not for the fact that nowhere at all can there be seen acting of Wilde and Shaw in the original, by teams with a nucleus of actors thoroughly on terms with the style required in the way Comédie Française actors are on terms with Molière and Feydeau. It is not some vague ideal one refers to, but reality: Gielgud, Ashcroft and Evans for Wilde; Richardson, Hardwicke and Clements for Shaw. Tony Britton on television comes over as a born actor of Wilde. The context in which he might consolidate does not at present exist.

Gielgud has referred to style, in his terse way, as 'knowing what kind of play you're in'. The attainment of it would seem to require conditions of a stability unknown in our theatre at the moment, or else a wasteful process of self-realization carried out among more distractions than actors have ever been subjected to before. Not to generalize tediously, we may consider the cases of Peter O'Toole and Wendy Williams, both of whom showed outstanding promise at the Bristol Old Vic. At 24 O'Toole embodied a collector's piece of a Hamlet, as near to the Osborne type of protesting young man as could be gone without travesty of Shakespeare. It had to be done once, and it was fascinating. A beard and tall, squeaky boots, along with harsh diction at headlong speed, removed all traces of aristocracy from the part; but the instantaneous neurotic fusion of thought and feeling often worked aptly. Never have I seen Hamlet's abstention from killing the king at prayer so plausibly managed.

Miss Williams as Ophelia gave the girl a demure Jane Austen poise, not without grave mockery at the expense of Laertes, so that her later insanity was more than the striking out of a cypher.

Because we had enjoyed her balance as a positive achievement of character in the decadent court, the loss of it hurt more. She made an equally good Viola, and never fell into the common error of emphasizing the burlesqued man more than the latent woman, whose feelings blend with the subtler textures of the play. Although there is much more in Viola than she found, the two performances had a repose, a grace in the attitudes and a lyrical enjoyment of the lines beyond anything I have seen since Ashcroft's early Imogen.

A well-ordered theatre would have supplied a recognized ladder of promotion for two such actors. When they left the Bristol Old Vic I expected to see them at Stratford-on-Avon or Waterloo Road. Instead I saw that good naturalistic actress Mary Ure playing a waspish Desdemona, that even better naturalistic actress Googie Withers playing a tough Beatrice, and several very pretty actresses who were not ready for leading Shakespearian parts. Of those who were ready, Dorothy Tutin, looking like the Cavalier child in 'When did you last see your father ?', and Barbara Jefford, looking like his elder brother, both played Viola passably without raising their verse much above the status of linking passages to the fertile stage business.

Meanwhile there was no doubt as to what O'Toole and Miss Williams were in need of as classical actors. He needed parts drawing largely on rhetoric and musicality—Brutus, Theseus, Joseph Surface, perhaps—parts not requiring the staying power and high tension he excels in, but static, hardly to be done without much relaxation and conscious attention to the phrasing. He chose or got the part of a soldier in *The Long and the Short and the Tall* who is rarely at rest in thought, word or deed and in whom slovenly diction is basic to the character. Miss Williams, who had mastered the essential outline of two Shakespeare heroines technically, needed little more than practice, the enrichment that comes from repeated performance within a sound framework, the logical extension from Viola to Rosalind, Beatrice, Desdemona. She was to be seen often enough on television after leaving Bristol, and once at least in a second-feature film, a classical actress of promise, gracing scripts from the naturalistic assembly line.

These two give one an idea of the sort of distracting versatility expected of present-day actors. Together in *Hamlet* they also illustrated the confusion of style it can bring about. Since Hamlet was raucously Royal Court and keyed up, Ophelia limpidly deliberate and lyrical, you had the extremes of reputable contemporary acting as practised in England. In between, of course, there lie the drab stretches of West End and Hollywood behaviourism, or frank exhibitionism, which feed the entertainment machine, skilled, meticulous and futile as the work a compositor puts into printing worthless fiction. Never before has there been so much dramatic activity directed to advertising, habit formation, canteen farce, melodrama, and to the ultimate debasement which drama can undergo: a cult of anxiety, of indiscriminate violence without catharsis. These misuses are so widespread that a major temptation for the new playwright is towards making concessions to them, in the fear that otherwise he may achieve no communication with present audiences at all.

Drama, more than other arts, is responsive to the society which produces it; being so public is both its essence and its limitation. In its developed mid-century English form it is one aspect of a consumer society, steadily changing since the Second World War in the direction of subtopian conformism on the American pattern. The quickest way to understand what was happening in 1956 at Coventry or Tunbridge Wells was to consult sociologists like Riesman, writing of American trends ten years before. The effect of these social changes on the drama was both external, on public demands, and internal, on the attitudes of those concerned with writing and staging. Just as actors tended to become versatile technicians, scurrying from one medium to another, so writers adapted themselves to demands rarely more exacting than those of women's magazine fiction.

Being the most potent influence on the human consciousness since the invention of printing, television has had its effect on mid-century drama. It came to power in England with the consolidation of the commercial channels by the end of 1956, and its immediate function has been to fix and maintain among millions of people the consumer values they were moving towards already. The receiving set itself even became a status object, displacing the hearth as a domestic focus for the first time since the Middle Ages. In many homes it usurped parental authority, conversation and social initiative to such an extent that criticism of any programme was construed as a reflection on the hospitality.

Here I am only concerned with television in relation to live drama, on which its effect has been peripheral and artistically insignificant. It comes, indeed, into the same alienating class of gadgets as the microphone. Whenever a theatre comedian or, as now happens at Olympia, a circus clown, resorts to the microphone, he makes a fatal compromise. Chaplin and Tati are in command of their technical sources of production, can re-shoot and cut, whereas the televison performer is enfeebled. He has neither the deliberation of the film-maker nor the direct contact of the theatre. The great personalities of television are non-dramatic: manipulators, expositors, revealers of the self or projectors of an anti-self. They do not suffer, they never learn anything and they do not change. What they exert is the reassurance to be had from a family album.

There is, of course, a great deal of quasi-dramatic activity on television, most of it in a drably naturalistic vein of domestic, keyhole drama. It has siphoned off the dregs of behaviourism and prompted a new respect for the impact of live actors in public. As epic breadth is denied to the small screen, *An Age of Kings* was at its best where the action of Shakespeare's histories narrows to one person's emotional state or the talk round a conference table. The intimacy imposed is unkind to self-dramatizing men like Falstaff and Hotspur, characters built partly by rhetoric which needs a live audience. Shrunk to naturalism and speeded up, they take second place to wily schemers like Worcester. Battles in this medium tend towards horse opera, the barons to modern gangsters.

If grand designs are fatally diminished, at least the mass audience is in tune with the idiom of new wave playwrights like Owen and Arden. Viewers are not fixated on worn out inter-war forms of drama. But one still fails to distinguish the end-product from that of the cinema in any way favourable to television.

Where television's own heights of drama are simply cinema writ small, its diffusion of work designed for the live theatre bears the relationship of vitamin tablets to a square meal; we know they take skill to produce and are good for us, but they remain a substitute. When something like Paxinou's Mother in *Blood Wedding* or Wolfit's Volpone takes the screen, people say that television drama is justifying itself. As a public service, it is, but we forget that it is only drama by courtesy. You cannot transpose great works of art from one medium to another without serious loss. The screen gave Paxinou's agony very well in close-up, without the effect her presence would make at the wedding on stage. It was like detail photographs of a large composition, valuable for research purposes provided you knew the original. Chekhov, on the other hand, is totally intractable. So much in him depends on simultaneous vision of the patterns of ensemble. Obliged to divide action for different cameras if it is not to be held at too great a distance, television destroys the organic harmony of the construction, which comes from sound and movement contrived within the range of a fixed point of view. Although less obvious violence is done to Ibsen, Stockmann haranguing a meeting is not the same as Stockmann speaking at the same time to a meeting and a theatre audience. Again, in *The Master Builder* Solness's climb up the tower is a matter of suspense conveyed by watchers from stage to audience. On the screen you can show him climbing, trite, or obey Ibsen, contrary to the logic of the medium.

Negatively, like this, television has done drama the service of showing how well the masters knew their theatre. Almost any realization in action is preferable to a reading of the text. Unfortunately, though, the screen is allergic to heightened language and all attempts at Shakespeare have been deplorable vocally. When even Prime Ministers are coached into the casual form of delivery, away from rhetorical breadth, what hope is there for tragic declamation? Speed up verse beyond a certain tempo and the result, as in the theatre, is intolerable. Shaw and Wilde, expository wits, make excellent viewing, but Synge at the same tempo loses half his meaning. Nothing between prose and song has yet taken hold, for it is precisely poetry, not only dramatic but unaccompanied lyric, that the screen rejects. Whether cause or effect, it corresponds to the taste of the mid-century public.

This public is unique in English history for its exposure to calls on the attention, incessantly made from print, screen and radio with the object of inculcating the quantitative and conformist values of a consumer society. Something in the individual has to suffer, and it seems to have been the ability to listen, to be affected by the unaccompanied human voice in a manner taken for granted by most of the great dramatists until this time. The exception—Jimmy Porter, O'Toole's Hamlet, Dr. Billy Graham —is language riding on a high emotional change, in which the interest comes from the speaker's state of feeling rather than his state of mind or what he says. It is the kind of symptom one would expect if there had been widespread impoverishment of the power to imagine and visualize.

Cinema and television, of course, do away with the necessity to visualize. More and more of what used to be the audience's job is now done for it; but compare the befuddled eyes of children after a long viewing session with their high spirits after the theatre and you are reminded of the drama's essence, its element of congregation and dispersal, the going to take part in an event and the coming away. Drama on tap in the home may also be a ritual, but only in the sense of putting the milk bottles out and winding the clock. So screen drama lacks the sense of occasion as well as starving the imagination and the plastic sense. It leads to that dull thing, a relatively passive audience, whose reactions are further enfeebled by the fact that no direct interchange between audience and performer can occur.

None of this may prevent the mass media from developing valid art forms of their own, as the cinema has already done, or from providing the drama with valuable records like Olivier's Richard III and the Comédie Française *Le Bourgeois Gentilhomme* or from predisposing the masses to better-quality experiences. But these distinctions are necessary if we are to understand the mid-century background. In making them, as all responsible actors, directors and writers are compelled to do, we often gain insight concerning the drama itself. When several experts agree that audiences are now so used to the screen close-up that they resent the absence of it in the theatre, the relevance of screen 'drama' is manifest.

Artistically null, except as a stimulus to revaluation of essential drama, the effect of the mass media so far has been a dispersal of energy. Having debased the response of audiences, tired, tempted, inflated and retarded two generations of actors, they remain a substitute. It is more than ever plain that the theatre functions best when protected from interpenetration by the media which often, as in the case of the Royal Court and of repertories endowed from television profits, seem to be its salvation. If we needed any confirmation of this it is provided by the way the Compagnie des Quinze still fires the imagination of people as different as Joan Littlewood and Gielgud, who saw their performances twenty-five years ago.

The perfection of their achievements came from privacy; they would rehearse for months in the country. The prowess of the foreign companies which showed us up from 1956 to 1959 on their visits came from State recognition. Protected by subsidy, their energy was not dissipated; and so we were given an experience like Robert Hirsch's Scapin. The gymnastics of that performance presupposed a training discipline unavailable here. In addition, it alluded to the present-day Neapolitan layabout and to the Commedia dell' Arte formula, still very much alive in the Piccolo Teatro di Milano production of Goldoni seen at Sadler's Wells a few months before. Hirsch's direction, on a set which contained nothing, from a boat to a flight of steps, not organically relevant to what was done, may serve as a standard for revivals of the classics in a modern idiom. Finally these are artistic discriminations. The environment he worked in only came to mind when you compared the results with the Old Vic's stodgy and lumbering *Tartuffe*.

Les Fourberies de Scapin, unwisely attempted by the lively 59 Company at Hammersmith in Otway's version, is a clinching argument in favour of assessing drama in performance; the student who could estimate its full effect from the text alone has not been born. No drama is richer in borderline classics than the English, but in these years even the B.B.C., which had at least kept Tourneur, Massinger and Middleton alive in our ears, yielded to competitive pressure and drastically reduced the time given to them on its Third Programme. The commercial theatre, dominated by the rise in Shaftesbury Avenue land values from seven pounds a square foot in 1938 to eighteen to twenty pounds in 1957, still bet on Agatha Christie, the middlebrow's Compton-Burnett, on the Whitehall farces, canteen humour without finesse, and on Pineroish flirtations with social problems.

And yet the final impression left by these years of transition is one of vitality and hope. Somehow, in spite of anxiety, distractions and bitter opposition from entrenched conformity, the new drama was launched. By the summer of 1959 Theatre Workshop had two productions, *A Taste of Honey* and *The Hostage*, running simultaneously in the West End. The Royal Court had penetrated there several times, and its example had encouraged orthodox commercial managements to sponsor *Flowering Cherry* and *Five Finger Exercise*, both of which contained material of a type acceptable only in musicals, or under the excuse of American and French origin, before.

The new drama had also gone so far as to influence mass media. A film of *Look Back in Anger*, directed by Tony Richardson of the Royal Court, was reaching audiences beyond the minority of theatre-goers. Commercial television's Armchair Theatre series frequently transmitted playlets conceived and acted in the Royal Court style. The critic's task was no longer to peer desperately in search of creative vitality but to estimate the strength and weakness, the potentiality, of a movement. Only one aspect of it needs emphasizing here. It stems from people too young to have enjoyed the privileges of British imperialism, often too old to have suffered maximum exposure to television in childhood. This sets them apart from both the Establishment and the younger, Americanized, English adolescent.

Since mid-century conditions tended to keep masters of classical style away from the people with most to learn from them, surplus energy from the new drama spilled over into Shakespearian revivals, where it was usually out of place. Porterism, for example, provides few clues to the aristocratic approach without which the major classical themes would be meaningless. It is easier to act or direct naturalistically on a basis of classical training than to attempt the reverse. But here again there were encouraging tendencies. However unsatisfactory their results, such directors as Tyrone Guthrie, Michael Benthall and Peter Hall had become sensitive to criticism of inadequate verse-speaking, as the interviews I have included show. Style had by this time been so frequently demonstrated by foreign companies that the lack of it in English revivals could no longer be denied. There was more talk of providing by subsidy the necessary conditions for its growth; claims to be refreshing the classics for a modern audience, when style was absent, took on a more defensive tone.

Finally, on successive days in July 1959, Olivier and Gielgud came before the theatre public after lengthy absences and some bizarre critical responses confirmed that their reappearance was long overdue. These actors, complementary in their gifts, are two of the mid-century's main points of continuity with tradition. Appreciation of them will be attempted in Chapter III.

Chapter II

THE AUTONOMOUS ACTOR
Individual Performance in Major Drama

———————————— ⋆ ————————————

By classical acting one means what is done by performers of the masterpieces. It will, like criticism, reflect individual talent and changing climates of opinion, but that does not reduce discrimination to an exchange of subjective impressions. There is the text, raw material of performance, to serve as a control; and there is the acting of it. Unless a Hazlitt or a MacCarthy happens to be in the audience, any artistic experience transmitted will have gone beyond accurate recall in a few weeks' time. We are left, all the same, with the known attributes of the actor concerned and at least the contours of his approach. Consciously or no, the other actors on stage with him night after night absorb these externals. When he is much admired they copy them, and so his work enters into tradition.

Mid-century classical acting in England is in a chaotic state, with Stratford-on-Avon anxious to pull in newly-rich factory workers, the Old Vic bearing in mind what Texas may be expected to like and Theatre Workshop winning prizes abroad for realistic versions of Jacobethan plays not wholly designed for such handling. Add to this the wandering free-lance status of Gielgud, Olivier, Wolfit and Richardson, potential nuclei of tradition, and you have a situation too fluid for quality. The tendency is for directors to set up surface agitation in lighting, décor, movement and speech in ways to be illustrated in a later chapter. They then justify their results by claiming to have refreshed the plays for a new generation of theatre-goers, although the originals may in fact have been weakened. Surface activity, effective only up to a point even in the new plays which call for it, is an obvious substitute for classical style; it is easy to direct and to act, and the public is geared to it. Sometimes, however, the effect is offensive, as if

Jackson Pollock had let his paint drip intertwining spirals on to a Cézanne or a Titian. Elegance of mind (Hamlet) and elegance of person, a factor in many of the classics from Marlowe to Wilde, are two of the dramatic effects completely resistant to such an approach.

It has been reinforced by Tynan, the most influential post-war critic, so that young actors, condemned anyway by the conditions of their profession to swim with the tide, have only the Marlowe Society and the Youth Theatre as pointers in another direction. Not that activity is vicious. It carries more essential drama than photographic naturalism, but the practitioner is an incomplete instrument. Too ready to dismiss other styles than his own as ham, he scurries athletically from group to group in well-drilled ensemble, often incidentally under the direction of an ex-officer, regimented into efficiency. Given a speech of any length, he rattles it off unpunctuated like a policeman in the witness-box, or pickles it in emotion. Subservient to ensemble, perhaps to a director more interested in décor and lighting than in the actor, almost always to a director much concerned with budget and time schedules, the beginner is unlikely to learn about speaking and gesture merely by acting in the classics as now performed.

Therefore, although the conception and total impact of classical productions are often brisk and intelligent, there is weakness along the sectors at which great dramatic writing depends on the sensibility and technical equipment of the actor; and not all the mechanical smoothness of ensemble can hide it. The inadequacy cries out when opportunist casting gives a Shakespearian lead to Miss X, who was so charming in such and such a light comedy or film; it is absurd to launch her in anything bigger than First Gentlewoman. But the classics, ours at least, often spread their riches over the minor parts and so are vulnerable throughout to bad habits widely diffused. Two mincing lispers or throaty beefwits can undermine an entire Tudor court on the stage and dissolve the whole issue into costume fantasy, if the set hasn't done so already. Lacking an institutional background for classical acting, we put up with unforgivable inequalities of performance within a single production. We rightly refrain from panning bad actors in minor parts, just as fast bowlers withhold bumpers from opponents low down in the batting order at cricket. There still remains danger in letting indulgence become a fixed critical

35

habit. It could lead to forgetting that there has never been a relatively satisfactory production in our time of a classic needing a large cast. There have never at one time and place in England been enough of the requisite actors on tap.

Although people may say there has probably never been that in the past either, it is a reasonable assumption that the great dramatists did not plan major effects likely to be botched on the stage. Fortinbras is a case in point. Unless he is manifestly seen to be noble and resolute, Hamlet will appear stupid to take so much notice of him. Fortinbras is given very strong lines, too, and at the end the way he delivers them can determine between tragic serenity and anticlimax. The night I saw a recent Old Vic production a single wrong emphasis lowered the tension, when he says:

> *This quarry cries on havoc—O proud Death,*
> *What feast is toward in thine eternal cell,*
> *That thou so many princes at a shot*
> *So bloodily hast struck?*

Out of this famous threnody the actor chose to emphasize the word 'feast'. Experiment will show that it's difficult not to, more or less. Done *sostenuto* on a single breath, from 'O' to 'cell', however, the words convey feasting as an activity marginal to death and eternity. If Fortinbras overemphasizes 'feast', coming in from outside as he does, he can convey the impression of being hungry. Eagerness, instead of stolid surprise, can be enough to confirm this unfortunate impact of the word picked out. We are not interested in Fortinbras himself at this moment. The actor must know what kind of play he is in, that he has now become the mouthpiece of tragedy itself, that the speech is frosting over a court littered with bodies until the stage picture carries a hint of durable sculpture. Characterization, the inner feelings of an extrovert soldier intruding on a Borgia party, the predicament of a man who has walked unexpectedly on to a throne, are beside the point, and with them most of the present-day actor's armoury. Fortinbras has to keep still, do justice to the lines and hope that his facial expression will not be too trivial for them. Some characterization, of great and congruous beauty, is in the imagery; and there it should stay.

Where a subsidiary actor's responsibility can be so vast, one need not dwell on the quality required from a lead. Ideally one would begin by casting the minor parts first and building from that foundation. The reverse is what happens, as in the days of Edwardian actor managers, and our much vaunted ensembles are rarely anything more than quasi-military and balletic sleight-of-hand to cover wide areas of text beyond the capacities of the cast. When the star system assigns leads as well to classical novices the danger of decline is obvious. It could end in the new generation of theatre-goers forming their standards from learners, from actors of inadequate technique directed either by men of small experience or by veterans inured to imperfection. Yet the exciting truth is that the remedy is within reach: a drift of public opinion in favour · of some national showcase for the performance of masterpieces and a constellation of great actors not far past their prime.

It seems, then, the right moment to recall some achievements of the established classical stars, first as a reminder of the insights to be gained from the actor and nobody else, secondly as a pointer to ways in which tradition is vitally redirected and, thirdly, to bridge the gap yawning between the star in his fifties and the Welfare State teenage audience while there is still time. It was the generation between, having taken the full strain of war, social revolution and their artistic sedatives, which overlaid classical revivals with thick layers of gimmick, ran amok on décor and reduced verse to the level of orders barked on parade. Meanwhile Olivier was in direct contact with articulate teenagers as Archie Rice and with the masses in his Shakespeare films. The cancellation of his Rank organization *Macbeth* was a disaster because it destroyed an important bridge. I had not, myself, understood the full seriousness of the break in tradition until I read the following assessment of Gielgud's poetry recital in 1959: 'But the deeper, the more mature the emotion the less Gielgud himself seems to be with it. To hear, with eyes closed, Lear's dying speech was profound and disturbing; but to watch it was simply distracting. The language seemed undercut by his angular, almost pettish movements. In a sense, Gielgud is at one with the old style of Shakespearian criticism which deferred continually to that indefinable essence, "verbal magic".'

Coming from the *New Statesman*'s dramatic critic,* that disconcerted me. Gielgud, it is true, can seem as angular as Leonardo's

---

* A. Alvarez, *New Statesman*, July 18th, 1959.

Saint Jerome, but 'pettish' is not the word for his movements in Wilde, Congreve and Shakespeare on stage. We have it on his own authority that his approach to the verse has been progressively more austere the older he gets, and on that of George Rylands, in a Third Programme talk illustrated by recordings of others, from Waller to Edith Evans, that Gielgud hits a nice compromise between sense and sound. Furthermore, the Lear episode complained of was as near as the actor could get to the requirements of Granville Barker, under whom it was rehearsed; and I don't remember any complaints of 'verbal magic' when Gielgud delivered the Cassius speech in the Hollywood film of *Julius Caesar* exactly as he did in his recital.

One way and another the *New Statesman* critic's remarks are an interesting reflection of contemporary taste, notably where they refer to Gielgud being 'less . . . with' his emotion. There is plenty of room in tragedy, as in the case of Fortinbras, for alienation effects. Here, though, a divergence of critical opinion is brought in to justify some digging into the past. To know that Gielgud's movement is not generally pettish and that he has never been a vague devotee of 'verbal magic' all you need is to have seen him sufficiently often. Something, therefore, can be done towards clearing the ground of grosser misconceptions fostered by the scarcity of classical acting in a country not willing to house it properly.

From the late nineteen-twenties, when I first saw Shakespearian touring companies in Yorkshire, to the present confusing situation, one person's memory is well able to supply data objective enough to serve as a basis for discrimination. The purpose would not be to reach a definition of classical style, but to recall some performances which instantaneously lit up a great play or else took on a satisfying aptness in retrospect, so that all subsequent interpretations referred one to them. Either of these would be fine classical acting, with the material for practical purposes confined to Shakespeare and a handful of comedies of manners. Olivier would be an obvious provider of the revealing flare-up, Gielgud of the immovably definitive study.

What was the soil they sprang from like? Within my own experience, arid. Seeing Benson playing Macbeth when over seventy at the Leeds Grand, the aged Martin Harvey as Oedipus, a veteran Lady Macbeth anticipating the Method by snores in the sleep-walking episode, is probably no fair way of estimating the actor managers' epoch. Nevertheless there was a discrepancy between classical acting and the drama an interested schoolboy expected. The stately tempo, no bad thing in itself, gave time for diction to do its worst. To my ear it combined a sacerdotal booming with a gobbling, masticatory action of the jaw muscles. Worst of all it reduced the lines to a ritualistic drone, as if actually making them heard was enough. It is characteristic of the folksily amateurish aspect of drama between the wars that controversy about style centred on audibility and not on intelligibility. Given the taste of that time, there wasn't much wrong with the gesture and movement of the actors. Presence, a thing beyond fashion, was exceptional in an actor like Henry Ainley, and I can think of few present-day stars who would not look ridiculous in the enormous wings he assumed at the close of Bridie's *Tobias and the Angel*. His voice, superior to any now to be heard, was acceptable in Antony's rhetoric if not for Hamlet. The style adopted, however, turned intellectual activity into mere sententiousness and measured out emotion line by line. But assuming the actor managers had comparable physical qualities in their younger days, it is possible, from Ainley's example, to understand why they were respected.

As actors, not speech therapists, were training beginners in diction, the raw material of revivals was an actor using an imperfect instrument in a bad declamatory convention. I take this to be the authentic ham tradition, nowadays more often found among street entertainers, orotund, condescending and false. One good thing the cinema and television have done is to mop up the remnants of it, though it still falsifies the diction of some sergeant-majors, toastmasters and clergymen. Fortunately my school at York was immunized against it by possessing an English master who read verse well. When we saw Henry Baynton as Hamlet at the Theatre Royal, we recognized at once that the speaking we heard in class was more musical and based on a better understanding of the text. And we were none too pleased to find the last entrance of Fortinbras cut, so as to leave Hamlet histrionically dead at Shakespeare's expense.

It would be nice to report that the way to better things was pointed by Gielgud's first performances at the Old Vic. For me, unfortunately, it wasn't. Offered a treat one evening in 1931, I had a grim conflict from choosing between his Lear and an Ald-wych farce. Although the farce won, and led to priggish remorse for a few years, I now approve the choice, gloating over memories of Robertson Hare as a judge laughing alone at his *obiter dicta*, Tom Walls as a barrister floundering in his own ignorance of procedure and Ralph Lynn handing his topper and cane to the usher. *Marry the Girl* came from the same Edwardian world as liked Benson's company all the better for forming a cricket team. That world was not really shaken until the first German bomber flickered in the sunlight above the lawn of a Home Counties country house and evacuees from Stepney swore at the butler. Its attitude to classical acting was gushing and snooty, just as the acting itself was done in a tone of condescension, as if aristocrats were putting on a show in the servants' hall. Something or other was being taken seriously, a ritual tied up with social status per-haps, but not the play.

Even in the provinces, however, where tatty tours competed with the last of the silent films, hints that better standards existed came through. *The Times* was laid on in our classroom. Having read all the sport, you could turn to Charles Morgan's notice of an 'all star' Shakespeare revival in the West End and find out who had been miscast. It was all lucid, polite and obstinately critical. Famous actors, one learned, were now and then biting off more than they could chew. Outside our classroom the plays really did enjoy life of a kind.

Then came the Old Vic, at the age of responsiveness which is likely to determine theatrical preferences forever—a possibility which every critic should bear in mind. It was *King John*, with Robert Speaight as the king and Richardson as Faulconbridge. The subsequent careers of both these actors confirm that it was no subjective aberration to think they spoke well, Speaight as the equivalent of an operatic tenor, though always with intelligence, and Richardson in the genial growl of a reminiscing sailor who rather likes the sound of his own voice, fruity but assertive. They made you listen. Although he was visually far more impressive than Speaight, Richardson upset one's preconceptions of a Shakespearian star. There was a Rowlandson craftiness, some-times a moonstruck look, about his eyes. His nose could hint at a cider apple or the rounded end of a gaffer's walking-stick. But here, as it turned out, was a whole territory of the Shakespeare canon covered: Bottom, Falstaff, Sir Toby, Henry V, an army of assorted barons and the weatherbeaten warrant-officer version of Iago. And here, at last, for me, was verse given a tidal surge. When he leered or chuckled through it, it was still heightened language.

Harcourt Williams was directing the plays with what one now recognizes to have been a praiseworthy reliance on the text well spoken. I cannot remember a set or a grouping, only the embodied action, coming across excitingly because I took care, whenever possible, not to have read the plays first. Ashcroft's performances had the effect of very sweet woodwind interludes in a robust symphony. Viewed by goggling students from the gallery, she had some of the glamour of the West End society most of them would never mix in, together with a kind of distilled essence of sex which humanized the lyrical heroines, who seem too hearty or too knowing when the average actress attempts them. This enabled her to carry off the bedroom scene in *Cymbeline* without a snigger from anyone. Incapable equally of a memorable gesture or an ungraceful one, Ashcroft defined an acceptable standard for this range of parts which has never been attained since. Her voice fluted away with a quality of eagerness peculiar to her and subtly feminine. The objections to her Juliet, as too slight in the later stages of suffering, have turned out to be academic; it is the definitive performance of our time.

The bearing of these two examples on classical revivals in general is that much depends on the specialist actor, for whom elaborations of décor and ensemble are no substitute. In the thirties two important sections of the national repertoire were saved from neglect or distortion because Richardson and Ashcroft happened to be available and because Harcourt Williams allowed actors elbow-room to develop in. Although none of the three was a dealer in the shock of recognition, they embodied transmissible qualities of dependability, integrity and respect for their material. After seeing something of the old hams, it gave one a feeling of security to know that Richardson, Ashcroft and Harcourt Williams were at work. Another of the same type of reclaimer was Tearle. His territory adjoined Richardson's where it touched Henry V, a part he played only three years before Olivier's revolutionary performance of 1937. This makes Tearle of fourfold importance: as a Shakespearian actor aged fifty in 1934 who was not ham, as an exemplary noble Roman from North's Plutarch, as a bluff, patriotic Tudor and as an aid to the appreciation of Olivier.

Tearle's own achievement in relation to the immediate past was made clear in 1932 when an 'all-star' *Julius Caesar* was put on at His Majesty's. The production by Oscar Asche, a disciple of Tree, was a stately, cumbersome affair with eminent heavyweights such as Basil Gill, Lyn Harding, Lily Brayton and Asche himself giving the lines all they could and taking their time about it. There was no nonsense about individualizing the mob, an enormous mass of players most of whom probably thought that Stanislavsky was the name of a Polish anarchist. Outside of a DeMille film it was the most convincing, because the biggest and noisiest, theatrical crowd I have ever seen. One member of it, Felicity Lawford, fell off a rostrum as soon as the curtain went up on the first night. A few years later she was to appear in the chorus of *On Your Toes* and so become a link between Edwardian classical acting and the American musical, so fast was the tempo of theatrical change in the thirties.

The first thing one noticed about Tearle was his presence. On a big stage packed with actor-managerial self-confidence, he concentrated the attention at once. It was not grace; he was too big. It was not mental energy; he was, if anything, sluggish. Simply his head was everybody's ideal of a Roman, his heavy body moved with a decisive, athletic certainty, and when he stood still he was 'there' in the manner of a portrait by Hals or actors of the Moscow Art Theatre. He had the sculptural gift of annexing space, and it went with an ability to seem alone with the audience, for instance when Antony conversed with Caesar's corpse. Then there was his voice. The funeral orations were done as a separate act, bracketed between intervals. Great care had obviously been taken to time the crowd's interruptions, but they were so wholehearted that Antony's speech might easily, as often occurs now, have been a series of interruptions of the crowd. Resonantly, within a range of tone not wide by present standards, he built the speech up according to its sustained emotional logic. It rose gradually to its climaxes, gathering strength from one's confidence that nothing would be snatched or strained. The diction was bluff and severe, the gesture and facial play innocent of nuance, congruent with the Antony of 'plain, blunt man' and 'I only speak right on'. Altogether it was the happiest of meetings between an actor suitably equipped and a very demanding text. It was also unexpectedly and wildly exciting, not from any startling insight or innovation, but from a straightforward delivery of stage rhetoric taken at its face value.

Later in the run Tearle took over the part of Brutus, with no apparent change of manner, and again made everyone else appear dim. In 1934 at the Alhambra, a theatre of 1,650 capacity, he played Antony again, this time relying less on the rhetoric and more on the character's powers of dissimulation. His more subdued approach carried to the back of the gallery, where I sat, more firmly than anyone else's acting in an experienced cast. It was followed by Henry V of the traditional 'Bluff King Hal' type, which contained no surprises and conformed to the author's valuation of an epic royal personage no longer much concerned with his Welsh extraction.

Was Tearle a ham? In the face of disagreement from a high authority, I refuse to believe it. Although I'm glad I never saw him play Hamlet, Tearle's forthright, heavyweight virility corresponded to an important element in Elizabethan drama, one which revivals will neglect at their peril. Actors of quicker reflex and finer sensibility are likely to reach only a decadent rendering of the parts he excelled in. Comparison with, say, the Henry V of Richard Burton and the Antony of Ronald Lewis would reveal a decline. Also, Tearle was more than audible, dignified and intelligible. He was able to project one of the most exacting pieces of rhetoric in the English language with lucid *bravura* and faithful observance of its architectonics. Sooner or later the classical actor must face that kind of test, a demand outside fashion, inherent in his material.

If these claims for Tearle have been substantiated, we are beginning to draw some conclusions about the scope of Shakespearian acting. An actor with certain physical and mental attributes will find himself working from play to play in a logical enrichment of himself and them. None of the three already dealt with, as it happens, did much filming on his way to maturity. All of them were allowed time and space enough for considered and meaningful speech. Like most continental actors, they conveyed, without ranting, a pleasure in the interchange of rich language as such, a relish of shared appreciation. Reference to Ashcroft's Beatrice or Richardson's recording of *The Ancient*

43

Mariner will quickly show that a vague addiction to 'verbal magic' has no part in it at all.

By taking only three actors into account, we have shown, then, that by the middle thirties windy declamation was on its way out and bluff Englishmen, noble Romans and lyrical heroines were provided for. So were the clowns, by Leslie French, who had the unusual repertoire of training in the ballet, a well-controlled light tenor voice and a pert sense of humour. In 1960 it is difficult to think of a candidate with more than one of these accomplishments, let alone all three. One mentions it, with no intention of dwelling on present deficiencies, just as a matter of fact, and the kind of fact which any community with a respect for its masterpieces should bear in mind. It means, for example, that the successes gained by the Old Vic and the Memorial Theatre, in America and Russia respectively, cannot have been artistically complete. Both did *Twelfth Night* and neither had a fully qualified Feste.

It is to be understood, of course, that the commercial theatre and niggardly Old Vic finances prevented any ideal concentration of the forces available at the time our great actors were developing. By means of a little patience and selection you could, all the same, piece together a satisfactory experience of the masterpieces without so much as opening a book. So far we have looked for a solid level of interpretation such as the organizers of a National Theatre will have to provide, asked who embodied it, what they had in common and, in broad outline, what ground they covered. We have considered only acting, where it becomes autonomous and bears, as in Imogen's bedroom scene or Antony's oration, the final responsibility; and we have still not touched on the more complex and demanding roles or mentioned isolated achievements made in the others.

If there already existed a National Gallery of Acting, such as will one day be collected on film, two of the exhibits would be lyrical heroines performed with inimitable brilliance. Evans's Rosalind (New, 1937), supported by Redgrave as Orlando and Guinness as Touchstone, was in theory too old, too worldly, too robust and too plain. In practice it was glowingly feminine, full of moodiness, caprice, gay deception, wit and frank sensuality, much of this with the equivalent of a wink at the audience, as in 'Now I will be in a more *coming on* disposition.' Within the situation, that Rosalind is in love with Orlando but must go on pretending to be a boy, she made transitions and variations not even sketched by other performers yet embedded in the lines. There was genius at work, of course, but also a great deal of intelligence and technique, more of both than should be let slip into the dumping ground of jaded memories and old photographs where great English acting so often finds the equivalent of Mozart's grave. Moscow or Paris would have codified that performance. It convinced me that the claims made for Ellen Terry in similar parts may well have been just, that Shakespeare, for some inscrutable reason, could load boy actors with parts drawing on the full resources of a High Renaissance woman and that many admired performances never properly get to grips with the text.

The Viola of Jean Forbes-Robertson (New, 1932) conditioned one's attitude to the play just as surely, though with less of a shock. Outrageously beautiful, with black hair and a complexion both pale and rich, she was a voluptuous and catty Hedda Gabler, the best I have seen. Her bone structure makes sense of Yeats's affected line about the lady who was 'hollow of cheek, as if it drank the wind'. She presented herself, as the disguised Viola, dressed in white, and spoke the verse in a steady contralto which never allowed one to forget that she was a woman; nor did her figure, although she now suppressed one and all of the tricks it was capable of as Hedda. A grave, candid innocence was recognized by all as the tone of this Viola, and indeed it is frequent in the lines. 'There seems a fair behaviour in thee, captain', became, as Jean Forbes-Robertson said it, a reflection of Viola's integrity, a considered opinion by no means irreversible. When she came to the 'willow cabin' outburst, an extreme Renaissance conceit, she had already committed the audience to a poetical relationship with the character and the passage did not seem extravagant. It might well be that she built the performance round it. All other approaches seem, by comparison, a long way from the pagan sadness interpenetrating this very sophisticated play. *Twelfth Night*, even in the drinking scene, is not farce.

Again, working in reverse of the director's and the actor's way, backwards from performance, we have been taken to the textual roots of great drama. To make this possible, even necessary, is the actor's highest function; the rest of his work, in practice most of it, is entertainment. As it happens, the performances of Tearle, Evans and Jean Forbes-Robertson discussed were products of the commercial theatre, which has a heavy debit, all the same, as a suppressor. London has never seen Fay Compton's Juliet or the Cleopatra undeniably latent in Margaret Rawlings, on the strength of her work in *The White Devil* and *Phèdre* a superlative tragic actress. Much could be said about the wastage involved in our system, especially when one thinks of the handicaps under which an actor like Wolfit has presented masterpieces. But we aim here at an ordering of recent classical tradition, when conditions are against a full appreciation of it and contemporary practice is the poorer in consequence. Instead of debating Wolfit's obvious defects, which include relapses into the kind of Edwardian portentousness we have already rejected, this is the place to define him as the master of Renaissance excess: in *Tamburlaine*, *Volpone* and *Malatesta*. Nobody else possesses the exorbitant gusto these parts require; nobody else can, as he does in *Malatesta*, turn plausibly from killing his fencing master to the worship of a Roman statue. Although he is our best Lear and Iago, it is wrong to think of him primarily as a Shakespearian actor. Call him a classical actor and you take in his Lord Ogleby, too. Wolfit and extravagance strike up a creative relationship anywhere, often with results unobtainable by the most expert director.

Lear, extravagance imprisoned in senility and beating its head against the dungeon wall, is not an illogical candidate for the best use of Wolfit's particular gifts. At times he knows what kind of part, if not always what kind of play, he is in. On the whole, though, it would be difficult to distinguish him from a reincarnated actor manager if one were foolish enough to be content with a surface approach. He hectors, frowns, licks his lips, sometimes rants; he has often tolerated supporting casts who looked unable to support themselves. Yet his Iago held its own with Valk's volcanic Othello blow for blow, and there are great parts, including Solness, which yield up their most intimate secrets to his flamboyance. These are facts to which theorizing about contemporary acting must be accommodated. Those who persist in calling Wolfit ham are misusing a valuable word.

Redgrave is another great actor who would elude any hard-and-fast definition of classical style. A schoolmaster before he went on the stage, he excels all his rivals, including Gielgud, where pedantry is at the roots of a character. Compare his Crocker-Harris in *The Browning Version* with Gielgud's teacher in *The Maitlands*. In such roles, however, Redgrave is suppressing a gaunt, craggy glamour, which by itself, as in Antony, is not memorable. He always seems to be suppressing something, an effect which communicates banked-up intensity, alarming in so big a man. He takes the Method in his stride and is the ideal Nordic Hamlet, perhaps the only one who can give a lecture on continence to his mother without appearing deranged, priggish or prurient. He brings Hamlet's advice to the players, often a break in continuity, well inside the character and the action.

Judged from their diction, Wolfit and Redgrave illustrate extremes admissible within the Shakespearian tradition. Redgrave's, very slightly nasal, is remarkably supple and sophisticated without dropping into prose, Byronic at the level of *Don Juan*, which he reads incomparably in just the right tone of ironic reservation. It is also the tone of an intellectual of Auden's generation, earnest, disillusioned and cosmopolitan. While the new mid-century drama was consolidating in the West End in 1959, Redgrave was to be found there as adapter and actor of *The Aspern Papers*. At the same time Wolfit put in an appearance on television as one of Hugh Walpole's meaty clergymen.

Chapter III

THE SHOCK OF RECOGNITION
An Estimate of Gielgud and Olivier

------------------------------ * ------------------------------

Redgrave and Wolfit lead us to the summit of classical acting. There the ultimate in technical skill, experience and glamour yields limited results unless it goes along with some personal affinity with the material, with texts of a richness, verbal, intellectual and emotional, often too great in any one role to be entirely within the compass of a single performer. No wonder the line of least resistance is to leave responsibility to the director and spread the load thinly over a group of able journeymen; for the drama of, say, Greece and France, however great its logic and intensity, tends to respect human limitations and ours does not. What dramatist outside Elizabethan England would construct a Cleopatra of anything like the Shakespearian complexity for performance by a boy? In this country, we must accept a discrepancy of ends and means from the start. For example, in our time the modulation into impersonal grandeur required of Cleopatra before her death has been beyond the range of actresses held to be qualified for the rest of the part. Evans, who projected the tragic climax magnificently, was elsewhere not happily cast.

If analysis of the stars can be made in terms of their failures, it can be seen how little reason there is for complacency about Shakespearian acting, even at a time when there is said to be too much of it. It remains the supreme test in this country, and those who pass it can adapt themselves to most of the material contemporary dramatists have to offer. Nobody wants only a theatre of revivals, but they are a valuable foundation. The best Anouilh, for example, seems to come from a man accustomed to seeing Marivaux well done and his summary of tragedy at the beginning of *Antigone* is from a country in which it is a recognized institution, so much so that in 1959 the Comédie Française was deprived of one of its theatres for neglecting tragedy. Conversely, many defects in American writing and acting stem from the absence of a native tragic or comic tradition in the classical sense. How to be cynical without brashness, intense without hysteria, are things they have yet to learn. The exception, O'Neill, was an addict of classical Greek drama as well as of alcohol.

Gielgud and Olivier are supreme among contemporary actors because of the relationship they have established with the stored riches of dramatic writing. The relationship is such as to go beyond the normal approximations and routines of acting. What they have done is raise their work into the domain of art where it sometimes carries as much authority as that of the scholar or critic, although it is the actor's mysterious blend of intuition and technique which has brought them there. I count it the special glamour of the theatre that the servitude of greasepaint, repetition, demoralizing grapples with rubbish and daily intercourse with competitive mediocrity can bring men to such a pinnacle. Although his traffic in entertainment can lead one to forget it, the great actor is one of nature's miracles. He brings aspects of music, poetry, literature and sculpture within the capacity of a human being and transmits them to the crowd, who later disperse and make what they can of it.

From my experience I can understand Olivier's hold on the mid-century adolescent. It is not only a result of accessibility reached on the cinema, with *Henry V*, *Richard III* and *Hamlet* regularly revived in the West End and even the suburbs. More likely it is his faculty for producing the shock of recognition—things like Richard's fussiness, Hotspur's stammer and the Oedipus howl—which rivet a generation bombarded with calls on the attention. It is not something demanded by the text we are recognizing but a variation the text can tolerate, a guarantee that the actor has made up his own mind about it, raided headquarters instead of going through the usual channels. A parallel would be with Vladimir Peniakoff, who provided his Army Commander with exact intelligence of the enemy's numerical strength in Southern Italy (1943), by seizing a rationing list from the quartermaster's office. Speed, decisiveness, an absence of gullibility, together with violent blazes of self-assertion, are qualities admired in present urban society. They may admit rest periods of knowing calculation. Olivier, meditative at slow tempo, is usually up to mischief. But the *Hamlet* film, introducing him as a man who could not make up his mind, handicapped itself from the start. We knew that in reality he would have sawn his uncle in half before the Ghost had time to explain how the poison worked.

Here I need only discuss three other aspects of Olivier: his revolutionary impact on the classics, his relationship to Tearle's equally valid approach, and the central stability which underlies the fireworks. My own first sight of Olivier in person was on the stage of the Central School in 1933, when he had been adjudicating a student performance. Shorter than one expected, he was compact, wirily alert from head to foot and briskly contemptuous about the standard of make-up that afternoon, a matinée idol martinet, the last person one would have thought of then as a potential classical actor. His performance as an amorous schoolmaster in *The Rats of Norway* was glossy and vigorous, with American intonations presumably acquired in Hollywood. By the time he played Romeo at the New in 1935 they had changed to a variation of Ernest Milton's idiosyncratic wail—'Farewail thou canst not teach me to forgait.' Although Milton uses his off-beat intonation with exceptional intelligence and expressiveness, it spoilt Olivier's Romeo for me, especially in direct competition with Gielgud, who alternated that part and Mercutio. Combined they would have made a good Romeo, and Olivier's Mercutio was excellent, but I did not want to see his Hamlet of 1937.

The first shock came that year with *Henry V* at the Old Vic, in a way any schoolboy could have recognized. There sat the king as the prelates got down to expounding his claim to the throne of France, and there was I, ready to watch a matinée idol's growing-pains. Having seen Tearle and Richardson, I expected to learn nothing new about the part. Sooner or later the legalistic drone would end and Henry would ask, in the stately manner of Tearle, or as near as a classical novice could get to it: 'May I with right and conscience make this claim?' It would, of course, be essential that the claim was just. Any doubt, and Henry would call off the war at once; if the play was not staunchly and reputably patriotic it was nothing. And then I noticed that the King was getting restive. Olivier was showing the same cross impatience with the prelates as he had shown to the students about their make-up four years ago. Generations of persecuted schoolboys were being vindicated by a Henry who had no more time for that dreary speech than they. That was the revolution, consolidated when Olivier spoke the enquiry very clear and fast on a rising, hectoring inflection. It was plain that he was going to war anyway. Right and conscience were being given the value they had in 1937 when speeches relative to the international situation were made.

Other points to note about this performance were the vocal range and the minor inspirations. Originally trained by Elsie Fogerty, the pioneer of stage diction on a sound physiological and anatomical basis, Olivier had released the unused resources of his voice. It was his own now, and could hit a rhetorical climax by climbing to the actor's equivalent of a top C in a way best appreciated by listening to what happens when other actors reach the invocation: 'God for Harry, England and Saint George!' One should add that the effect on a live audience was many times more thrilling that what you hear on the film sound-track. At one extreme of his range of expression was this trumpeting diction and at the other a quirky habit of striking casual sparks from moribund lines:

> Good morrow, old Sir Thomas Erpingham,
> A good soft pillow for that good white head
> Were better than a churlish turf of France.

Could anything be flatter? Yet Olivier paused after 'turf' and threw in 'of France' like a contemptuous afterthought which made the old knight's privations and their common predicament more severe.

Unexpected aptness, as of a man excited by discovery and fitted for it by coming from films and the commercial theatre without stodgy preconceptions, was at the heart of these performances. It galvanized the Old Vic Coriolanus of 1938 in what was the first unmistakably grave and contained interpretation, though bursting with Olivier's explosive impatience. Where Tearle would have showed his contempt for the mob with a statuesque disdain, Olivier gave it nasty overtones of distaste. He enjoyed calling them a 'common cry of curs' with a relish that almost brought him down to their level, and fleeting twitches of the nostrils hinted that physical revulsion had as big a part as aristocratic pride in his rejection of them. They had not washed.

When did the noble Roman begin and the embryo Fascist dictator leave off? They were fused by the actor's personality in the unique amalgam which has led to so many misguided attempts at tackling the classics without basic equipment. Olivier, though James Agate complained that he walked like an all-in wrestler, had now the voice and the presence of a noble Roman or a king. There was never any suspicion that his readings were modern because he only knew how to act in a modern idiom. The tradition had been expanded, not ignored or disrupted. It is as well, too, to remember the intention of the dramatist. Boring as it now seems, the prelates' exposition of Henry's claim has the important function of legitimizing what otherwise would be unprovoked aggression. Tearle's reading was therefore more in keeping with the original and not to be despised. We know that the Elizabethans, chronic litigators, liked a slice of legal argument.

Olivier's most valuable lesson for his mid-century successors is not his wilful originality but the kind of skill he applied to his second Macbeth under the direction of Saint-Denis (New, 1937). It is a part which had brought out the worst in many actors, all rant, haemorrhage and melodrama if the intellect is lacking and a ghastly parody of *Hamlet* in kilts when the actor is sensitive without seeming military. One can imagine the old ham's approach to the speech where Macbeth convinces himself that he has been condemned to insomnia: it's about sleep, so take it gently. As it's about the withholding of sleep, a terrible prospect, Olivier brought the speech to a howling climax, accepting the invitation clearly given by the open vowels of 'sleep no more'. He was equally terrifying in the little night-piece before Banquo's murder, that small bomb of atmosphere which starts with a homing crow and lets loose the agents of night two lines afterwards. In another key the briefing of the murderers had already revealed a Machiavellian motif just as relevant as the northern gloom. Olivier went about the business of persuading these ruffians as if it was a dangerous move which could misfire. Watchful, insinuating, crafty, he made a Renaissance intrigue of a scene which before had not seemed able to bear such weight.

In dealing with an actor of such magnetism it is doubly necessary to keep the solid level of achievement in mind. Olivier's fireworks are in danger of blinding one to the very high order of his intelligence and poetic expressiveness. Where the Renaissance mind and the contemporary mind are alike, as for example in political intrigue—*Macbeth*, *Richard III*, perhaps *Coriolanus*—his mental agility is dazzling and relevant. Sometimes, as in his Lear, described by Professor Wilson Knight in an exemplary piece of observant and informed theatrical criticism,* it gets out of hand. I admired the tasteful and sensitive parade of symptoms with many reservations, for Olivier had decided to attenuate his voice, which is the most emotive on the contemporary stage, and to do Lear in water-colours, in arabesques of gentle pathos. He was impersonating an elderly psychopath, as he was later to impersonate a seedy comedian, but also impersonating Lear right out of the tragedy. It is an amazing gift, less useful in classical acting than the resonant voice, arrogant bearing and quick thinking he uses to such happy effect.

The reminiscences in this chapter and the one before are partly offered in reproach of the sprawling eccentricity rampant in mid-century classical acting. War, social revolution and the dispersal of energy over different media have created a situation in which the generation of proficient actors over fifty is still active but imperfectly understood. Their mature work, on the rare occasions it can be seen, is absorbed at a personality level, so that, for example, Olivier's successful experiments are construed as a licence to modernize. In practice that means bringing the young actor's limitations to a classical role and cutting it down to size. As the new drama, to be discussed later, makes no call on anything like the disciplines of tragedy, high comedy or romantic comedy, the classics tend to be burlesqued in a mid-century idiom. There has been a series of kittenish Olivias, bouncing Violas, a Cassio with a thick provincial accent, a Macbeth who looked and spoke like a high official on the National Assistance Board, all acceptable to a new audience, many of whom regard Olivier as Vivien Leigh's husband, Marilyn Monroe's leading man, the best living Hamlet and the name of a brand of cigarette. The chaos is not reduced when guest stars are miscast. Paul Robeson's beautiful speech rhythm was never adaptable to Elizabethan drama and Charles Laughton's range was defined in his Old Vic season of 1933–34. It includes Angelo and Prospero, memorable work, but not Macbeth and therefore, because of vocal limitations, not Lear.

The middle generation, of from thirty to forty, has progressed very slowly in this field, though sometimes magnificently equipped. Richard Burton, to my mind the most promising, was deflected

* *Principles of Shakespearian Production* (Penguin, 1949).

into films, as was Guinness, supreme in whimsical comedy. Paul Scofield, who came out in *Venice Preserv'd* with a ringing heroic voice, was soon tied up in a musical, like Keith Michell. These are typical of the tendency towards dispersal, whereas Olivier and Gielgud came back to the great roles again and again with the dogged humility of Ingmar Bergman, who told me he had directed *Macbeth* three times and hoped to succeed at the fourth.

In any case the hit-and-run approach to classical acting, so often a hasty approximation of personality to conform with some director's gimmick, has led to a widespread loss of power and intelligence in interpretation where these have to be focused on a single part or speech. As we have seen, good diction and average intelligence can go a long way. Revivals are now quite free from the static sermonizing of the Edwardian hangover, but they are often so eclectic and colloquial that they fail to communicate vital aspects of the masterpieces. Orsino, to harp on *Twelfth Night* which is so often regarded as a dated romp, is central to the mood of the play—in fact, if you accept Dr. Hotson's claims, its pre-text—and unless he is played as a sophisticated aristocrat we are being subjected to burlesque. Gielgud's importance at the moment lies in his command of these areas of the repertoire worst handled in mid-century revivals. From his Hamlet of 1934 (New) to his 'Ages of Man' recital (Queens, 1959), I have seen Gielgud play Shakespeare, Congreve and Wilde with such authority that criticism becomes more dangerous to the critic than to him. He is equally the master of civilized introspection and gay persiflage. Whatever he may say about always being himself, the man supreme in Lear's pathos and John Worthing's cut-glass effrontery, not to mention Prospero's isolation, is extremely versatile. Agate went so far, at one time, as to think his temperament more suited to comedy than to tragedy.

Indeed, Gielgud's achievement in the classics has outstripped the supply of criticism competent to deal with it and develops like the output of some great creative writer, inexorably. I saw his Richard II (Queens, 1938) with an actor who had played in the earlier Old Vic production and regretted the undercurrent of suspicion Gielgud now put into the line: 'Dear earth, I do salute thee with my hand . . .', which before had carried joyous rediscovery. There was excessive stress, too, in his 1934 Hamlet, not all a result of the absurdly exacting run of 155 performances, though wear and tear was obvious at a second visit. Yet at the Lyceum (capacity 2,800), fired by memories of his Terry ancestry and the knowledge that its temple was about to be dismantled, he electrified that great auditorium in the same part. At the New each scene had been separately perfect, without the continuity of progress towards resignation which Ernest Milton so notably projected.

Apparently Gielgud was in his prime in the Haymarket seasons of 1944–45, which I missed on service abroad, but he developed still further, towards a Lear, a Leontes, an Angelo and a Prospero steeped in Virgilian pathos and diluted sunshine. Tynan's conclusion that 'his acting lacks stomach and heart'* is of little use in estimating the process in operation here and would more aptly refer to qualities required of a fighting bull. To end this summary, I need only mention Gielgud's delivery of the soliloquy in *Much Ado*, when the audience knows that Benedick is the victim of a practical joke and he does not. The balancing of it, so as to convey conscious enjoyment of the comic irony while maintaining the illusion that Benedick has been taken in, is beyond the powers of any other contemporary actor.

This inventory of achievement isn't, perhaps, the digression it may have seemed. Negatively, it has exposed deficiencies in the routine output of mid-century revivals, where they rely on the irreducible actor. In a positive sense, it has isolated good diction and intelligence as prerequisites. The models, under present conditions, are elusive, but enough of their work is available on gramophone records to repay close study. Finally, not only from the relative popularity of Olivier and Gielgud, but from the implied attitude of younger practitioners to the masterpieces themselves, one may draw conclusions about mid-century drama in general. It is extrovert, emotional, impulsive, impatient of introspection or deliberation, tone-deaf to nuances and always on the move. In the golden age of the Lambretta, an extreme form of dismissive criticism is to call a performance or a production 'static'.

* *He That Plays The King* (Longmans, Green, 1950), p. 37.

Chapter IV

THE POTENT INTRUDER
American Drama and its Influence

---*---

In August 1959, at the miniature British Drama League theatre in Fitzroy Square, Odets's *Waiting for Lefty* was given two performances under the direction of Charles Marowitz. Sitting next to me was a West End theatrical agent, there to spot talent. The play opens with an irruption of actors into the audience through the pass door, talking loudly, as if they were assembling for a trade-union meeting. When these came in, the agent mistook them for members of the public and indignantly told them to keep quiet. His mistake helped me to reconstruct the impact this play about a New York strike of taxi drivers must have made in 1935, when the Group Theatre first performed it, and also to recapture the thrill aroused by their *Golden Boy* at the St. James's in 1938.

Yet we are now so far from the strenuous political feelings of the thirties that strikes arise from abstruse grievances too trivial to engage the sympathy of those not involved, votes are cast with an eye to luxuries unexpected by the proletariat of those days. Arnold Wesker has already looked back, in *Chicken Soup with Barley*, with indulgence on the generation which was passionate about politics, and Marowitz was careful to describe *Waiting for Lefty* in his programme as a period piece. But on that August evening it still came across with the impact of anger rooted in hunger and the instinct of self-preservation. Heckling from the infiltrators among the audience and the speech of the trade-unionist on the stage conveyed a brutal, sinewy vigour which had survived twenty-four years of political upheaval since the original performance. The declension from this to the exhibitionist hero of William Inge's *Picnic*, in conflict with a desperate schoolmistress whose advances he has repulsed, is steep and depressing; like the

56

decline of the American musical from *Oklahoma!*, which celebrates
the superiority of the farmer to the cowboy, down to *West Side
Story*, a gangster version of *Romeo and Juliet* drawing more of its
vitality from violence than from love.

Sentimentality and violence, opposite sides of the same debased coin, are now on the increase in American drama* to a
degree that reflects favourably on the new English playwrights,
deeply indebted though many of them are to American models.
To my mind Arthur Miller was mistaken in having one man
forcibly kiss another in *A View from the Bridge*, just as Pinero was
wrong to let one of his heroines throw a Bible in the fire. In both
cases the appeal is not of the kind a dramatist wants to exert on
an audience when he is at the top of his form. The type of person
who reacts strongly to such incidents is unlikely to appreciate
anything less frivolous the play may be trying to communicate,
while the others will at once be on the watch for a failure of
inspiration. It is nothing to do with morality, simply a matter of
right and wrong ways of putting an audience on the alert. Although
it contains material of great sociological interest I was quite unable to take *Tea and Sympathy* seriously, because it ended with a
teacher's wife seducing one of her husband's pupils. If the comic
aspect of an episode like that is not to dominate all others, it
should occur while there is still time to quell the ribald associations aroused.

The raping of Blanche du Bois by Stanley Kowalski in *A
Streetcar Named Desire* is in the same class of sensationalism,
because it occurs after the theme of the play and its central
character have been fully explored. It brings us down abruptly
to the level of pulp fiction. So does the prominence of the bed in
the setting of *Cat on a Hot Tin Roof*. As Tennessee Williams is
careful to point out in his notes to the designer, it should be
slightly raked so that people on it can be better seen. Like his
finicky stage directions about details of female dress and its
accessories, these examples illustrate an aspect of Williams as a
playwright which suits the taste of a consumer society content
that its films and television programmes should be mostly directed
at a feminine audience. But the foreground of dramatic action

* ' . . . most playwrights are devoted to dramatizing situations which grow
more hysterical and rarefied with every passing year.' Robert Brustein in
Harper's Magazine, October, 1959.

can absorb only a limited degree of sensationalism without loss of total impact; what was hailed as the century of the common man has become in mid-course the century of the common woman and the playwright is faced with new dangers as well as new subjects.

In American drama the surface agitation we have already noticed in contemporary revivals of the classics now tends to obscure deeper conflicts which are the backbone of O'Neill, Miller and the early Odets. What could be simpler than the dramatic axis of *Golden Boy*: a young man whose hands can both box and play the violin? Once you have granted that unlikely premise, the personal tensions crystallize neatly and something about conflicting ways of life can be said. The framework will carry a great deal of personal emotion, including the refinements of Method acting, as Morris Carnovsky and Luther Adler proved at the St. James's, with little danger of the actors swamping the play. What could be bolder than the notion, in *Waiting for Lefty*, of turning the stage into a trade-union platform and the audience into involved participants? The device automatically produces involvement of some sort, like the question: 'Who are you neutral against?', said to have been hurled by an Irish brawler at spectators on the sidelines. And what could be richer, in contemporary terms of social and moral conflict, than Miller's idea in *All My Sons* of having a manufacturer fit up an entire squadron with defective engines, then wash his hands of the consequences because the cylinder caps *might* have got by, and, anyway, he didn't happen to know the fliers personally? In all these cases the playwright has firmly decided what is to be the centre of gravity, has raised his work above the caprices of directors and future audiences, laid down conditions from which everything else will flow. Whereas in *A Hatful of Rain*, admittedly built as a showcase for Method acting, the interest is in the parade of junky symptoms. In *Orpheus Descending*, *The Rose Tattoo*, *Picnic* and *The Rainmaker* the decline in creative control is a lesser one, but perceptible. All four stem from a sexual catalyst, dropped into the stagnant water of a torpid community. The construction depends on a formula which cannot fail to produce action of a kind, any more than it can avoid novelettish appeal to fantasies of wish-fulfilment such as cling to the ending of *Tea and Sympathy*.

It is a matter of some urgency to make these discriminations, because American drama springs from the society which sets the pattern of life in mid-century England, and is diffused by television and the cinema as well as the theatre. From the social point of view it elucidates our own behaviour and may even determine it. Moreover, it has been ahead of ours for two decades in social criticism, psychology, animal spirits, in all the elements, except acting and classical revivals, which go to make up a mature dramatic art. The London commercial theatre, smugly rooted in economic opportunism, weakened its defences against the new English mid-century drama by letting in on an American ticket work which is radically subversive. Political and sexual taboos were lifted to admit Miller and Williams. Precedent after precedent was established, until the new native drama was able to swim into the West End over obstructive groynes on a high tide. Since few people now in their twenties could have seen any vital new plays not of American, or now and then French origin, it is surprising how quickly some of them, including Shelagh Delaney and Arnold Wesker, have developed an English accent.

For practical purposes American drama has won a place in the European tradition and the playwright's licence to draw on it sensibly is inescapable. The fact that it is, at any rate temporarily, in decline, need not obscure the achievements, of which the most fruitful has been of special relevance to the public art of drama, a genius for *keeping in touch*. First Odets was in touch as a dramatist with the pragmatic thirties, then Miller with the economics of hot war and the fanaticism of cold war. Now Williams, in touch with the primitive urges of half-educated people maladjusted to prosperity, reflects Subtopia and the Beat generation; while O'Neill, posthumously at that, is crowned laureate of the tranquillizer, the romantic dreamer's escape from stimuli too spicy for his digestion.

Meanwhile, in England, many laid their bets on the revival of verse drama initiated by T. S. Eliot and carried on by Christopher Fry. It built up a respectable circulation in cathedrals and training colleges, but has remained obstinately on the margin of public taste in spite of eminent sponsorship. One reason is that the movement was closely related from the start to ecclesiastical policy, for two decades in which churchgoers were a very small minority. It also suffered from an academic approach to theatrical form, and the assumption, common to a similar movement in

America, that the next significant advance would come as an act of grace by the literary establishment, from above, instead of, as actually happened on both sides of the Atlantic, from the working classes. The initial indignation aroused by John Osborne reflected the jolt he had given to that assumption. How seriously the 'poetic revival' was out of touch was clear at the time in Fry's *The Lady's Not For Burning* (1948). Not only was the title and much of the tone lacking in tact at a time of ruthless persecution, but the verbal arabesques, at play above the vacuum where a dramatic situation could have been, were proofs that a promising subject was in the wrong hands. Miller's *The Crucible*, in touch with both contemporary and historical issues latent in the same subject, gave it an artistically richer treatment in plainer words. As in *Waiting for Lefty*, the action would have lost focus if an author's verbal dexterity had been in the foreground. Nobody wants to read a murder trial or a declaration of war in elaborately allusive language.

The spate of imitators in three different media tends to obscure the outlines of Miller's place in the scheme. Hence the necessity to define it again. There is the working-class childhood, the professional education in the drama department of the University of Michigan, and there is the Marxism, controversial, of course, which backs his work with the authority of an intellectual tradition, as well as leading him to points of collision between contradictory claims, between conformity and self-expression, conscience and the profit motive. These qualifications might add up to no more than a blueprint for committed drama of the kind eroded by every change in the political climate, were it not for Miller's ability to perform the initial act of selection so many others evade. He goes in with a scalpel, dissects the morally diseased tissue at the roots of his theme and describes in human terms the damage it does to the body as a whole. There is a parade, not of symptoms but of people exhibiting symptoms, and there is no gloating, nothing like the persecution Williams inflicts on Brick, Blanche and Big Daddy. Everything depends on the kind of relationship Ibsen establishes in *An Enemy of the People*—of which, incidentally, Miller has done an adaptation—between various forms of vested interest and the challenging fact of a polluted sewer. In Miller's plays the direct source of corruption is a specific human weakness: Loman's insistence, disastrous in its effect all round, on being 'well liked', Keller's on pushing family ambitions to an anti-social extreme which even his own son can't accept.

Just as, in Ibsen, Rosmer's weakness turns out unexpectedly to have been the main structural support of the play, because it is plausible, representative, incurable and not wholly unsympathetic, so Miller builds firmly on rifts in the social fabric. Compared with others, four acts of brutally expressive façade enclosing a void, his plays put one in mind of contemporary architecture when it relies for stability on central pillars unseen from outside. Confidence increases the further you penetrate, for Miller has a particle of Ibsen's gift, which Shaw never understood, in peeling away the more rigidly political implications of a subject until we are dealing with human problems no longer limited by the original social context. *All My Sons*, which seems for a time to be developing on the lines of a denunciation of war profiteers, justifies its title by coming out with an attitude, difficult to separate from the Christian one, in favour of extending love and protection beyond the limits of the family. The action of great drama has always been in this sense interior, and a parallel would be with Ibsen's gradual dismissal of its political line-up to the background of *Rosmersholm*.

Having seen Frederick March on the cinema, Albert Dekker on television, but not Muni on the stage, in *Death of a Salesman*, I cannot tell how far the 'turbulent longings' demanded in the stage directions could be acted in such a way as to bring Willy Loman nearer to King Lear and further from Zero, the central figure in Elmer Rice's *The Adding Machine*. Loman, an ageing drummer, is licked from the start and not helped out by anything like the self-assertion O'Neill allows Hickey, his counterpart in *The Iceman Cometh*, before he crumbles. Although this time he seems to have let his diagnosis of weakness weaken the dramatic effect, it may be mere pedantry to fault Miller because he fails to give Loman tragic stature. What has tragedy to do with Subtopia? Perhaps the whole point is that Loman, the main support of the action, is horribly disintegrating before our eyes. His brother Ben, 'the only man I ever met who knew the answers', had to deal with an altogether different set of questions, and Loman, as one of his sons remarks at the funeral, 'never knew who he was'. Lear did.

The limited degree of insight available to such a character, pitiably conditioned, as his creator recognizes, by commercial pressures, is a handicap not only in this play but through the whole range of American drama and of the new English drama as well. I have often suspected that Shaw, so very articulate, was ill at ease in landing himself in *Saint Joan* with the equivalent of an uneducated spiritualistic medium as his heroine; the part lapses badly into dialect and pseudo-poetry. The interest is not in her personally, nor Miller's in Loman. At one point his wife has to say: 'He's not the finest character that ever lived. But he's a human being, and a terrible thing is happening to him. So attention must be paid.' She calls twice more for attention, and it sounds like the appeal a dramatist makes to the audience when he's not quite sure they are with him. Both plays have an epilogue, of course, always something of a let-down because it is in the nature of theatre audiences to resent anything which abruptly destroys continuity and has the flavour of an afterthought. Resolution, following at once on a climax, taps deeper sources of response.

With these reservations, *Death of a Salesman* (1948) is a masterpiece of concentrated irony and controlled indignation. One of Loman's sons throws his father's ethos away after a protracted struggle; the other pursues it in a more corrupt form. Biff, the recalcitrant one, draws his rebellion in Miller's best manner, more from disgust at one of his father's infidelities than from any reasoned objection to what he has been taught. Nothing short of a slur on that universal idol, the American's mother, could have roused this character from his mental lethargy, and a suitable occasion is provided. The idol herself learns nothing; we leave her puzzled because her husband chose to kill himself at a time when they were free from mortgage and hire-purchase obligations for the first time in thirty-five years. Her other son has 'an apartment, a car, and plenty of women. And still, goddammit, I'm lonely.' All this when Bernard, the neighbour whom Loman has taught his sons to despise and who may be a projection of the author, is a happily married executive. Then again, Biff is well suited to life as a cowboy on twenty-eight dollars a week and only resents it when home influence taunts him with failure. The ironies intercross in scene after scene, always in the sense that there exists a mature solution for the problems but that none of this family knows what it is. Loman has seen to that, by transmitting to his sons only the narcissism of a salesman, a target of dollars, and success fantasies born of increasing disgust with his own servitude. Now old age, fatigue, obsolescence and the backwash of his mistakes are brought to bear on him ruthlessly. It would be an ugly sight if Miller were not dissecting a sick society rather than one man.

Altogether the texture of this play, although the lines are austerely naturalistic and the surface action frequently explosive, is of a close-grained allusiveness not to be found in minor works of art. Some of Biff's actions take one straight to known sources of juvenile delinquency; numerous episodes seem to bear out Riesman's sociological findings in *The Lonely Crowd*, and so on. Add this to the constructive ability and moral preoccupations already referred to, which invite some comparison with a master like Ibsen, and the conclusion must be that Miller is a dramatist from whom all others now living could learn something to their advantage.

Fortunately the new English drama shows many traces of his influence, most of which can be inferred from the above analysis by anyone who cares to consult, say, *Flowering Cherry* or *The Entertainer*. To list them in detail would need a book. But one further point about *Death of a Salesman* has to be raised: its scarifying relevance to English life in the year 1960. The ritual washing of the family car, the instalments on the washing machine, 'Do it Yourself', the record album of children's prattle compiled by their proud father, the cliché 'personality wins the day' which lies behind so much television programme planning, the hope that the mediocre Biff may be a late developer 'like Thomas Edison'—by all his carefully selected social debris Miller demonstrates the drift away from values which help a man to know who he is. It is precisely the drift against which the new English drama has to struggle, and a decade later the environment here is the same. Loman, hemmed in by cars and apartment houses, no longer enjoys the urban slave's atavistic escape to his own gardening. He says: 'They massacred the neighbourhood.' In Riesman's jargon, inner-direction has given way to other-direction. Suburbia has become Subtopia.

Nothing I have yet been able to discover in the plays of Tennessee Williams comes up to Miller's combination of social perceptiveness and organically rich dramatic construction. One is always suspicious of an author who repeatedly drives criticism back to defend him in terms of his 'sense of the theatre' or of how much better the American production was; and, in any case, reference to the film versions can rectify many injustices done by faulty interpretation, just as reference to the printed text, especially the flatulent prefaces, tends to confirm defects obvious on the stage. The fact is that Williams is more representative than Miller of mid-twentieth-century taste, as we have seen it coming into focus during our examination of classical acting. Compared with Odets and Miller, who must seem to many of them as remote from their concerns as the Bostonian novels of John P. Marquand, Williams speaks to the young in a more sympathetic dramatic idiom. He deals, for example, in the shock of recognition —two shocks for the price of one in *Cat*, when Brick exchanges a diagnosis of cancer for Big Daddy's diagnosis of homosexuality. Williams is also concerned with every nook and cranny of the immediate stage effect, with lighting, costume and music, insisting in the production notes to *Summer and Smoke* that 'colour harmonies and other visual effects are tremendously important'. One result is that his plays never bore one at a first visit. The stage is alive in the sense that something vigorously expressive is always going on somewhere, if not on the cyclorama, then in the dialogue, and if not there, perhaps in some prop like Blanche's paper lantern or in a snatch of song.

This resembles the way tachiste and action painters animate a canvas with incontrovertible proof of artistic activity. Bursting on the chatty naturalism of the West End commercial theatre's postwar routine, Williams reminded a new generation of many almost forgotten things the theatre is for. He bombards the senses in such a way that attention must be paid; he doesn't ask for it, he grabs it. And these profuse strains of premeditated art are nothing if not expressive. Expressive of what? With that question, which has to be asked, the critic is at once in danger of being called a square, and when that happens his usefulness to the public art of drama is reduced, for he will be assumed to have opted out of the creative energy of his time. In evaluating Williams he will reveal how he is likely to respond to the new English drama, which, apart from direct imitation, draws on the same neo-romantic assumptions, the same cult of primitivism, exoticism and violence. Three considerations, however, lessen the critic's risk of creating a chasm between himself and his readers instead

Finney as Luther
Photograph: Sandra Lousada

Olivier
Photograph: British Theatre Museum Association

Tearle
Photograph: The Times

Gielgud's Prospero (with Doreen Aris)
Photograph: Angus McBean

Olivier's deathfall in *Coriolanus*
Photograph: Angus McBean

All's Well that Ends Well. The court
Photograph: Angus McBean

The camp
Photograph: Angus McBean

Marlon Brando as Stanley Kowalski
Photograph: Warner Bros Pictures Ltd

ANGRY YOUNG HAMLET
Peter O'Toole (with Wendy Williams)
Photograph: Desmond Tripp

Gielgud's Mirabel (with Pauline Jameson)
Photograph: Angus McBean

Jacques Sereys and Micheline Boudet in *Les Femmes Savantes*
Photograph: Bernand, Paris

The Three Sisters, 1940

The Three Sisters, 1958

Serjeant Musgrave's Dance (Theatre Royal, Lincoln, 1960)
Photograph: Hartley Laurence

The Dumb Waiter (Royal Court, 1960)
Photograph: Helen Craig

Arnold Wesker

Photograph: Roger Mayne

Shelagh Delaney

Photograph: Ida Kar, Camera Press, London

Peter Hall

Photograph: Tony Armstrong Jones

Alec McCowen

Photograph: Angus McBean

Ingmar Bergman (with Gunnel Lindblom)

Photograph: Keystone Press

Katina Paxinou

Photograph: British Broadcasting Corporation

of a bridge. Whereas Williams is in his forties and seems to be maturing even less noticeably than Anouilh, with whom he has something in common, his imitators are in an early stage of development, still in a position to pick and choose. Secondly, the best of them are, in my opinion, sounder in their dramatic approach to human relationships already. Thirdly, their attention is increasingly drawn to the Romantic Movement itself, and there is no need to freeze one's responses to that at the level of Mrs. Radcliffe, early Keats and Fuseli.

Drama is about people, and the most humane aspect of Williams as a dramatist is his determination to speak up for the emotionally underprivileged. 'Oh,' says Alma in *Summer and Smoke*, 'I suppose I am sick, one of those weak and divided people who slip like shadows among you solid strong ones. But sometimes, out of necessity, we shadowy people take on a strength of our own.' It is a kind of strength very difficult to render in theatrical terms and perhaps only Chekhov has yet found an acceptable way. Vershinin, of course, is a classic example of the sexual catalyst who justifies the chemical analogy by remaining virtually unchanged himself after the stir he has caused in a backwater. The Moscow Art Theatre now renders Lopakhin as if he, too, had something of this function. One sees how useful the formula is, for shadowy people fall below the minimum degree of outline stage characters normally require if their conflict is to hold an audience. The potent intruder can give them definition in relation to each other and to him. You find him, where the rest of the characters are not shadowy but merely conventional or out of stock, in work as different in other respects as *Amphitryon* 38 and *The Passing of the Third Floor Back*.

The use Williams makes of this formula gives a fair indication of the way in which he has developed from the twilit quietism of his earlier pieces towards an increasing sensationalism. In *The Glass Menagerie* the intruder is treated on the lines suggested by his suburban status as a 'gentleman caller', while in *The Rose Tattoo* he has coarsened into the clownish truck driver who drops a contraceptive on the floor, just as the genteel earlier heroines have given way to strident Serafina, boasting of her late husband's virility. Although there is no longer anything shadowy about either of these contestants, the dust they raise is so blinding that we find it difficult to decide whom or what we are asked to be neutral against. They give us, not the Odets feeling of being caught in a street fight, but the more detached one of overhearing some domestic squabble in a tenement. There has been a gain in turbulence, with less impact than comes from a collision of rival causes.

What is being expressed? What is all the fuss about? In a *coup de théâtre*, Serafina smashes to pieces the vase containing her late husband's ashes, but that only tells us she is now ready for another man. Yet Lea Padovani's magnificently realistic performance in London pointed towards a more interesting statement, towards a creature of abounding vitality running to seed because of primitive Catholicism misapplied ('To me the big bed was beautiful like a religion'). If this is the theme, her scene with the local priest misses a chance to focus it and peters out in Serafina's contempt for local society; and if that is the theme it is sketched, not realized. The suspicion is that Williams is overwhelmed by his own creation and not in control. Instead of enrichments the ambiguities are a distraction, born of episodic profusion which lacks the shape an initial act of selection by the playwright would impose. Are we, for instance, to believe Serafina's claims for her husband? Padovani delivered them rather as one scoring a point against two silly women who accuse her of envying their success with men. You had no obligation to take the claims literally, but the text wants them to be made 'suddenly and religiously'.

Alvaro, the catalyst truck driver, is given here as much as he can handle in the way of dramatic resistance and the hero of *Orpheus Descending* too much. Foreshadowed by the postscript use of the device in *Summer and Smoke*, where Alma picks up a stranger in the park, their loss of face corresponds to a steady increase in rampant femininity, from *The Rose Tattoo* to *Cat*. While the atmosphere of neurosis and sexual privation thickens, it becomes less and less helpful to approach these plays as the investigations of loneliness they are often held to be. The characters are, it is true, lonely people, in the sense of being cut off by repressed instincts clamouring for discharge. They drug themselves with superstition (Serafina) or alcohol (Brick), yet are scarcely shown to be suffering from anything which the appropriate tussle in bed cannot cure. Such predicaments, however robust and complicated the surrounding action may be, bring them closer to the persecuted college boy in *Tea and Sympathy* and his casual mate than to the conscious loneliness of Chekhov's people. Too many human factors are left out, and though Williams relates his characters to the wider social context that affects us all, he tends to make it romantically atmospheric, like the flower-seller in *Streetcar*. How well he could work in another direction he shows in the cash-nexus aspect of *Cat*, which yields more mature results than his melodramatic use of Brick's crutch and the bed. In a different way Pinero can offer the same frustrating mixture of insight and gimmick. But *Cat* leaves us in fatal doubt as to the author's valuation of what takes place. Maggie, the deprived wife, triumphantly asserts her marital rights at last, in reward for the energy and intelligence we have admired throughout. Our assent to her success remains naggingly modified by suspicion of her motives, which seem to include a mercenary greed as repulsive as anything her opponents exhibit. Based on experience of poverty, it is greed rooted in fear and would repay much exploration. This problem is never resolved. Instead our attention is occupied, or diverted, by the jubilant ending of her sexual drought.

In *Cat*, Williams at least got clear of the catalyst formula and shadowy people, the last of whom—Blanche in *Streetcar*—is explored very thoroughly, then lingeringly blotted out. Working in an opposite direction from the former one, the playwright here brings the shadow to the substance. Now it is the shadow of personality stretched to breaking point between gentility and nymphomania, the substance of Stanley's mating call, a popular equivalent of Olivier's howl in *Oedipus*. Although *Streetcar* succeeds in transmitting a *frisson* of one kind or another from start to finish, the sensationalism which invades Williams's later work strikes here very crudely on too vulnerable a victim. The real crisis comes when Blanche confesses her nymphomaniac exploits to Mich, the timid wooer who is her last hope, and he rejects her. After that, there is the dramatically false crisis of Stanley's assault on her, followed by the sadistic episode of her dismissal to a mental home. If Stanley were to be anything more than the most dangerous of many factors working against Blanche's pretensions, then he deserved an opponent nearer his own fighting weight: Serafina or Maggie the Cat. The playwright's exchange of a rose-tinted microscope for a battering ram, at this point in what ought to have been the resolution of *Streetcar*, reflects in one play the decline traceable since in American drama as a whole. Stage violence, except perhaps at the box office, is subject to a law of diminishing returns.

No amount of emotional power, expressiveness in mood and atmosphere, sense of the theatre and eye for the arresting conflict can reach major drama if, as seems to me the case with Tennessee Williams, there is uncertainty or perversity in the handling of human relationships. That is why, though you automatically refer to Ibsen during a discussion of Miller, it is Pinero who comes to mind in relation to Williams. Extended comparison of *His House in Order* with *Cat* might be revealing in more ways than one, but a deeper affinity lies in comic talent very much underrated. To me Blanche du Bois is even more of a comic figure than the wife in *Tea and Sympathy*, with the very big difference that something in the attitude of Blanche's creator connives at such a view. After all, he gives her unlimited supplies of the self-deception and social pretension which lend themselves to a comic purpose. Perhaps that is why *Streetcar*, with its perversely Strindbergian ending, looms in the memory like a monstrous offspring of *The Father* and *Portrait of a Lady*. And comedy is demonstrably within Williams's range. Amanda, the mother in *The Glass Menagerie*, is extremely funny, the author who makes her speak of 'the hand-writing on the wall' an expert in conscious bathos. This talent is on the prowl later in *Cat* and *The Rose Tattoo*, insufficiently nourished. What I believe to be its proper function as a solvent in the lush fertility has been usurped by booster injections of emotion and by an intellect not up to the job.

As we are dealing with a major influence, if not *the* major influence on contemporary English drama, time may have been saved by following Williams to the dead end he seems to have reached. For a decade he has, in fact, occupied the place in theatrical history staked out for itself by the abortive poetic revival. The result is that a new generation of theatre-goers take it for granted that the stage should vibrate with light and busy action, that metrical skill is no substitute for a strong situation, that dialogue is fluent prose enriched by colloquialisms and that poverty is a mine of local colour. All these, except perhaps the last neo-romantic assumption, represent an advance on the tired commercial drama. The exception is revealing, for where the problems treated in *Waiting for Lefty* and *Death of a Salesman* are closely concerned with economic survival and work, the characters in plays by Williams are at grips with an overriding mid-century problem: leisure. They are face to face with themselves and the U.S.A. Since their creator, who has expressed a preference for the Hemingway of *The Sun Also Rises*, has neither the Odets-Miller Marxist discipline nor O'Neill's Freudian solutions to offer them, but only a vague admiration for D. H. Lawrence, is it any wonder that they find each other difficult to live with? Proletarian drama in an era of prosperity drops easily into picture-postcard romanticism or toothless quarrels between the half-educated and the unteachable.

This may account for the surprisingly warm welcome given to late O'Neill when *The Iceman Cometh*, brilliantly directed by Peter Wood, was put on at the Arts in 1958. Here was the old master of neo-romanticism, who had used the ballad 'Shenandoah' in counterpoint to Puritan guilt in *Mourning Becomes Electra* a quarter of a century before, introduced Captain Brand as a sexual catalyst in the same play, anticipated Stanley Kowalski in *The Hairy Ape*, run the entire post-war course of stage neurosis with precise Freudian accuracy, squeezed 'African' local colour till the pips fell out in *The Emperor Jones* and found, in recent history, a suitable soil for Greek tragedy, which is more than Cocteau ever did. And now O'Neill was exploiting the drugged inertia sensationalism takes refuge in as the only alternative to its rioting luxuriance. Younger playgoers at once pronounced his Skid Row alcoholics authentic; they had seen them in *On the Bowery* on the pictures.

The Iceman Cometh is an old man's play, colourless, defeatist, written in the no longer fashionable naturalistic convention about social outcasts who have opted out of reality. Why did it appeal to the imagination of a gifted young director and gain instant success with an alert minority of mid-century theatre-goers? The answer seems to be that all audiences, including the television audience which responds well to Ibsen, develop a craving for dramatic experience organized in depth every bit as insistent as their more obvious craving for surface colour. It is wrong to assume, as commercial interests and creative theatre groups equally do, that any one line of approach to the public can be relied on. Something like late O'Neill or *Waiting for Godot* appears. Then everyone wonders why it takes on, although there is cool jazz as well as hot, the black and white violence of Swedish films alongside Hollywood scarlet, not only Turner but Caspar Friedrich catching all eyes at the Romantic Movement exhibition.

Close to proletarian drama in subject, though not in treatment, *The Iceman Cometh* is a major work which sums up the American achievement and offers a technical standard for the new English playwrights to keep in mind, although O'Neill's pessimism is in the end a crippling subjective limitation which, happily, this young movement rejects. New Orleans local colour and Sicilian squabbles are healthier imaginative diet in the early stages of growth.* Drawn to *The Iceman Cometh* by its documentary authority and the topical relevance of Hickey to the salesman installed by television in their homes, young addicts of drama may still become curious about the play's fascinating use of apparently drab material. Isolate some of the elements in its construction, and we indicate the important place systematic planning can have in the impact of mature drama; we need not harp on it later, in the chapter on Theatre in the Raw.

Apart from the astonishing narrative skill which brings first one and then another of a crowd of sluggish deadbeats into prominence and keeps up the hypnotic motion of creatures in an aquarium tank, O'Neill draws on a modification of the potent intruder formula. Hickey, the salesman who sells the alcoholics a cure which turns out to be worse than the disease, derives from Gregers Werle in *The Wild Duck*, alludes pungently to the wider social context of which Miller is the spokesman, and goes one better by relating its attitudes to those of evangelical religion. Ian Bannen's unctuously glib rendering of this part in the Arts Theatre production reminded me forcibly of Dr. Billy Graham's expert use of mass-media technique on his congregation at Harringay Arena.

Hickey, it turns out, is sucked deeper into the despair he seems to conflict with than any of the others. Such irony has no bottom; but Hickey's behaviour, on which the entire action of *The Iceman Cometh* arches steadily to a climax, is only one of two major themes. The other is the relationship between Larry, the lapsed syndicalist-anarchist, and Parritt, the renegade who has betrayed his own mother and wants to transfer the guilt. Hickey's arrest,

---

* ' . . . the Sicilian, Giovanni Grasso, who exemplified a violent emotional acting that positively stunned us.' *The Fervent Years*, by Harold Clurman (Dobson, 1946), p. 18.

which disposes of one theme, is closely followed by Parritt's suicide, which resolves the other. Larry is in conflict with both Hickey and Parritt throughout, so that the two knockout blows are delivered in harmony. In addition, Larry is an educated man. He still retains enough reasoning power to prevent drab realism from getting in the way of everything else and sprawling all over the action until it becomes incoherent and only shock tactics can beat it into shape.

I do not believe that any reading of the text, which lies on the page repetitively colloquial and colourless, could demonstrate the high quality of such a play. Perhaps that is why O'Neill was so often dismissed by poetic revivalists as too mediocre in diction to merit serious consideration. On the page, he is, and on the page, where much of their own work has since remained, the poetic revivalists were right. The new mid-century dramatists are in a stronger position. Although they have come up from below, with a bias in favour of the cruder stage effects, it has been acquired in the theatre. At least, like their American predecessors, they know where the issues are decided.

Chapter V

THREE COSMOPOLITANS
Brecht, Beckett and Ionesco

———————————— ⋆ ————————————

The aim of Stanislavsky was to make audiences forget they were in a theatre. That of Brecht was to remind them by every possible means, and in this preoccupation he typifies writers who resort to the drama when they have already achieved some status, or at least a personal attitude, in literature: Eliot, Yeats, Claudel, Cocteau, Pirandello, Chekhov, Synge and Shaw. Twentieth-century men of letters approach the drama in the first place as something outside them. Their repugnance for the concessions demanded by an art of the market-place is offset by humility, which comes from finding out how far the pursuit of literature has removed them from the general public. The drama becomes a challenge, a final test for their powers of communication. How many people had heard of Dylan Thomas before the appearance of *Under Milk Wood*?

Inevitably these self-conscious grapples with a resistant medium bring out a sweat of theorizing and other by-products easily mistaken for the end-product, the plays which result; and equally inevitably, the by-products are eagerly seized on by students because they are more accessible than performance and are already in a conveniently malleable academic shape. In terms of what I believe to be the false antithesis between naturalism and vital drama which has persisted for half a century, tidily superficial and plausible conclusions can then be drawn. At this level solemn discussion of Wilder's debt to the Nō plays, Anouilh's to Pirandello, Cocteau's to Sophocles, and for all I know, that of Williams via Gluck to the Orpheus legend, take place. Meanwhile some 'expressionist' fantasy like *Camino Real* may be holding the stage and leaving one convinced that the author is well out of his intellectual depth, or a verse play with the forbidding title *This Way to the Tomb* may have failed to attract as many of the public as a film called *Some Like it Hot*. We might as well be discussing a trial in terms of *obiter dicta* without knowing either the charge or the verdict.

This critical substitute for more precise assessment of drama is now crystallized, like the floating vote of progressive, vaguely dissatisfied, academic or merely amateurish practitioners, on Brecht. Both Martin Esslin* and John Willett† agree that Brecht jettisoned and modified his own theories whenever it suited him. Yet his diffusion was hampered by debates on theory when criticism ought to have grappled with the plays. Even in translation they reveal the breadth, complexity and structural hold of the master Brecht was. You scent his influence everywhere in the contemporary drama and some aspects of the new English work would be unaccountable without it. Fortunately we are under no obligation here to discuss his liking for posters, projections and other eye-catching gimmicks of the expressionist twenties; and if you have ever spent two hours nightly as one of the servants in *Lady Precious Stream,* alongside a property man who smoked cigarettes and dropped paper around to represent a snowstorm, then you may not be bowled over by the oriental techniques either. To the young mid-century drama, however, such things are excitingly new, and Brecht is the channel.

We have seen, from comparison of the poetic revival fiasco with predominantly naturalistic work by Miller and O'Neill, how slight the relevance of formal experiment to mature achievement can be. What matters is the power or complexity of the message, not the origin of the code, although scholars content with lumping Ibsen and Chekhov together as naturalists are probably ill-equipped to probe further. Brecht's subject matter, more even than his technical influence, has an international appeal, because it touches at so many points on the conflicts of a divided world. While Miller's Marxism has clarified his analysis of a superficially stable society, Brecht's Marxism, forged from living in the Weimar Republic amid social bankruptcy in collapse towards Hitlerism, has a more urgent, wider and sometimes looser application, yet a similar effect in hitting on essentials. Thus *Mother Courage* appeared before the Second World War began and

* *Brecht: A Choice of Evils* (Eyre & Spottiswoode, 1959).
† *The Theatre of Bertolt Brecht* (Methuen, 1959).

73

Brecht's use of Far Eastern subject matter anticipated the rise of Communist China.

One result of these interests is that many of Brecht's characters have a crude over-simplification, well illustrated by contrasting photographs of a heroine and a villain in Willett's book, which gives them a period flavour to be found in even the best Soviet inter-war films. Another result of his didacticism is an emphasis on lucid narrative. These disciplines emerge in later work, such as *Galileo* and *Lucullus*, in the form of a mature control and selectivity ultimately more useful to imitators than the expressionist gimmicks which can have limited impact on a public accustomed to Todd-AO and Technirama. From this aspect of Brecht one looks, too, for a corrective to the excesses of neo-romanticism. He seems to know exactly what he is doing in the garishly Byzantine episodes of *The Caucasian Chalk Circle*, for example, and never to let its abundant local colour swamp the action.

Seeing the Berliner Ensemble in this play at the Palace in 1956, I had no doubt that here was the best ensemble acting I had seen in London since the last visit of the Compagnie des Quinze. Here Brecht deploys two long narratives in turn, then makes them intersect. The first concerns Grusha, the kitchen maid who earns the right to adopt an aristocrat's child. She is like a staunch, picaresque heroine of the silent films. Sharing the structural load of the play with her is the rascally scribe Azdak, anti-hero of the second story. He is given not only the off-beat judicial wisdom of Sancho Panza but Brecht's own irony and adaptability. Kept apart until the end of the action, they embody two modes of survival, two wisdoms, of nature and the intellect. To get this message at the Palace Theatre we had to drop the habit of approaching drama as a mesh of clockwork crises screwed up in a room. That would have been too tense an attitude altogether. Sometimes the entire depth of the stage was exploited in balletic weaving movements, much as the Quinze had done when half-a-dozen soldiers represented the Battle of the Marne, and the German actors often projected themselves with the touch of conscious vanity and pride all virtuosi possess. The general effect was life-enhancing, professional in a way unattainable under present English theatre conditions, and about as far as can be imagined from the scruffy charades which often claim Brechtian origin.

Twenty-eight years after it was written, the B.B.C. Third Programme gave a broadcast of *The Exception and the Rule* which offered the chance to estimate Brecht's merit as a dramatic constructor. Two of the characters took pains to inform us that the merchant, racing one of his rivals across the Mongolian desert to win an oil concession, was a very bad man. Deryck Guyler's delivery, the vocal equivalent of raw steak mixed with sandpaper, had already made the point, and the earnest, buttonholing content of the interpolated songs seemed equally repetitive. But the story has enough suspense to satisfy the most square-eyed television addict and steadily peels off its melodramatic accretions until the merchant is left alone with an anxious coolie who cannot find the trail. The distance between these two men is as great as the distance between Prussian militarism and common decency, although their desperate situation might be expected to reconcile them. That is the first ironic statement, and Brecht makes it appear to be an inevitable result of the Capitalist system. The coolie at length offers his tormentor some water and is killed because the container is mistaken for a stone. Estrangement has gone so far that the humane gesture is interpreted as a threat. Irony deepens. Although the facts come out at his trial, the merchant is acquitted on the grounds that nobody could have expected a friendly gesture under the circumstances. Irony is rammed home.

Written in 1930, *The Exception and the Rule* is an example of drama with glib propagandist elements riding on the surface of profound insight and constructive skill. One of its subjects is the cruelty which so very soon afterwards became the rule in Germany. Brecht shows how it can be inflicted and condoned as a matter of course in a society which relegates some of its members to less than human status, and in doing so he draws on the clearly motivated violence which is more acceptable in responsible theatre than violence indulged in sadistically or for surface effect. The merchant resorts to violence only when his life and his winning of the oil concession seem directly threatened.

We find the same basically healthy avoidance of gratuitous violence in *Mother Courage*, where the theme of war might have been expected to invite a return to the sensationalism of the twenties, especially in one to whom the hectic squalor of Döblin's *Alexanderplatz* had been part of everyday reality. Instead we have a statement about war made in what seem to be the only terms which could rescue it from contamination by mass-media treatments of the subject, that is to say, by the exclusion of romantic associations. In *The Life of Galileo*, the statement is about scientific method; that if you block it in one place it will break out in another. Galileo himself shrinks to a senile food-addict who has let the team down at a crisis but still has wisdom to offer. Although Bernard Miles's Mermaid production of 1960 kept schoolboys fascinated for three hours, some older critics mistook the whole thing for a history lesson or an exercise in deflation. It is in fact a model of taut construction which draws its strength from keeping to the point and avoiding theatrical short cuts to effect. Characters neither swamp the theme nor reduce the actor to a Shavian mouthpiece. The effect of suppressed emotion, when a romantically inclined personality submits to vigorous self-imposed discipline, may be one of the lessons learned by Brecht from Büchner.

These examples may have served to illustrate the intellectual atmosphere of Brechtian drama at its best and, more specifically, to emphasize a phenomenon very rare in the twentieth century: the steady development of a playwright in creative, and not merely technical mastery. Few literary artists have chosen the theatre as a preferred means of communication without sooner or later asking, like Shaw, Pirandello, Claudel and even Lorca, for rather more indulgence than the average audience is prepared to give. Other dramatists who submitted themselves to a standardized progress from naturalism through various forms of expressionism have tended to lose fibre on the way and to merge with the entertainment industry. One thinks of Rice and Priestley in this connection; and, higher up, few of us are entirely satisfied with late O'Casey. Reputations have leaked imperceptibly to dissolve on one side into literature and on the other into the history of gestures almost lost in the current of routine commercial plays. Brecht, closer than any of those mentioned to the practical mechanics and professional mystique of the theatre, is the only one of them to have kept ends and means in harness; you might almost say, the only one to have stayed the course.

As renunciatory self-discipline, aimed at the control of material liable to trigger off tawdry responses, Brecht's conception of epic drama makes immediate sense. He begins by distancing *Mother Courage* in the Thirty Years War and dispenses with the unities of time, place and action which, from Aeschylus to Ibsen, have been something more than a pedantic fashion, because they are tested aids to concentration and the softening up of audiences. Thinking, perhaps, that contemporary audiences have been more softened than is good for themselves or the drama, Brecht calls for a considered response. Hence 'alienation', which fits his own intention, invites a responsible attitude answering to his own, and could be a substitute for the religious context of Greek performances or the court context of French classical drama, factors which modify their audience's response to performance and have to be allowed for by the dramatist.

Although Shakespeare's historical epics also renounce devices which have been shown to correspond with the psychological needs of audiences, they exploit the Tudor craving for a stable monarchy and float on a known reservoir of anxieties and hopes. They also gain continuity from the rhythm of short scenes and counterpoint from the double plot. When Brecht renounces this rhythm, too, and hangs self-contained episodes side by side, like exhibits in a gallery, one is entitled to wonder whether he may not be asking too much of an audience. But he lets us have the wagon, an epic symbol hallowed by the cinema, and Mother Courage herself, a traditional stage 'character', as witnesses of Helene Weigel's performance were quick to point out. One cannot entirely rule out prophetic reference to the consumer-society matriarch, her car and caravan, for social mobility was an aspect of our time which Brecht experienced himself. War is very much a matter of dreary journeys and the symbol of the wagon recurs in Ingmar Bergman's films. Both *Mother Courage* and *The Seventh Seal*, though distanced in the past, convey the Second World War's atmosphere time and again. In both, the soldiers, professionally relaxed and cynical, spend most of their time idling in an impoverished countryside, as if battle were an indigestible meal and leisure the time it takes to recover before the next. Brecht, a displaced person, and Bergman, a neutral, are immune from the infantile cult of the fighting man which overtakes almost everyone directly involved in war, and the effect is to make their soldiers more, not less, sympathetic. On the other hand, American stereotypes on the cinema, always anxious to prove something, and English stereotypes, tight-lipped with the effort to avoid subjects taboo on the golf course or in the officers' mess, offend one by their implied ignorance of facts known to every child old enough to have played on a bomb site or begged candy from a G.I.

Party critics in East Germany, so Willett informs us, found the shabby tone of *Mother Courage* particularly objectionable. We may regard them as completing the iron circle of vested interests with a stake in glamorizing war and conclude that Brecht in this play has broken out of it by the most deliberate of creative acts. By abstention from romantic and heroic devices he risks a breakdown of theatrical communication; he goes as far as to withhold the final emphasis which could be made by having Mother Courage reject her means of livelihood, war. Her imperviousness would make sense in terms of the play's structure if she represents the mythical immovable body in contact with war's irresistible force, and she would be one explanation of society's ability to survive the major threat to its existence. Then the austere means to the creative end would be justified, the drabness most theatre audiences instinctively recoil from become positive. We are, in any case, dealing with a bleak, knotty master with whom the only temperamental parallel in contemporary drama might be Betti.

However bad our theatre-going habits have become, however closely we are called on to re-examine them in terms of Brecht and the popular hysterical surface agitation he denies us, *Mother Courage* offers attractive bait to offset its austerity. It seems to be the playwrights of exceptional intellect who create the most Rabelaisian characters. Here is one the great actress Paxinou can have her eye on while her immediate task is Lorca's Mother in *Blood Wedding*. Mother Courage's care for her dumb daughter is an elementary humanizing trait, the daughter herself an orthodox expressionist symbol of passive suffering who at last becomes shockingly active. Brecht, called on by the nature of the subject to make full use of his disciplinary techniques, also makes traditional concessions, loosens his theoretical rigidities in just the kind of creative situation which is apt to leave literary dramatists airborne beyond the ordinary playgoer's reach. Ends and means keep in step.

Naturally it is the means which so far have gained most attention, and everyone must come to grips with the V-effect, or alienation. As Brecht was alive to the dramatic possibilities of professional sport, one may be excused an example taken from football. It was at a match between Tottenham Hotspur and

Birmingham that a boy of about ten years old, sitting behind me, said to his father: 'Mackay, Brown and Jones are all right. I don't think much of the others.' Predisposed in favour of Tottenham, he was sufficiently detached to discriminate between degrees of skill without becoming coldly *dégagé*. The assessment, confirmed by more than one Press report on the following day, remained an audience reaction; he was brightly watching every move in the game as he spoke. Perhaps all that's expected of us is not to leave our brains in the box office.

More specifically, Michael Woods, who played Shu Fu in Hull University's production of *The Good Woman of Setzuan* at St. Pancras Town Hall in 1958, projected the character by three distinct routes. Without a trace of corny buttonholing or hamming he went through the words and motions necessary if the action was to make any sense at all. At the same time he let one know, by various oily smiles and gestures of petit-bourgeois vanity, that here was a type not confined to the Far East, and thirdly, that he, Michael Woods, was holding up Shu Fu to public ridicule in St. Pancras Town Hall and thoroughly enjoying himself while doing so. I take this to be the authentic alienation effect, so near to the normal relationships set up by all skilled comic acting as to be almost indistinguishable from them. The degree of detachment an actor chooses to convey can also, as we have already observed in the case of Fortinbras, be a decisive factor in undertakings greater than the projection of any one character. By stressing this matter for his own creative purposes, Brecht may have cast light on a traditional element in performance neglected by students manacled to the text.

It will be enough if these brief indications of Brecht's technical skill and maturity of attitude have shown him to lie beyond the reach of criticism or sponsorship mainly interested in his political commitment: several supporters of the new English drama use the label 'Brechtian' as a mark of vaguely progressive respectability, to cover experimental techniques in general. This habit limits responsiveness to work scarcely less significant than Brecht's, by shifting discussion away from performance on to a political or philosophical plane. Ultimately it is as lazy and inconclusive an approach as that of the amateurish academic theorizers, who volubly debate alienation and the like without having studied the elementary problems of getting drama across. Criticism, which should enlarge responsiveness rather than restrict it, has raised barriers against the appreciation of experimental drama by such episodes as the Ionesco-Tynan controversy, which told one little about Ionesco's practice and a lot about the personalities of the two contestants. Tynan's notice of *Endgame*, in the form of a facetious parody, struck me as significantly evasive. Nobody can accuse neo-romantic drama of neglecting the Death Wish, but Beckett exploits it without local colour, hysteria or any of the fashionable palliatives and disguises, so that *Endgame* is hangover drama. Probably, the more one is addicted to theatrical riots of the senses, the more intolerable Beckett is.

In illustration of the literary playwright's tendency to become self-absorbed beyond a theatre audience's tolerance, *Endgame* fails in performance because it demands the wrong kind of attention, not because it offers no joy. The sustained monotony and closely interlocking dialogue, virtues at a reading, are too exacting on the stage. Respectful attention is what we give them, feeling cheated, all the same, as if we had come to the wrong address. The pace is so slow that we have time to react cold-bloodedly to Hamm's bloodstained handkerchief, to wonder whether we are being got at; and everything done or said bears the author's signature. It's Beckett again, from minute to minute: an impersonal appearance, so to speak. It might not be going too far to claim that this is theatrically a negative drabness, in comparison with the positive drabness of *Mother Courage* which is arrived at by many conscious acts of exclusion. You sense the indignation, pity and disgust banked up behind Brecht's matter-of-fact tone, whereas Beckett in *Endgame* is so evidently speaking at the top of his voice, so obviously putting everything in. This particular exploration of the human condition, unflinchingly honest and uncompromising as it is, demands more privacy than the theatre permits. There we tend to dwell on the explorer's weakness rather than his lonely heroism, to see only the beads of cold sweat, the fear and the effort. The scale is unsuitable, as it would be in a recital of Leopardi at Madison Square Garden, for Beckett has ignored the limitations of a public assembly. He pays the price of seeming to rely in this play on an intellectual sensationalism as corrupt as the emotional shock-tactics of extreme American drama.

Waiting for Godot avoids this mistake, and Brecht paid it the compliment of planning to write a full length play by way of answer. Although Beckett's means in this case do not go beyond a rehash of Joyce, vaudeville and orthodox expressionism, a sense of theatrical integrity missing from *Endgame* comes over. At the height of the pre-Osborne drought, reactions in England lent *Godot* the fatuous notoriety of 'problem pictures' at the Royal Academy and the play's tour took in Blackpool, like an Epstein in the fun fair. Joycean ancestry gave it immediate status alongside the poetic revival. Yet it communicates its Pascalian interrogation as pithily as a Biblical strip-cartoon at more levels than one. Anyone who can't understand Lucky's speech is entranced to hear him speaking at all, and anyone who can is aware of the ultimate in consumer-society morons, conditioned to respond with the jargon inculcated by his persuaders. Pozzo's self-pitying violence and Lucky's passive suffering have the direct Brechtian validity on stage and are prophetically in touch. We like Lucky better when he doesn't speak. When he does, there are painful associations with children conversing in the slogans of commercial television.

The throwing of a bridge over the gorge which appears to separate Brecht from Ionesco might be thought too ambitious a project and Ionesco has not made it any easier by calling Brecht's "un théâtre de Boy Scout". Nevertheless, I can claim to have chanced my arm on Ionesco earlier than some by giving my opinion* that *The Lesson* might do well at the Palladium just before the Royal Court audiences packed in to see that little coiled spring of contracted violence. The revue-sketch handling of an elderly professor's maniacal assault on a girl student, which serves to disinfect an inherently squalid subject, blinded a number of critics to the play's psychological truth and social relevance. Among other things there are references to brain-washing, to the infantilism of killers so constantly emphasized by knowledgeable crime-writers like Hammett and Burnett, and to maternal connivance in delinquency, here shown in the servant's indulgent attitude to her master's crimes. Something in the English character, from the Third Programme downwards and perhaps in the consumer society's established persuaders everywhere, deeply mistrusts the treatment of serious matters in a comic tone.

Ionesco brings us back to the literary dramatist's dependence on mastery of the medium. He is a most profound, though eccentric

* *Encounter*, April 1958.

student of it, and spent many hours of his childhood watching the Punch and Judy show in the Luxembourg Gardens. Unlike his often frivolous theoretical pronouncements, his practice is altogether too skilled to be neglected on the grounds of 'committed' distaste for avant-garde attitudes. *The Chairs*, however bleak its conclusion, which hinges like Lucky and Mother Courage's dumb daughter on the inability to communicate, is a masterpiece of wide allusion in simple terms, an epic charade. Other literary dramatists of the twentieth century have been much concerned with the nature of theatrical illusion. It is a preoccupation which sometimes throws a smokescreen over the playwright's lack of confidence and always tends to deflect the critic. But Ionesco has probed the matter of illusion to the roots when he can effectively fill the stage, as he does in *The Chairs*, with a crowd of people who are not there. By that capture of the audience's active imagination, Ionesco entitles himself to a place among the contemporary models available to younger writers with other things to say. Like Beckett, he has more in common with Brecht than any classification based on a philosophical estimate would suggest. Brecht, for example, wrote a poem about Weigel's props, and laid great emphasis on the importance of these inanimate things. Montherlant's use of a book, a statue and a dagger in *Malatesta* is exemplary. Ionesco bases an entire play on props in *The Chairs*, and the only midcentury parallel to the giant legs invading a household in his *How to Get Rid of It* is the classical theatre of China's dionysiac dragon. I always enjoy the sight of lofty minds trafficking in such toys. It is proof of a respectful approach to the drama.

Chapter VI

DIRECTORS AND DÉCOR

———————————— * ————————————

Whe director, formerly called the producer, but better described as *metteur-en-scène* or *régisseur*, is the man who makes or mars contemporary drama in performance, in any medium. Therefore it is a fallacy to believe that scholarship and criticism can responsibly ignore his contribution. As we have just seen, the weight of expression may shift at any given moment away from dialogue and gesture to some dead object, to rows of chairs, to Serafina's urn, to Blanche's paper lantern, not to mention Yorick's skull and Bottom's asinine head. Always it must have been somebody's business to see to such things and to regulate the way actors occupy space. He may have enjoyed the status of car-park attendant, drill instructor or monarch assured of precedence, but he existed. Not even Pinero, whose scripts, like Feydeau's, are precise drawing-room choreography, could do without some personal intervention.

Consider what can happen when actors are weakly directed. A schoolmaster, conducting interviews with boys across a desk, turns his chair towards the West End audience, full face in sight, while his interlocutor shows part of a mouth and an eye in profile. A star baritone Mephistopheles sings all the scenes between them upstage of Faust. An amateur Sir Toby persuades Malvolio to interrupt the *Twelfth Night* carousal by entering diagonally from the O.P. corner, less and less of his face in view at every step.

Admittedly we are scraping the barrel for these examples, yet it is surprising how few of the more outrageous malpractices are detected by assiduous playgoers, far less expert than most enthusiasts of sport. Illusion still counts for much, though a vague idea that somebody is in control has developed and we no longer meet with the attitude of the old lady who invited an actress I knew to tea, was told rehearsals prevented it, and asked: 'Do you go through it first?' Many amateurs have now got to know what it feels like to be exposed to the public with only an overloaded memory and a few bits of stage furniture between them and humiliation. They worry about masking one another, about speaking their lines on a falling inflection, about what to do with their hands. Meanwhile the graver risks are not suspected. Their director will send the curtain up on a farce without warning them not to speak through the laughs; he will let them pile so many wrong stresses on everyday phrases that illusion is drained to its dregs after half an hour. The Light Brigade was well briefed in comparison.

Actors in the conformist commercial theatre are given better guidance than the amateurs, at a price. In transmitting either their personalities or the inanities supplied by a popular playwright—for a big success, probably both—they are likely to be in the hands of a diplomat. His business will be to eliminate friction and he will do it very well, so well that nobody concerned, except perhaps the playwright, will learn anything. Not to learn, for an artist of any kind, is to stagnate, to ossify in repetition. That is the danger of the continuous long run and the fate in store for directors too closely committed to the kind of drama which depends on it. Quantitative success breeds respect for the customers who provide it, until finesse within an arbitrary conception of public tolerance is as much as can be achieved. The work of many West End directors and of some of the best repertory directors stops short at this point. They may be better artists than the authors they are called on to interpret, in which case all they can expect is appreciation from a very narrow circle of insiders who can recognize the sleight-of-hand disguising some flaw in construction or poverty of conception. Often they are not so much interpreting as creating piecemeal, within a rickety framework designed by somebody else for a purpose the director himself cannot respect. The actors are probably doing the same, for this is not art but entertainment, an inhibitory flow of calculated concessions—to an actor, an author and the public—which may become habitual. Use of the telephone, plausibility of movement, ingenuity of grouping, changes of mood and tempo, pungency of phrasing, can all witness to great professional skill in productions of this kind. It may have taken the better part of a lifetime to achieve them. Lavished on a whodunit in which the convention may require responses meaningless outside the rules of the game or on a 'starring vehicle' which reduces drama to a refined form of personal publicity, the director's experience is not made use of creatively. The public usually assents to what is effectively his subordinate status by forgetting, or not even bothering to find out, his name.

The moment drama rises above ephemeral entertainment it is in the hands of the director, and so, to an alarming extent, are we. Ultimately, a great drama depends on the author, as playwright, composer or choreographer, and in this sense no director can be better than his material. In another sense, the one in which all drama lies fallow until it is performed, adequate direction is indispensable to it. Imagine what might happen to a recent masterpiece like *The Iceman Cometh* in the wrong hands. The richness of organization O'Neill achieves we have already demonstrated. What he asks of his interpreters is not, we may feel, our business. But his demands are exigent. For more than three hours a drab crowd of alcoholics is expected to hold our attention on a stage drained of primary colours other than those worn by the tarts. Each of these bums is repeatedly to come into prominence and then merge in the squalid ensemble. Hickey, the activator, is to be recognized as such on stage by the positions assigned him in a large group. Larry, among other things an author's mouthpiece, is to be in the group but not entirely of it; so is his persecutor, Parritt. The degrees of perspective required are most exacting, and these are only a few of the visual problems. What about the props? What about the manipulation of glasses and bottles, any one of which can become emphatic? A possible list of breakages in continuity would make any but the coolest of directors take to the bottle himself and would appal the laziest of part-time waiters in an English provincial hotel.

Then there is the dialogue, obstinately naturalistic and almost entirely in an American idiom. Somehow it has to be varied in mood and pace, now given the iridescence of stagnant water and now the viscous turbulence of a whipped-up canal. Peter Wood's handling of all this at the Arts was such as to hold one's interest from point to point and still leave the play's majestic inner structure as explicit as the central supports of a skyscraper before the floors are hung on. In other words, it was worthy of the author; and when that is achieved with a major dramatist, the director has ceased to be entirely a subordinate. Like the perceptive literary or theatre critic, he has to some extent retraced the creative path his author took. Unlike them, the director is necessary to the effective continuance in being of the work of art concerned, for by its nature as a theatrical project it cannot function without his intervention. There is no need to point out what would happen to *The Iceman Cometh* if its performance were left to the results of negotiation between the actors. Two directors, unless the degree of collaboration were superhuman, would be equally disastrous. It is one man's job, and he needs for it a combination of critical and technical skills which, applied to worthy material, entitle him to the status of a creative artist. This does not hold good for anyone else concerned in drama other than the playwright and, exceptionally, the actor. Again I am assuming that drama is about people. If so, it follows that décor is a means to an end and that Picasso himself would be subordinate to Massine in staging *The Three-Cornered Hat*. Roger Furse constructed a winding staircase on purpose to aid Olivier's conception of Osric's interview in the *Hamlet* film. It is the correct relationship between the designer, no matter how eminent, and a play's director.

Wood's direction of *The Iceman Cometh*, followed by a respectable staging of Schiller's *Mary Stuart*, illustrates the range to be expected of a creative director and also leads to the axiom that this position requires a high standard of academic education. Press coverage of star directors tends to concentrate on their mastery of the modern theatre's exciting technical resources, which run from stage machinery proper, by way of lighting, to the latest experiments in recorded sound. But whether these amount in the end to anything more than sophisticated gimmicks depends on the use made of them by one artist, the director, interpreting another, the playwright. This is no sphere for the half-educated trouper or the inspired technician, and the mid-century drama in England is enriched by a constellation of directors with an academic background behind them. Tyrone Guthrie, Michael Benthall, Hugh Hunt, Peter Brook and Tony Richardson were at Oxford, Peter Wood and Peter Hall at Cambridge. Each one of them is equipped to grapple with problems of meaning and literary intention beyond the average actor's competence. Joan Littlewood, who won scholarships in painting and drama and had a long spell with the B.B.C., draws authority from a compound of Marxism, Nonconformist radicalism and respect for models as varied as

Harcourt Williams, Saint-Denis and Brecht. Considered as educators, illuminators and stimulators of the prosperous, but often bemused and passive mid-century public, these are among the key names of our time. I see them as champions of the good life, against the false values explored in *Death of a Salesman* and sedulously fostered by the mass-media persuaders. When Miss Littlewood speaks of actors being as necessary to the community 'as bread and wine and libraries' she states a fact taken taken for granted by most governments abroad.

Bread and wine on the Costa Brava, then back to the assembly line and a tramp round the Useful Arts section of the public library in some conurbation, on your way home through the smog to the telly—that sequence recurs in so many lives that the contemporary director cannot disregard it. In England he, too, must be a visual persuader, until more efficient State education, the volubility of the younger dramatists and his own example have spread a 'Do it Yourself' attitude to language widely among the newly-rich proletariat. It is true that the square-eyed hear the recorded conversation of Bertrand Russell and A. J. P. Taylor as well as a flow of language prostituted to commercial use, but they can't ask a question or answer back. Nor are they likely to switch off when one item is finished and form the small discussion groups which crystallize among dispersing theatre audiences. Trailer announcements or one person's interest in the next item usually prevent that. They are set in their ways, their own powers of conversation held in abeyance, usurped, and the theatre director has tended to distrust his ability to hold their attention by means of dramatic speech. This negative attitude to speech, arrived at in deference to the limitations of the mid-century audience, has been abetted by the positive trend of the last two decades towards balletic ensemble, a thing of intrinsic beauty and vitality. Michael Elliott's direction of *As You Like It* in 1961 went some way towards a literate fusion of moves, décor and text. Yet Vanessa Redgrave's extravagantly praised Rosalind, a splendid first attempt, was only a shadow of the high spirits and sexy humour the lines convey time after time. There is no short way to success with Elizabethan dialogue.

As we shall see, English directors were aware of this deficiency, at least where it stuck out inescapably from revivals, by the summer of 1959, and, from Guthrie to Hall, John Barton, Toby Robertson and Michael Croft, gave signs of overcoming it. At this level we are not dealing with incompetence, but a maldistribution of the director's creative riches, one of criticism's more enjoyable tasks. Of two equally spectacular Shakespeare revivals at Stratford-on-Avon, for example, which is preferable: Douglas Seale's *Much Ado* of 1958 or Guthrie's *All's Well That Ends Well* of 1959? The settings for both were designed by Tanya Moiseiwitsch with sumptuous elegance and shifted the period more than three centuries forward from Shakespeare's time. Yet one of these productions, although it made a colourful and civilized evening's entertainment, seemed to me a glossy burlesque and the other an intelligent contemporary restatement of one of the Bard's less successful works. Call it the difference in relation to the original between elaboration and collaboration.

Several acquaintances thought my notice of *Much Ado* was guilty of being too elaborate, but the terms of reference were laid down by the production itself, beginning with a programme note about Verdi and Puccini. Redgrave turned in a Benedick like one of Manet's reclining dandies who look at you with lazy indolence as you walk past their elongated frames in a picture gallery. I found it enchanting until he had to speak the words 'on my allegiance', guaranteed to put Renaissance audiences in a dither of apprehension, from a lounging position, seated while his overlord stood up. Beatrice, in the society of jaded wine-bibbers aquiver with epaulettes and unlikely to tolerate a virgin for any length of time, could not deliver her bawdier witticisms without sounding like a dissolute woman with more experience and staying power than her friends. Her dress and her surroundings, the period in general, worked against the type of person Beatrice is and the things she has to say. Horns and marl, the comic Shakespearian subsoil, were sprinkled around in the conversation uncomfortably. They were no more appropriate to this salon than mud off the gardener's boots. When we came to the Dogberry episode, social realism which still holds good for a type of Englishman obsessed by the enforcement of regulations, the visual emphasis on Messina was hopelessly distracting. Beautifully disposed though they were, I could not tell what was gained by the display of onions, Chianti bottles and rococo volutes, other than irrelevant allusions to espresso bars and continental holidays.

The result of Seale's immensely accomplished, but in my view misapplied direction was enlightening, all the same. The one undoubted success was Richard Johnson's Lermontov version of Don John, which revealed the director's essentially romantic approach to his material and was an enterprising transference of Tudor misanthropy to a later period of history. *Much Ado*, however, is obstinately rooted in Castiglione. Too intense an approach, by way of the villian's envious destructiveness, obscures the condemnation of Don John's breach of courtly etiquette when he devises a stratagem at the expense of a woman's good name. When Benedick says of his own wit, 'It will not hurt a woman', he is pointing to a major conflict of attitudes, even, perhaps, to the contrast between Machiavelli, as understood by the Tudors, and the aristocratic ideal. Since a play as deeply embedded in Renaissance habits of mind as this one is not lightly to be set in an environment where they no longer have currency, Seale's production compared unfavourably with Gielgud's, which was slanted in favour of the traditional duet between Beatrice and Benedick, dressed in period, prettily set without intrusive ornamentation and founded on the easy good manners Castiglione insists on all through *The Courtier*. The impression was that, to return to the definition of a director as key intermediary between author and public, Gielgud had appreciated *Much Ado* as closely as Wood was to appreciate *The Iceman Cometh*.

In the case of *All's Well*, you might, at some risk of encouraging a disrespectful handling of minor masterpieces, welcome Guthrie's uninhibited face-lifting operation, performed on a text admittedly corrupt and sagging in many places. As I have always found Boccaccio's *Giletta di Narbona* one of his most boringly didactic fables and think few of us would willingly attend any performance of *All's Well*, it seems to me that here is a promising field for experiment, Shakespearian insight being only fitfully present. Guthrie's direction went all out for three bridges between *All's Well* and a mid-century audience: the predicaments of a dying man, a jilted wife and soldiers on service abroad. He cut characters out, telescoped others, dressed his soldiers in the khaki drill tropical kit and black berets of something very like an Eighth Army tank regiment, his court in Edwardian styles. When an equivalent of the 'Tudor' inner stage was called for, it would appear as a little French drawing room or an Italian hovel, furnished for naturalistic acting. In the army scenes, soldiers would openly wheel it on.

For the vital business of casting, individual acting and the deployment of courtiers and soldiers, Guthrie's inventiveness was matched by an intuitive sympathy with mid-century taste. The line-shooting post-war *miles gloriosus*, target for Amis and Osborne, was here vested in Parolles, who flaunted a handlebar moustache, canary pullover and striped tie. Cyril Luckham gave him the right slurred and nasal accent, filed his nails during a conversation with Helena and after his exposure declined to the abject seediness of Graham Greene's Minty in *England Made Me*. Wherever a choice was open to Parolles he wore the wrong clothes; among the muted greys and blacks of the ceremonial uniforms, it was a scarlet jacket on the way to a faded orange. Social satire was transmitted visually by the resources of a crowded stage. One of the courtiers resembled photographs of the younger T. S. Eliot.

Helena's love, her devotion to Bertram, the young sprig who despises her, exceeds its object in a way little short of disastrous to both Boccaccio's story and Shakespeare's play. Guthrie dealt with it by casting Helena sympathetically in the person of Zoe Caldwell and giving her earlier scenes with her guardian, the Countess, a distinctly Chekhovian background. Possibly in conscious parody of the Moscow Art Theatre's set for Act IV of *The Three Sisters*, Miss Moiseiwitsch provided a background of wan, leafless trees and a summer house. Rinaldo, the steward, was played as a doddering old family retainer in the last tremors of senile gentility, rather on the lines of Fiers in *The Cherry Orchard*. It all seemed a plausible environment for the sprouting of Helena's passion; for it made Bertram's youth, no matter how closely allied to arrogance, an attractive contrast and obvious escape route. Guthrie's direction of the illustrious Evans, as the Countess, was ingenious. Sometimes he used her face as a reflector. The play of its expressions pointed and enriched the effect of Helena's gushing speeches while Evans sat listening to them in full view of the audience, an ageing aristocrat, caught like Prospero in the crossfire of memories we endure when impulses tamed in ourselves reappear on the doorstep with our children.

At the other extreme of expressiveness from this fine grain of sensibility was the uninhibited burlesque of the military episodes in a modern idiom. It was mainly on the stereotyped lines of *Sergeant Bilko* or *The Army Game* on television, but carried off with unflagging high spirits, right down to the failure of the public-address system before the Duke of Florence's pep talk. Having assisted at ceremonial parades abroad in uniform almost identical with that worn in this production of *All's Well*, I was able to savour the detail. Guthrie, for instance, had noted that the ridiculous aspect of such occasions is seen in the inspectors rather than the inspected. When a microscopic stain was found on one soldier's kit, it was the gawky, bending attitudes of the commanders he emphasized and the vulgar triumph of the warrant officer who took the offender's name. The slow march, in shorts a hopeless anachronism, was not spared; neither was the over-zealous type of salute, properly assigned to Parolles, nor the idiocy of compulsory cheers for a V.I.P. There was also inspired contrast: in the technician in charge of the public-address system who looked down from his platform contemptuously as the parade assembled, wore the same uniform as the others, but in a state of squalor, and smoked a cigarette like the property man in Chinese drama. If not exactly Brechtian, the approach to these episodes was certainly expressionist, and as they draw what cohesion they have in the original mainly from the trick played on Parolles, already defined in mid-century terms as a tempting target, Guthrie was within his rights in setting the tone by that. Without departing from the cynical tone established, he was also able to gain sympathy for Bertram's pursuit of Diana, the Italian girl Helena adroitly replaces in bed, by presenting it as the compulsive act of a young officer tortured by continence on active service. Angela Baddeley made of Diana's mother a memorable grotesque, and I would not put it past Guthrie to have had in mind deliberate parody of *Mother Courage*.

Chekhovian and then pseudo-Brechtian in two of the main themes selected, the direction was at its firmest, though least obtrusive, in the third theme, that of the King of France, supposed to be incurably ill. Spectacular ensemble was used to project beyond any doubt that the man really was a king, someone breathing the air of protocol, power and the caprices attending on them. Naturalistic acting and direction showed that the King was a man. It was as simple as that. Within the clear intention one was at liberty to recognize Guthrie's mastery of the expressive means involved. The grouping, to begin with, was balletic in its variety, precision and plastic sense, but never merely pretty or exhibitionist. If you cared to notice them, the paralytic tremor of a be-medalled courtier or the degrees of scandalized reaction to despotic caprice were details to be savoured at repeated viewings. They never swamped the action, which relied here on the kind of direction which takes effect unobtrusively. The King, for example, having begun in a Bath chair, took part in a dance when he had recovered. In the final altercation with Bertram it was the rejuvenated King who covered stage ground in long, excited strides. As Bertram, young Edward de Souza had little more to do in these court scenes than take up the positions assigned and look handsome, sulky and detached. Nobody, least of all Shakespeare, gives him much say in the necessary unravellings of a tiresome plot, and at one time Guthrie had him standing with back to the audience on the brink of the stage, watching the stately proceedings like us. The exception, his unexpected refusal to marry Helena at the King's first command, came over as the reflex action of any young man of the Edwardian period asked to wed a family dependant. So much for the spectacle. As for the naturalistic realization of the King, an aged man with more energy than anyone else in his court, it hinged on an actor, Robert Hardy, young enough to have played David Copperfield only a short time before. During Helena's eloquent plea about her remedy for his illness, he went on scrutinizing documents without looking at her until she annoyed him. Then he lifted up a hand bell to call for her removal, held it poised as she began to convince him. The turning point of the scene was marked by a most restrained action: his slow putting down of the bell.

In order to distinguish between the artistic function of direction and its external mechanics and embellishments, we have spent some time on the virtuoso handling of an uninspiring play. The points to bring home are the mastery of several styles and the critically informed estimate of the text which leave this production outside the category of wanton experiment and make of it a creative act. It is the work, if you count that of Craig and Granville Barker as incompletely carried out, of the greatest director yet to emerge from English drama. The strength and the weakness of all but the very youngest of mid-century directors broadly resembles his. That is one of many reasons why mid-century revivals leave out what Castiglione stands for, why verse is mangled and visual appeal emphasized. Directors have kept up with Guthrie's faults, especially those inherited by disciples such as Michael Benthall, and been deprived of any National Theatre which could have shown how those faults become virtues in collaboration with actors like Olivier or in Guthrie's later work, spread between Edinburgh, Tel Aviv and Ontario. One need not point out the abuses open to his *All's Well* approach if it were misapplied.

An extremely unkind decoding of Guthrie's conversion to open-stage production would read it as an admission of failure to get Shakespeare generally well spoken by English actors in English theatres, in both of which tasks Harcourt Williams succeeded, and to rely on Canadian audiences only too glad to hear the classics spoken at all. A visit to Edinburgh, at any time in the past decade when *The Thrie Estaitis* was on, would go far to offset the suspicion—and it is a disgrace that a Londoner should have to travel so far. What Guthrie had achieved became clear to me when an Oxford graduate in the train back explained that she had studied Lindsay's text of 1540 and been left with no desire to see it performed. As directed by Guthrie, it was, of course, irresistible. Entrances made down the aisles, actors within touching distance, are not intimate in effect as many advocates of this type of staging maintain, any more than the boxing ring is intimate. In fact, Guthrie's production of Priestley's *Dangerous Corner*, near the start of his career and on a picture-frame stage, probably conveyed the illusion of intimacy far more closely. Involvement is what occurs on a good open-stage production, as in *Waiting for Lefty*, and when Correction made his entrance in *The Thrie Estaitis* the entire audience seemed to share the alarm of gamblers interrupted by the police in a vast, illegal casino.

Distress was slightly reduced by the fact that the lances of Correction's escort were all pointed towards the revellers on the stage, three couples interlinked a few seconds before in the untidily vulnerable attitudes of sensual exhaustion—I would have given a lot to have heard Guthrie directing them—and relatively static, a state as ominous in one of his productions as the meditative passages of Olivier's acting. When Correction came in, it was down one of the aisles to a *fortissimo* from the orchestra, reinforced by the Assembly Hall's organ, held in reserve for this purpose, and a visual blaze of soldiers with lances and pennons. He was Tom Fleming, looking taller than his actual six feet one and wearing grey robes in contrast to the vivid colours everywhere. While two sergeants stood guard over the twin doors under the gallery, the men-at-arms rested their lances on the platform stage and their feet on the steps leading up to it. A deep, static silence pressed down. Then Correction, speaking the beautiful Middle English lines very quietly in a rich Scottish voice, began telling us who he was. Guthrie was demonstrating what can be done by the spoken word.

It is not from lack of data on other directors that so much of this chapter has been devoted to him. Two at least of the younger ones, Hall and Wood, saw Guthrie's Old Vic seasons at the New in boyhood and regard them as crucial experiences. Understand the practice of Guthrie, now sixty years old, and you have a standard for appreciating the others. They have learned much from him. But for the inaccessibility of his work of the past decade they would have learned more, for they are fantastically adaptable and energetic, continually on the stretch between television, the cinema, executive duties and the basic art of interpreting plays. Since the risk of becoming virtuoso entertainers bears as heavily on them as on the new dramatists, one wonders how much time they have to draw on the wisdom of colleagues like Glen Byam Shaw and George Devine, disciples of Saint-Denis.

At the Royal Court, Tony Richardson has developed a personal style, often in collaboration with Loudon Sainthill's décor, which includes garish neo-romanticism and a strident naturalism of the kind practised by such painters as Middleditch and Bratby. Raw, vociferous and highly emotional, it has close affinities to the Method, which we are to discuss in a later chapter, and is a theatrical equivalent of the scarlet and white sticking out of a Bratby canvas when he models a Lambretta in squeezed ribbons of paint. It suits the new drama admirably. To *Pericles* at Stratford-on-Avon, it gave a necessary face-lift, but in *Othello*, miscast and misrepresented on the lines of a Cassio with a northern accent, Richardson's style rang false. Yet he directed *The Lesson* with electrifying impact, typically reduced by making the professor instantly formidable, instead of inflating him slowly from mouse to murderer.

Miss Littlewood's mastery of Brechtian ensemble has been handicapped by an inability to pay Brechtian salaries and by the commercial theatre's greedy eye on her company as a source of

talent. Otherwise her limitations as a director seem to be mainly
self-imposed on a Marxist basis. She has not touched Ionesco,
and wherever I have seen an aristocrat in one of her productions
he has been guyed. This leaves a fatal gap in a minor classic like
The Dutch Courtesan, in which one character's Hamletish misogyny
is a major theme. But Miss Littlewood avoided working in the mass
media until her style was formed, is a creative collaborator with
new playwrights and is accepted abroad as the practitioner of an
international style.

By 1959 much critical sniping at the misuse of spectacle in
revivals had made heightened speech a problem which Hall,
Benthall and Guthrie himself, among others, were ready to discuss. Brook, in productions of *The Winter's Tale*, *Measure for
Measure* and *The Tempest*, had shown how a young director
addicted to spectacle could manage verse increasingly well by
working with a star Shakespearian, in this case Gielgud. Some
appalling travesties were still to be seen and heard right into 1962.
At most revivals to listen was a penance. It wasn't music that was
lacking, so much as the logical pointing of words in a speech. Down
came emphases at random; bubbles of 'inner feeling' broke up the
most obvious rhythms of the text. If anyone had done such things
to an opera score there would have been riots. Almost everybody's
breathing had become too gusty to supply the needed legato.
Directors seemed to have lost confidence in Shakespeare, but in
1959 one production measured up to him.

As it turned out, the reappearance of Olivier in *Coriolanus* was
not just a symbolic meeting of his achievement and Hall's promise.
It marked a noticeable improvement in Hall's own work as a
director. True, he had saddled himself and his actors with a set
of cramping verticality, all stairway, platform and Tarpeian rock,
which left no horizontal plane big enough to permit surging progresses, reduced the mob to a handful of individuals and made
the storming of Corioli seem a strategic impossibility. Why? To
echo Guthrie's recent enthusiasm for grouping at different levels,
to please the Memorial Theatre's upper-circle patrons, already
treated to an exceptionally good view of Desdemona's bed by
Richardson, or simply to induce vertigo in the cast of a play rooted
in insecurity? Boris Aronson's stage architecture did at least
convey an archaic savagery of pre-classical columns, cavernous
doorways and angry bronze, while Michael Northen, foremost of

English lighting experts, linked the necessarily abrupt goings off and comings on.

Hall's major success lay in basing the action on four human supports: Olivier, Evans, Harry Andrews and, graduating in such company for the first time, Anthony Nicholls. In terms of our discussion about revivals, this meant that, where the play can no longer be entrusted to ensemble and depends on the autonomous actor, it held firm. The weight laid on Andrews as Menenius was exceptional for that part, and most impressive in effect. So was the verbal animation of comic passages often scamped in revivals of this play. If a former pupil of F. R. Leavis took to directing classics after a thorough grounding in theatrical practice, this was the kind of stimulating result you might hope for.

In the shifting of emphasis a little away from spectacle towards a dramatic projection of language, this production of Hall's confirmed a trend already discernible elsewhere. The Marlowe Society had given performances within the past year of *Edward II* and the two parts of *Henry IV*, all three of which, more or less under the influence of George Rylands, that connoisseur of speech, were vigorously and intelligently spoken and mounted with a minimum of visual fuss. Then, in the summer of 1959, which also brought Gielgud's recital, Olivier's Coriolanus and Wesker's *Roots* before the public, the schoolboy actors of Michael Croft's Youth Theatre made a West End success in *Hamlet*. They played it briskly and vigorously in the spatial freedom of an uncluttered stage, projecting the verse with an evident relish that kept me happy indoors on a hot August afternoon. By 1962, Croft was perhaps the best Shakespeare director at work. Starting from a nucleus of Alleyn's School pupils his company became a true ensemble. Such tests as giving *Hamlet* at the Théâtre Sarah Bernhardt matured the leads quickly and they went on acting for the Youth Theatre during drama school and university vacations. One of them, Richard Hampton, was a memorable Richard II at the age of 21.

The director of Shakespeare has three chief means of interpretation: verse, grouping and the management of crowds. Again and again, notably in the closing episodes of *Henry IV Part II*, Croft showed his mastery of all three. No doubt he would take time to do as well with an *ad hoc* company set in bad habits. If he can keep his ensemble together, or develop another one, it will be to the enormous benefit of acted Shakespeare.

To transmit a playwright's message through actors to an audience demands a rare combination of insights, technical, critical and creative. Sometimes, as in Croft's case, they may skip the orthodox ladder of promotion and appear, fully developed, from an unlikely quarter. Michael Elliott, Benthall's successor at the Old Vic, is an expert television director; David Thompson has had successes with Euripides, Ford and Alun Owen, wrung from mediocre casts at fringe theatres. These three combine literary discrimination with a fierce mid-century theatrical idiom. Rounding off a constellation of ace directors, ready to take over new playhouses as soon as they spring up, we can add William Gaskill, John Dexter and Anthony Page, all of whom have worked at the Royal Court and reflect the style evolved there by Tony Richardson.

Chapter VII

THEATRE IN THE RAW
The New English Drama

———————————————*———————————————

I f there has been some agreement with the discriminations in relation to American drama attempted in Chapter IV, several aspects of the new English work, including its primitivism, neo-romanticism, sensationalism and reflection of mid-century social pressures, will call for only incidental reference here. By the time these words are in print some of the new playwrights will have advanced; others will have receded or been sucked into the process which moulds the writer to the entertainment industry, surrounds him with the material comforts he once despised and redistributes him as a credit title among the other technicians who serve the profit motive. People say: 'Young writers have never had it so good', thinking of the overnight fortunes amassed by Osborne, Delaney and others. Having it so good so young can, of course, from the point of view of creative writing, be fatal. Yet if none of these playwrights should ever work for the theatre again, they already constitute a movement which has enriched English drama and will have to be taken account of by students. It is not the business of criticism to lay bets on their future.

Not forgetting, then, the influence of American drama, which offers answers to many problems arising from the Americanization of mid-century England, or the pioneering by Leftist groups like Theatre Workshop and Unity, I have no doubt that the credit for launching the movement should go to the English Stage Company, based on the Royal Court and founded with the avowed intention of encouraging new playwrights. Within three years the Royal Court had developed tiresome mannerisms, fallen at times to the amateurish ineptitude of an experiment like the pseudo-Brechtian *Eleven Men Dead at Hola Camp* and given the popular press many a pretext for its favourite habit of deriding the arts. The fact remains that it was the Royal Court which made the breakthrough with John Osborne's *Look Back in Anger*. It was submitted through their normal channels in 1956, read by George Devine, their Artistic Director, whose experience of European drama in association with Saint-Denis scarcely revealed a destiny as patron of Porterism, and accepted for production. The content of the play is such that it would have stood not the slightest chance of acceptance by any front-line theatre in Central London in 1956. In effect it would have been censored, not by the Lord Chamberlain but by the managements, on the grounds that it departed too far from their estimate of public taste to warrant the gamble of production. How wrong they would have been was quickly shown by the success of an excerpt on television, which boosted receipts at the Royal Court in time to rescue the entire English Stage Company venture.

Aside from Devine's act of selection, the breakthrough had been achieved strictly from below. It is most unlikely that the founders, Lord Harewood and Ronald Duncan, with a hopeful eye on literary establishment figures like Angus Wilson and Nigel Dennis, can have anticipated a shot in the arm for drama by way of a Redbrick failure who calls his brother-in-law 'the straight-backed, chinless wonder from Sandhurst' and derides the sacrosanct intellectual weekly papers. The historic Court Theatre seasons of 1904–7, in so far as they involved Murray, Masefield and Galsworthy as well as Shaw and impinged on the building's recent tradition of Pinero farces, were high-toned affairs. Half a century later, Eliot, who had once hit on a great contemporary theme* in *Murder in the Cathedral*, seemed resigned to addressing the more genteel West End audiences in verse they could no longer distinguish from prose. But something was banking up under the stodgy surface of life in mid-century England. While elections came increasingly to depend on the floating vote of white-collar workers uncertain what social class they belonged to, politics were conducted by Conservative and Labour spokesmen, sometimes from the same public schools, in the manner of arguing lecturers at the London School of Economics. It was not the State but the working class, having benefited from wartime mobility and post-war welfare legislation, which was withering away. Hunger, the prime mover of all radical politics, was no longer a major issue. It

* cf. Cardinal Mindszenty.

was soon to be replaced by galloping consumption and the era of organized greed. People were growing up to whom *Waiting for Lefty* was a period piece, war heroes a bore, the Royal Family an institution exploited with tawdry philistinism in the less literate magazines, the British Empire a dangerous fiction which got their brothers killed in Cyprus. State education was giving more and more of such people the intellectual equipment to criticize the society they had to cope with, and they were beginning to use it. Unless they intended to devote their lives to some form of artistic activity in England, hunger was something other people, in undeveloped countries, suffered from. Much more of a threat, to well-fed young people taking material welfare for granted, would be the known danger of nuclear destruction. Self-preservation would incline them to put that political issue above all others, certainly above the stresses of a shrinking empire.

People tend to rationalize their dislike of things which get in their way. 'Hell', in Sartre's words, 'is other people.' As parents get in the way of the young in any society, we shall not be surprised to find them targets of the new English drama, as they had been of the American. The Establishment, however, is a specifically English concept, the existence of which has to be taken account of if we are to distinguish these playwrights from their transatlantic masters and colleagues. If something of the kind, an élite with formidable powers of adaptation—enough to recruit two poets of pre-war Leftist sympathies to post-war professorships at Oxford —really does exist, it would function in a manner to be understood only by insiders or by people on close terms with aristocratic tradition. If it doesn't, it would be a convenient scapegoat for the frustrations of any impatient arriviste. Hence, perhaps, the contempt which mixes with any sympathy we feel for the hero of *Look Back in Anger*. The sympathy is aroused by Jimmy Porter's generous impulse towards a loyalty beyond the bourgeois family ideal. He shares his home with a friend and grieves at an old woman's death. His ill-treatment of his wife can partly be condoned as the by-product of a collision of values; she, after all, has been cradled in privilege and should, in theory, have the wider human sympathy. But his job selling sweets in a market seems a self-imposed misuse of education, a gesture of self-pitying exhibitionism. He is less angry than petulant, a reincarnation of Mackenzie's Man of Feeling in a Bratby setting. If the Establishment exists, we are not satisfied that it is sacrificing anything indispensable by excluding Porter; if not, then he is a failed arriviste with a chip on his shoulder. Three years later we are to feel much the same about Walter Lee in *A Raisin in the Sun*, a Negro chauffeur whose only criticism of the dollar philosophy arises from the fact that he resents his employer getting a bigger cut. Both Osborne and Lorraine Hansberry are putting a valuation on their characters above what is made good in the theatre.

Although *Look Back in Anger* may date as quickly as Coward's *The Vortex*, just as *The Entertainer* is a kind of *Cavalcade* in reverse, it tapped sources of resentment which could be turned to creative theatrical use. A young Australian painter brought up in a remote mining community tells me that Porter's sardonic quotations from the Sunday papers at the start of the play gripped his attention instantly, because they expressed feelings which he had long been disturbed by himself. This artist, who has worked in an advertising agency, scorns civilized leisure in England as 'pottering about in a rose garden under a leaden sky', admires the neo-romantic novels of Lawrence Durrell, enjoys the most lavish Stratford-on-Avon embellishments of Shakespeare and considers Mary Ure the ideal contemporary beauty, is of working-class origin and represents the livelier elements in a mid-century audience. What he found in Osborne was a kind of safety-valve, a spokesman of protest. But I think we can already claim two dramatic, as opposed to sociological virtues in Osborne: his diction, and his compassionate rendering of characters he believes to be misguided. In repertory theatres all over the country Porter's tirades, longer than anything recently tolerated in English plays for the commercial market, were listened to with rapt attention even by people who strongly disapproved of him. The Colonel, his father-in-law, who might so easily have been a stereotype on the lines of Low's Colonel Blimp, is treated sympathetically enough to give older people a foothold in the disorder.

This triumph of tolerance on the part of the playwright has to be appreciated in relation to the new drama's anti-militarism, not at all the same thing as pacifism, which it shares with a number of contemporary novels. We have noticed how closely Guthrie's version of Parolles conformed to mid-century taste in the matter, and the parallel with a post-war English type is obvious. Many a saloon bar had been dominated for a decade by reminiscent officers whose conversation tended to be increasingly boastful and nostalgic as their technical skills became obsolete, time dimmed their victories and the Empire shrank. Since the British film industry had failed to project the war at anything much above the level of brisk understatement in action and horseplay off duty, and Kenneth More's alcoholic R.A.F. charmer in *The Deep Blue Sea* was of limited interest apart from his sexual hold on the heroine, it is easy to understand how a contemptible image of militarism came into currency.

Before extracting it from two recent plays, one may refer to this image in *That Uncertain Feeling* by Kingsley Amis, where the owner of a car involved in comic scenes at a road house conforms to it, and in John Braine's *Room at the Top*, in which Jack Wales, the hero's rival, is an R.A.F. officer etched in acid, exaggeratedly so in the film version of the novel. It is not very far from this to the curtain of *Epitaph for George Dillon*, Act I, which falls when the hero has picked up the photograph of a young man killed in action, looked at it steadily and said: 'You stupid looking bastard.' The son in *Flowering Cherry* refers to his father as a phoney and adds, as if in corroboration, that he was decorated in the Great War. Earlier in the same play, we have, however, a clue to one explanation of this kind of resentment, when Cherry says to him: 'My word, boy, you've got a rude awakening coming; they'll teach you quick enough in the army. I only hope you get an R.S.M. like one or two I've known. There's no State Scholarships there.' This refers to compulsory National Service, regarded by both as in conflict with benefits conferred by the Welfare State. Military life, not war, is the subject at issue; and it is one which may reveal a deep cleavage of attitude. For one thing, the disciplines which often led their fathers to a more stimulating life were undergone by the sons as an interruption of cushioned civilian progress, rendered more irksome by the contrast between advances in nuclear armament and the residue of feudal ceremonial still to be found in British military routine. Moreover, his National Service may well have been the only contact a young playwright ever had with the Establishment until he came up against the Lord Chamberlain as censor. It is a contact which can disconcert. Around 1945 an order could still go out with the reminder that saluting derives from the freedman's privilege of looking his liege lord in the face.

Having considered two causes of banked-up resentment, the

Establishment and the officer type, we should remember that they powered the new drama as emotive images, variable in their relationship to the facts of mid-century life. For example, Lord Harewood, co-founder of the English Stage Society, would find a place in almost any list of Establishment insiders. Sometimes it seems there are more ex-officers directing plays than being scolded in them. Theatre Workshop reports that the only newspapers which gave adequate notice to their early efforts in London were *The Times* and the *Daily Worker*. We are dealing with a process caught up, as soon as it was visible, in contradictions of a specifically English kind, and the initial protestory phase of the movement was in this sense indigenous from the start, however great the dependence on transatlantic models. An American critic has demonstrated the extent of Osborne's debt in *The Entertainer* to *Death of a Salesman*. One may add an example of Robert Bolt's, apart from the basic idea of a boyish extrovert throttled by the commercial grind, in *Flowering Cherry*. The wife, under the same compulsion as Mrs. Loman to protect her husband from criticism by the children, says: 'He's been through a great deal and he's a fine man in all sorts of ways and you will treat him with respect! With respect! With respect!' Again, as in 'attention must be paid', it is an appeal to the audience. Cherry, like Loman, is too far gone in fantasy to carry the load demanded by major drama, and his creator as yet lacks Miller's ability to stack the weight of it round the character instead of on him.

And still Bolt's play is something more than a pale variation of Miller's or an excuse for Richardson, supported by Celia Johnson as the West End English suburban wife, to refine on the commuter equivalent of a punch-drunk heavyweight. For one thing, Cherry's pastoral dream mirrors historical reality and the sort of community to be found in the Cotswolds as recently as 1946, when a village postmaster at Temple Guiting could tell me he had never been to Winchcomb, which is bigger and five miles away. For another, the young people in *Flowering Cherry* have the authentic mid-century tendency to court the approval of what Riesman calls the peer group rather than the approval of their parents. You feel they merely pay visits to their parents, that more than one generation lies between the differences of outlook, that theirs is formed in coffee bars and cinemas among themselves. In *Flowering Cherry*, as in *Five Finger Exercise*, incompatible parents are under resentful scrutiny, and it is the more self-assertive parents who come in for the heavier punishment in each case. As it happens, these, Cherry and Mrs. Harrington, are also the deeper sunk in fantasy, that of Mrs. Harrington taking the form of pretensions to Parisian elegance based on retrospective upgrading of her grandmother's social status. In addition, Cherry and Mrs. Harrington both yield momentarily to sexual impulses aroused by people twenty years younger than they. Henry Green, in *Loving* and *Doting*, had prefigured this youthful censoriousness with much comic effect and an emphasis on its puritanical element. In the new drama it holds the whip-hand and gains authority from the fact that the parents are entirely plausible. We meet such people everywhere. They are less mature than the young playwrights dissecting them, in many ways less mature than their stage children. Bolt goes so far as to show how defects in one of them can spread delinquent tendencies to both son and daughter.

Perhaps enough has been said to indicate that the traditional target of parents has been hit with unusual accuracy, and not by chance. All these plays are naturalistic in treatment; social protest, rather than a preoccupation with literary or dramatic experiment, is their motive power. What neither the English theatrical profession nor the literary élite had been able to achieve since Shaw, some would say since Congreve or even the Jacobeans, a new generation did. First, after the lid was taken off their resentment at Sloane Square, came the phase of protest, popularly interpreted by the 'angry young man' cliché, itself misleading in so far as the stage behaviour of the protesters was critical, analytical, sometimes exasperated, but precociously shrewd. The thing to be emphasized was not anger, but the fact that they were articulate. Unless points of view widely held were being expressed, these playwrights would not so soon have gained a hold on the public; and in spite of its indebtedness to Miller, Osborne's *The Entertainer* presupposes a British public. Incoherent though it is, with expendable characters like the pacifist son and the enlightened daughter, with *ex cathedra* rhetoric about the Royal Family and the Suez invasion, admittedly the last stand of the pre-nuclear *miles gloriosus*, nevertheless *The Entertainer* shows an advance in structural organization.

I base the claim on Archie Rice and his wife, with a nod of recognition towards Rice's father, the Edwardian trouper conceived in this playwright's kindlier manner. To give Olivier most of the credit for Rice is unjust. This shoddy vaudeville performer is, first, the parent target we have already discussed. His marriage is a failure and he chases young girls. Secondly he is a boyish funster who drinks too much, thus incurring the espresso bar generation's contempt both for ageing neurotics and English saloon bars, which many of them regard as resorts for the maladjusted. Thirdly, Rice is, in spite of many signs to the contrary, capable of genuine emotion, something the young prize beyond intellect; Olivier shocks us into recognition of this when Rice learns of his son's death. Fourthly, and most important of all, Rice embodies the debasement of popular art which Hoggart and others have observed. Through him Osborne is facing up to problems greater than those presented by parents, the Establishment and rivals in uniform; he is coming to grips with the new drama's most dangerous enemy, which, as I maintained in Chapter I of this book, is the sterile conformism implicit in the values of mid-century consumer society and fostered by commercial interests with the powerful aid of psychologists and the mass media. Compared with his relation to these problems, Archie ('Thank God I'm normal') Rice's excursions through the fourth wall to direct contact with the audience in his music-hall acts are a secondary matter, though managed with great skill by the playwright.

The very real danger of young dramatists being assimilated by debased commercialism is a main theme of *Epitaph for George Dillon*,* and the connection between suburban values and popular entertainment is implicit in the action. Dillon's abdication when he vulgarizes his play on the lines of its new title, *Telephone Tart*, runs parallel with his assimilation by the family whose cocktail cabinet, a status object resembling a cinema organ, comes in for its share of his invective, like the 'bloody birds' on the wall. These, and this typical English mid-century family's addiction to 'the telly', prepare one for the way they react to the discovery that their daughter's seducer is already married. Any possible resentment is swept aside when they learn that Dillon's estranged wife is on the panel of their favourite television parlour game. 'What?' exclaims Percy Townley, in the tone of primitive man refraining from use of a deity's name, 'Not her!' In *The Entertainer*, one source of

* On West End transfer, the word 'Epitaph' disappeared from the title.

sympathy for Archie Rice is the fact that his wife is mentally crippled in much the same way as Townley. Addicted to the local cinema, she can return from it unable to remember the title, the name of the star, or whether he was English or American. But Osborne, helped by Brenda de Banzie's rendering of obsolete blonde glamour in decline, is not too unkind to Mrs. Rice and she exists, like the Colonel in *Look Back in Anger*, as more than a symbol of rejected values. So does Rice, founded on what Desmond MacCarthy called, in another connection, 'sordid aplomb'. Within the family framework it must have been easy for Olivier to project the character; the difficulty so brilliantly overcome lay in convulsing one with laughter at comic patter designed to be unfunny. Rice, we feel, more than suspects how bad it is, and the author knows; but what we are actually laughing at is complex enough to excuse immaturities, including the pacifist's lament for his brother, interwoven in the play.

Trying to recapture the sense of released vitality which accompanied the new drama's early progress, I remember queueing all afternoon at the Royal Court for standing room at *The Entertainer*. Probably because I happened to be reading *Room at the Top*, Braine's novel about the city I grew up in, the slick young enthusiasts in jeans, pony-tail hair styles, crew-cuts and gay blouses or shirts, made the long wait on the steps in Sloane Square as comfortable for me as possible. Though probably more familiar with outer space than with adults over forty, they accepted the novel as a passport and saw to it that I spent most of the time at ease in neighbouring espresso bars. Owing much to the stimulus given by the Festival of Britain (1951), hung with plants, onions and cradles for Chianti bottles, partitioned in stony surfaces enjoined by New Brutalist architecture, equally tolerant of conversation or skiffle, these places were in cosmopolitan reaction to the drab Nonconformist philistinism which social revolution carried out by the Labour Party since the war had done little to shake off. It was already being replaced by what Jack Kerouac, in *The Dharma Bums*,* calls 'middle-class non-identity in rows of well-to-do houses with lawns and television sets', but the coffee bars partake of neither. They often reflect the colourful neo-romanticism we have already discussed in relation to Tennessee Williams. One of them, in a London suburb, is typically called *El Sombrero*.

* Deutsch, 1959.

Their equivalent, almost an emanation of them, in the new drama, is the sort of work I call Theatre in the Raw, which is proletarian, vigorous, violent and hysterical in the vein of mass-media sensationalism. Its two evident limitations are the difficulty of organizing profuseness towards the structural balance of major drama and a temptation to stress the exotic aspect of squalor. The hero of Errol John's *Moon on a Rainbow Shawl* is a type of the West Indian who was increasingly to influence English social life during these years, and the action concerns events which cause him to emigrate. But one remembers chiefly the surge of emotion and the garishly ragged shacks of Sainthill's décor, just as, having lost interest in a mother who dominates her son into spinelessness and then trusts him with a large sum of money, one may remember only a dance in African costume from *A Raisin in the Sun*. Such plays attack one with the uninhibited rhetoric of surface texture to be found in mid-century painting and sculpture. If the new drama's phase of protest tended to be negative, Theatre in the Raw is positive. It asserts proletarian energy, a source of drama long banished in England to the music halls, the decline of which, as illustrated by Archie Rice, went hand in hand with the new drama's increasing resort to jazz and popular ballads, more or less under the influence of Brecht. Willis Hall's *The Long and the Short and the Tall* is named after a lugubrious ballad which conveys both the desolation of military service in foreign parts and a kind of cynical team spirit based on servitude to an oligarchy. It might not be too fanciful if we related this trend with Eliot's unexpected conversion to the Kipling of *Barrack Room Ballads*. His *Sweeney Agonistes*, in the use made of music and slang, had long ago anticipated Theatre in the Raw.

Again, however, the revolution came chiefly from below; and comparison of the song Hall drew on for his title with, say, the Eton Boating Song, would reveal a submerged world of vernacular poetry neglected by Shaw and Galsworthy in their stage treatment of the working class. Better late than never, I thought, as the West End which had silenced O'Casey for a decade resounded at last to the imagery and rhythm of English proletarian language. My theatre programmes lie scrawled with phrases as slangy and expressive as 'Lend me your ears'. By any estimate this enrichment of the drama's vocabulary is a major achievement. 'I write', says Delaney, 'as people speak.' It is a long time since anyone outside a highly educated minority of playwrights, addressing themselves to a restricted public, could justly claim that.

With an extension of vocabulary have come forms of behaviour new to our drama. Hall's play was directed by Lindsay Anderson, a distinguished creator of documentary films; but the documentary aspect of plays is marginal to major work in the theatre and few people are likely to care in a few years' time whether this or that subject was accurately rendered unless the artistic rendering can stand up to scrutiny. This brings us, without danger of joining the enemies of a movement undeniably on the side of life, to consider its present limitations, the first of which is inseparable from the adolescent phase of an art: it is emotionalism, dogged by those mangy mongrels, violence and sentimentality. Both are to be found in Hall's technically skilful treatment of the Japanese prisoner on whom the actions of his British rankers hinge, so that it is too early to judge whether he is a dramatist who graduated from television or a scriptwriter who has written a play. Then there is *One More River*, by Beverley Cross, an unusually promising work thrown up by Sam Wanamaker's too short Liverpool venture. In it the crew of a freighter mutiny, put their first officer to the parody of a trial and, in the original version, hang him at the climax of two acts which excel Hall for the interplay of melodrama and documentation encrusted with emotive speech. Cross, however, is not content with that. Well within his artistic rights, and building on three levels, he aims to follow his tribute to proletarian energy and his rejection of its collective authority by a vindication of the officer class. But the third act founders because the highly trained novice, who alone can solve the navigational problem posed, is a theatrical puppet. Unless you can back him with the kind of emotion which roused protest from the Secretary of the Mercantile Marine Service Association against mutinous treatment of the Red Ensign earlier in the play, he cannot be taken as seriously as Cross requires.

Still, here are two plays written about Service life from opposed angles, and both of them vibrantly Theatre in the Raw. Not for nothing has Tynan, pundit of the movement, written: 'We have artists afraid to affirm anything addressing an audience that believes either nothing or nonsense. When that kind of deadlock is reached, *it is time for the heart to take over from the head*.'* What we are getting, in terms of Nietzsche's distinction, is the Dionysian

* *Declaration* (MacGibbon & Kee, 1958). My italics.

THEATRE IN THE RAW

with only a hint of the Apollonian, the equivalent, in terms of this book, of Williams without Miller, of Olivier without Gielgud, of early O'Neill and Brecht. When Theatre in the Raw is 'committed', it can only be to authoritarianism or to a progressive Socialism inapplicable to most of the mid-century British working class. The soldier luckier than Hall's patrol will come back from Malaya to the consumer society just replacing the headquarters of an empire. He will find a city like Coventry aglow with prosperity, its workers on the automobile assembly lines fanning out through the rural Midlands as subtopian commuters. Commitment, as Lindsay Anderson's later philosophical position suggests, must henceforward be against the Philistines. To find an underprivileged class—apart from the old, who do not lend themselves to colourful treatment—it must look to the West Indies, to Ireland or to the unemployed fringe. It will be hard put to transmit any of these theatrically without falling into neo-romantic exploitation of local colour like John Arden, when he opposes gypsies to a Yorkshire Subtopia in *Live like Pigs*. Meanwhile State education in the nuclear age is opening channels which by-pass the Establishment, social realism and English proletarian tradition, on their way to the moon.

Granted that the new drama is a blessed enrichment, we must face the fact that the conditions which favoured its quick consolidation could also destroy it. Watching three tycoons on the Royal Court stage, sober against the *Moon on a Rainbow Shawl* colours as one of them made a gift of £1,000—not enough to buy a second-rate footballer—to the English Stage Company, I suddenly realized how immature the rousing new drama still is, how much of everyday experience is yet to be reclaimed. Any schoolboy on terms with a laboratory or science fiction is more closely in touch with mid-century life at the roots than the playwrights mentioned so far, and a gulf yawns between high finance and its treatment as a theatrical subject. Politics have yet to be handled at anything like the level of Sartre in *Les Mains sales*, a decade old. These might be set up as warnings against complacency. As possible targets for the future, they ought not to be beyond the capacity of those who have achieved so much already.

Taking a hint from Osborne, more in touch in the way Brecht and Miller were than any of the rest, we might regard the immediate task as an all-out attack on consumer-society values. They are obviously in the way of any playwright's progress towards maturity and they act incessantly on his subject matter, people. Within the framework of the play itself we are entitled to expect a more inward tension, such as comes from emotion matched by intellectual control in the creative wrestle one senses behind the writing of a Miller or a Brecht. Unless this can be acquired, the movement will be in danger of becoming provincial, a fate avoided so far by the adolescent exuberance of its first explosive phase. If recent American drama prompts the aphorism: 'Every artist his own psychoanalyst', and leads us to reject a protracted foisting of infantile symptoms on the public, then the new English drama suggests three more: (1) 'There is only room for one Strindberg', (2) 'Painting did not come to an end with the Douanier Rousseau' and (3) 'Brecht was committed, but also involved.'

To find out what philosophical assumptions lie behind the movement, one might invite answers to the following examination question: *Tynan and Koestler are committed writers familiar with Spain.* (a) *Compare the circumstances in which they gained experience of that country*, and (b) *Define the positions at present taken by them.*

What matters ultimately, of course, is not the controversial background of the new drama but results in performance. Three of the first new wave playwrights to make their mark were Behan, at thirty-seven the elder statesman of the movement, Delaney and Wesker. With an eye on the high standards set by O'Casey, O'Neill, Miller and Brecht, I think we can claim not only potential but achievement in these three cases. All three, if committed, are also involved, traditional products of the working-class backgrounds they represent; all have already written plays free from gratuitous violence and modish exoticism. To deal first with the most precocious, Miss Delaney wrote *A Taste of Honey* in a fit of pique aroused by what she regarded as the misuse of her favourite actress in a West End 'star vehicle'. Her own play is about a girl of sixteen left pregnant by a Negro sailor while her mother, an amateur tart, is on honeymoon with a car salesman. Nothing could be less wholesome in summary and more delightful in the treatment given. As well as an overdue transfusion of contemporary Lancashire speech, English drama receives at one blow the precious gift of four characters—the girl, her mother, her lover and the gentle homosexual she turns to for company—realized on stage with a tolerant compassion in my opinion beyond anything Tennessee Williams has yet to attain. In a situation bristling with opportunities for resentment and facile sensationalism, none of them, not even the mother, is denied a gay acceptance. Faced with that, it is frivolous to dwell on the casual construction and make hay of it by Archerian standards. We are dealing with a humorous talent emotionally mature at twenty years old.

Miss Littlewood's direction of *A Taste of Honey*, full of Brechtian elegance as against the too fashionable Brechtian overlays, amounts to the kind of creative collaboration we referred to in the chapter on directors. The praise I give to this play allows for an unknown degree of intervention and alludes to the author's creative marrow. For example, the mother would remain valid if played naturalistically and not made more palatable by 'alienation' into the vaudeville relationship with an audience. Behan's *The Hostage*, also from Theatre Workshop, is the product of similar collaboration. A distinct personality survives group work on the script. The maturity here can easily pass unnoticed behind its rollicking surface tone. It lies above all in the healing by music and the comic spirit of raw wounds in the social body: the Easter Rebellion, Cyprus, Kenya, death in reprisal, purple passages in the chapter of man's inhumanity to man. They remain exactly what they are, but soften to a golden haze as if someone we knew to be juggling with live ammunition did it so well that, charmed by his skill, we forgot the danger. And there is a better structure than might be supposed, especially in the way we first see the hostage only as a comic foreign intruder, then, ironically, as a soldier professionally indifferent to his I.R.A. counterpart's execution, lastly as linked indissolubly to the other's fate. For Behan, formerly of the I.R.A. and thus a committed enemy of the British, to have created the most lovable and authentic English ranker in the century's drama is one of art's miracles, an unlikely result of years spent in English gaols.

As signs of maturity are greatly to be prized in a new movement like this, I have to comment on Ray Lawler's *Summer of the Seventeenth Doll*, underrated, perhaps because its Australian setting and origin drew attention to secondary aspects. It deals with the increasingly urgent working-class leisure problem as it concerns cane-cutters living to a special alternating rhythm, all work for months on end and then all play. Lawler refrains completely from exploiting the primitive romantic side of the men's work; his solution of the local colour problem is to exclude colour, except from speech. What he concentrates on is the annual spending spree and the distorted domestic instinct which inclines men to return year after year to the same woman. One of the two women in the play rejects the equivocal status, part wife and part mistress, involved; the other, an infantile hysteric tethered to the pleasure principle, clings to it even when her stupid lover is ready for a more mature relationship. Although the Australian diction is new to our theatre, Lawler builds it towards a design applicable far beyond local conditions until he reaches a universal statement about people, valid anywhere.

In form, *The Summer of the Seventeenth Doll* is totally naturalistic, like Wesker's *Roots*, a representative masterpiece of the new drama which came to the West End by way of the Belgrade, Coventry, and the Royal Court in the summer of 1959. Again the surface, this time in Norfolk dialect, distracted many from a just assessment of the play. It was even held to be a one-acter spun out to three, an opinion which shows how disastrously a diet of surface action may blunt responses. In fact, the supposedly redundant first act establishes the first authentic rural community since the Tudor drama which I, for one, had yet seen on the English stage. To appreciate the aptness of making the householder a garage mechanic with the mental processes of a traditional farm labourer, you need, perhaps, to have seen these displaced rustics at work in English villages and country towns. Formerly slaves to the horse or the land, many of them are now unskilled or semi-skilled slaves to the machine. *Roots* deals with this transitional phase in which an old way of life, not without dignity amid its feudal superstitions, lies in decay at the mercy of mass-media values. Beatie Bryant, the heroine, returns to this environment after three years as the mistress of a London working-class intellectual; it is through her eyes that we see it. Act I focuses three points of view: hers, her family's, and that of Stan Mann, an elderly reprobate still singing the praises of drink and sex, though crippled and on the brink of death. It also gets us used to the fascinating dialect and shows Beatie's predicament. She is in a limbo between Norfolk and her boy friend's ideals. To say that nothing happens betrays ignorance of the nature of dramatic action.

In the first scene of Act II, Mann's death, off-stage in conformity with Wesker's essential gravity, dismisses with great dignity the old order he represents. Then we see Beatie's father and mother at loggerheads. The second scene, in which the mother says: 'Turn that squit off!' when Mendelssohn's Fourth Symphony is played on the radio, ends very subtly with mother and daughter in harmony. It is illusory harmony, for here, precisely, is a case of the half-educated at odds with the unteachable.

Beatie herself does not know this until the third act, when the family assembles to meet her lover as future husband. He sends a jilting letter instead; and here Wesker rises to his theme, for the mother erupts in aggressive spite, while Beatie, the injured party, looks for a cause of failure in herself. We now understand that Wesker has found a solution for proletarian drama's major difficulty, the provision of a character with enough intellect to point the action towards something more crucial than documentarily accurate behaviour. It is Ron, the lover, who does not appear at all. He dominates the action by proxy through Beatie's quotations. The climax comes when she speaks with her own voice instead of his; and what she says amounts to a rejection of this rural environment and an acceptance, in fact an assumption, of his.

Roots, one of the most enlightening experiences I have ever been given in a theatre, accords at many points with the mid-century situation as set forth in this book. Instead of luxuriating in outworn proletarian gestures of protest, it faces the fact that ignorance, not poverty, is the enemy now to be grappled with in Britain. In the allegedly inactive first act Beatie quotes Ron as follows: 'Well, language isn't words. . . . It's bridges, so that you can get safely from one place to another. And the more bridges you know about the more places you can see.' It is a plea for education in tune with Julian Huxley's opinion that language most removes mankind from the animals. The third act lists films and women's magazines among other media with a vested interest in ignorance. It also relates commercial practices to the prosperous workers as a source of profit. But Wesker goes further still, to arraign the passivity of the workers themselves, instead of laying the blame on a convenient father-figure like the Establishment. 'The whole stinking commercial world insults us, ' says Beatie, now speaking for herself, 'and we don't care a damn. . . . We want the third rate, we got it.'

The quality of *Roots* lies in the evolution of this accusation from a naturalistic drama; it emerges without the chilly, anti-theatrical flavour of something tagged on or schematic. Middle-class playwrights would be incapable of finding the objective correlatives for such a statement in a community dominated by 'guts ache', trivial family quarrels, threats of dismissal to casual labour and culture diffused by television. Most of those who did know the community would be incapable of dramatizing the statement. Wesker succeeds on both counts. Although he admits debts to O'Casey and Miller, the dramatic texture of *Roots* is interesting from point to point in its own way. Like his heroine, Wesker now speaks for himself, as well as for a generation still seeking its bearings.

That *Chips with Everything* should be Wesker's first resounding West End success is a decisive consolidation of the new drama, for it combines the anti-militarist and anti-Establishment impulses already referred to. It is an attack on the system upheld by the British officer class. The victims are R.A.F. conscripts under training in peace time, exposed to the brutality inseparable everywhere from the learning of a brutal trade. At times the dramatist's identity merges with John Dexter's ferociously visual direction, so that the personal voice becomes feeble or strident. Side by side with a bold change of technique there is a weakening of some crucial relationships; traces of defeatism and sentimentality appear. But indignation gets through, in the most powerful and subversive of protests.

Chapter VIII
THE SECOND WAVE
Developments in Formal Structure

————————————————★————————————————

To speak for one's self as a dramatist is to get rid of primitivism or Left Bank pessimism, the two crutches most readily available to young English playwrights before they find their own feet. That done, are there any critical terms which can help us to chart what progress there is? Not realism, now used as loosely as 'beauty' once was, and not tragedy or comedy, forms perfected in the past. As in the visual arts, expressionism really did enter, not only with Brecht but with a furious display of theatrical gimmicks, often morbidly romantic. The major influence seems to be Artaud's 'theatre of cruelty', advocated in the heyday of Fascism by an insane author. Its popularity in the fifties may have been caused by nothing more sinister than the anxiety to justify live theatre in terms of its power to shock. At the end of the decade Edward Albee could still bring on a bloodstained doctor in *The Death of Bessie Smith*.

All the same, progress beyond Theatre in the Raw could already be traced, apart from Wesker, in Harold Pinter, John Arden and Alun Owen at an early stage in their careers. These playwrights have discarded short cuts to effect by violence and have more to offer than the vitality, welcome though it is, of the regional dialogue they excel in. By the early sixties they invited non-partisan criticism at a high level; none has anything like the intellectual range of a Brecht, but they have gone beyond folk art. I found it helpful to consider them in the light of two formal concepts, one recent and one old: Compressionism and the Picaresque. A third form, which concerns acting and staging as much as writing, and keeps Theatre in the Raw alive in a wider context, is International Style. Again, as in abstract expressionist painting, there is a mid-century idiom common to younger people all over the world. It has formed in the drama partly as a spontaneous growth of sensibility and partly in answer to the needs of touring abroad. You may see entire plays governed by it or merely a single actor injecting it in the most unlikely place, as in Hirsch's performance in *Britannicus*. It can touch classical revivals anywhere from Moscow to Stratford, Ontario. The strength of it, seen at its best in Roger Planchon's version of *The Three Musketeers* or in Tony Richardson's direction of *Luther*, comes from a return to the ritual basis of drama, actors solidly present in three dimensions and released from the tyranny of static décor. The weakness of International Style is verbal, a positive gain when playing to foreign audiences but a threat to the integrity of great plays, oversimplified to fit the director's 'ruling idea'. Although the result can be enormous fun, what we get is Shakespeare cut down to the size of Planchon or Littlewood, Racine flouted in the interests of Hirsch, who decides to raise a laugh at the most sinister intrusion of Nero on the lovers. Some think Olivier's Coriolanus goes too far down this road.

The appeal of International Style is to uninstructed audiences. It resorts to 'total theatre' tactics more stimulating than the effete pictorial staging of the nineteen fifties. Sets tend to be spare and solid, with emphasis on features like Jocelyn Herbert's crucifix in *Luther*, the tree in Richard Negri's *As You Like It*, the bed in Planchon's Marivaux. Recorded sound effects are carefully fitted in. Wood and canvas are shunned and the stage floor is often built up steeply or used to lodge an acting area like Wieland Wagner's tilted saucer. Sumptuous costumes look well on actors who enter and station themselves with the swagger of prizefighters climbing into the ring. Eyes and ears gratified, we may be attacked by way of our noses too, by incense in *Luther*, by swirling vapour in *Troilus and Cressida* at Stratford-on-Avon. Planchon's booted musketeers, not content with their splendid bearing and dress, assert themselves by stamping loudly in unison. Within all this unabashed theatricalism, naturalistic effects take on a wicked charm. Cardinal Richelieu cooks himself an omelette on stage; Tony Richardson equips the retinue of Pope Leo with a live falcon and two Afghan hounds.

It seems churlish to question the dramatic value of experiences as richly enjoyable as these, yet that is the critic's duty. Actors and directors are on the spree; the playwright is in danger of shrinking to a provider of situations and themes. International Style doesn't often insult him to the extent of handing his text over to the actors as raw material for improvisation. Its awareness of the means of production does, however, tend to swamp any special attention to the author's words and to overlook the fact that those words may often carry the main dramatic impact. For the last two thirds of *Luther*, a Shavian or Brechtian subject outside John Osborne's range, I don't think the author's words are adequate to the job in hand and I was thankful for the drama put across by Albert Finney and his director. It's quite another thing to rejig *Henry IV* and *La Seconde Surprise de l'amour* on the lines of an idea outside the texts, in both cases good enough to stand on their own feet. The same applies to *Romeo and Juliet*, from which Zeffirelli elected to stress the theme of a hopeless rift between generations. He succeeded triumphantly in conveying this aspect of the play and in bringing out the drama of the potion scene, a masterly study of anxiety as written; he made nonsense of the built-in aristocratic sensibility of the young gallants, of the Nurse's vulgarity and of the hero's course to maturity, these being left by Shakespeare mainly to the verse. An opera director who got in the way of the score so obstinately would not be tolerated, let alone praised. Zeffirelli's *Romeo and Juliet* is a cautionary example of International Style's ability to debase a minor classic by neglect of its diction. John Whiting's *The Devils*, on the other hand, seems to me a case of mediocre writing inflated by International Style to an appearance of high quality. We are worked on by the broad contrast between a handsome hedonist and a gibbering hysteric. He happens to be a priest and she a nun. The parade of symptoms includes his muscular tremors after prolonged torture; like Osborne's *Luther* he is most real when most physically theatrical, although we are asked to take his faith seriously. Grandier, out for a life of sensations rather than thoughts, is the one possessed; first by lust for women, then by lust for martyrdom.

The Devils, like other work in International Style, is basically Theatre in the Raw, glossily packaged in literate dialogue and period costume. Something of a throwback to the sensationalism of the fifties, it also points forward to a more promising form, the Picaresque. This, I think, is the best result of Brecht's influence on English playwrights, the aspect of him most suited to our genius. The master himself seized on Farquhar's *The Recruiting Officer* as fit for the Berliner Ensemble, finding positive value in it at a time when Farquhar had long been thrown by scholars into a limbo somewhere between waning high comedy and the early novel. Seldom capable of epic, the English delight in its picaresque off-shoot, partly because of the relief it gives from our national claustrophobia. Film producers have long made use of the Picaresque; now it is the theatre's turn. Everything favours it: increased travel, social mobility and, in the drama, an impulse towards fluid staging and away from enclosed naturalism.

The new drama's picaresque masterpiece is *Serjeant Musgrave's Dance*, unrecognizable as such in Lindsay Anderson's original production, which led to a lot of acrimonious partisanship for and against. Some older critics were put out by the play's pacifist 'message' and its implicit allusion to recent events in Cyprus, while an atmosphere of conscious daring on stage may well have led to neglect of the deep feeling and strong narrative line. At any rate, the result was all handsome, incoherent surface and a tone consistent with the naive Royal Court idea of a Brechtian demonstration, already exposed by the abysmal *Eleven Men Dead at Hola Camp*.

This can be excused up to a point by the fact that John Arden off form can be very bad indeed. *Live Like Pigs*, for example, is like a parody of Theatre in the Raw, awash with rugged exoticism which blurs the excellent idea of conflict between families on a housing estate by importing gypsies and folk-song. In *The Happy Haven*, inmates of a home for the aged turn on their persecutor and inject him in the buttock with a giant syringe. But gypsies are picaresque material; and so are soldiers, as Arden reminded us by selecting one as the catalyst in an Italia Prize television play. In *Serjeant Musgrave* he brings four of them to a bleak northern town. We see them in the streets, in the pub and in a stable. They are deserters intent on denouncing war under cover of a recruiting drive. When the crowd gathers, the skeleton of a young local man killed abroad is offered for scrutiny.

First, it is a play with a good story which keeps on the move. It did that in Kevin Moore's production at the Theatre Royal, Lincoln, because the stage was left bare right up to its back and side walls and furniture was sparse, with Musgrave sleeping on the cart later used as a platform. Second, its message is not that of the deserters; they are unfitted to be emissaries of peace, for one kills another in a brawl and they propose to mow down their exploiters, the local Establishment. Third, it is steeped in compassion; and in the marvellous stable episode when the pub slut is wooed in turn by three men, it needs sensitive acting. And the songs must be sung well or not at all, just as the dialogue will benefit from actors at home with a northern idiom. Fourth, it has one of the theatre's traditional pitfalls, a clergyman satirized. At the Royal Court he was caricatured, at Lincoln brought close to the natural. Finally, Serjeant Musgrave himself can be the pretext for a virtuoso study in religious mania, but there's quite enough going on without making too much of that. So far I have liked best the performance of Mr. Frederick Hall, who played him as a stolid, half-educated, Victorian N.C.O.

Clearly this work is not to be defined as picaresque in a limiting way. It has a complexity of organization which cannot be fully described outside itself and I see it as a permanent addition to the national repertory. Nor is there any certainty that Arden will go on using the form; but a neat television play, *Jack's Horrible Luck* by Henry Livings, confirms how the Picaresque can give direction to low-life material otherwise merely quaint. There a sailor on shore-leave looks for a community which will accept him, disrupts the one he intrudes on and ends up knowing that the only togetherness he will find is afloat. Behind the Picaresque, of course, lie Farquhar and Brecht; in front of it is a mine of unworked dramatic material, past and present.

At a formal extreme from the Picaresque stand Harold Pinter and Compressionism. With very few exceptions, the history of English dramatic criticism over the last fifty years has been one of estrangement from modern literature. I can think of no other reason for the difficulty most critics had in placing early Pinter. His obscurity was not so dense as to deter an audience of more than ten million from digesting *The Birthday Party* on television, but obscure the play often is. Pinter lets the backchat run away with him in the manner of Ionesco at his garrulous worst, and there are obvious debts to Joyce, via Beckett, to Kafka and to the Hemingway of *The Killers*, perhaps to Eliot's Sweeney.

The result is often diffuse and pretentious, though not enough to hide this playwright's originality. It consists in his treatment of semi-illiterate persons without cheating. Instead of romanticizing them, sentimentalizing them or using them as the peg for a sermon, he places them before us in a drab English environment. Then he picks out the weakness of one or more characters and states the commonplace background in terms of that one's fantasy. In *The Room* a neglected wife's fantasy is actually projected as an acting part in the play. By the time we get to *A Night Out*, a gesture is enough to resolve the conflict of subjective worlds. The mother-fixated hero is left alone with a genteel whore, not unlike Blanche du Bois. Reared on Williams or Anouilh we might expect the situation to end in murder, rape or perhaps romantic love. Not at all; the poor woman is only made to go down on her knees and tie his shoes. Yet the incident carries more pity and terror than Blanche's exit to the mental home. Likewise in *The Caretaker* the crisis is a collision of illusions. Aston will endure almost anything from the aggressive tramp he has befriended; but when the tramp sneers at Aston's illusion of building a shed in the garden, it's over between them.

To isolate the dramatic tension peculiar to Pinter is by no means to have done with him. His diction alone is a factor which allies him to the other new English dramatists as much as it marks him off from the French avant-garde. Pinter's dialogue has no parallel for social accuracy outside the fiction of V. S. Pritchett; in addition, it is stylized in a way to assist projection in the theatre and it can carry scathing satire on the Affluent Society, the scruffy underside of which is Pinter's chosen subject. Not only has he brought in to drama the Welfare State's cast-offs, got inside the human wrecks too forlorn to claim their own meagre rights and found a shape in the monologues of eccentrics who startle the public in street or bus; he reflects the everyday language of office parties, football matches and advertising as well. As in the dramatic play-off of tensions, so in the diction there is always a firm anchorage in the commonplace. It is the commonplace given anecdotal polish, the way actors do when they make fun of provincial life as seen on tour, more than a little Dickensian. Add this diction to human relationships conducted with cast-iron logic, fuse action and diction indissolubly, and you have *The Caretaker*, a masterpiece.

On the way to this mastery, it is interesting to see Pinter trying out and discarding a number of the new drama's unrewarding devices. At the close of his first play *The Room*, the unhappy housewife is visited by a gentle, blind Negro who stands for everything her husband is not. To see this helpless man struck by the husband is so shocking that the crude violence blurs the dramatic point. It is an assault on the audience which may cause them to lose the key to the action, given in a speech of the husband's where he reveals that his truck receives the affection denied to his wife. *The Dumb Waiter* also ends with imported violence, with one of a pair of hired killers revealed as the other's victim. This may be justified as a resolution of suspense, but it is synthetic compared with the interest we feel in the analysis of the two men. They are ignorant, suggestible, as ready to obey orders for food as orders to kill. Above all they are commonplace. The terror comes from the closeness of their world to ours. As we are never allowed to forget that they trade in killing, nothing is gained by making the violence explicit.

On the other hand, violence in *The Caretaker* is rigidly functional. The owner of the hovel, not knowing that the tramp is there by invitation, pounces on him from behind and twists his arm. That is the tramp's biography in a gesture. His own aggressiveness is summed up in a compulsive stabbing motion, made at the climax with a knife. It is, if anything, less disturbing than Aston's account of licensed violence when he recalls his treatment in a mental home. There the playwright is content to let the words do the work in one long speech. Among other things the passage offers a social criticism of public squalor, in counterbalance to Mick's solo about private affluence and the passion for interior decoration, a bizarre mid-century fad.

By a different route, Pinter arrives at social comment every bit as relevant as Osborne's or Arden's. But what exactly is Pinter's route? He has explained that the sight of people in a room has three times given him the idea for a play and that he plans in terms of a picture-frame stage.* We think of his people as enclosed. This ties up with the notion of Kedrov about Chekhov's characters and their essence squeezed out under pressure.

The compassionate rendering of isolated beings, unable to get through to one another, is an evident link between Pinter and Chekhov. What Pinter intensifies is the element of compression, a device which deserves a name to itself. You can see it at work in Francis Bacon's portraits of political prisoners. In the drama, its lineage is from Sartre's *Huis clos* and *Altona* to Beckett's *Endgame*, with Sherriff's *Journey's End*, set in a dug-out, as a familiar

* *Twentieth Century*, February, 1961.

example. From one point of view it is a naturalistic economy device to avoid changes of set; from another it favours the classical unities of time, place and action. As used by Sartre and Pinter, Compressionism is more on a par with Stendhal's preoccupation with the wall as a symbol, a vital response to the times. Like any other index of sensibility it may wear out. Perhaps Beckett's Winnie in *Happy Days*, buried up to her neck in a mound of earth, is the end of this road.

Drama alternates between what is miscalled 'loose' and 'tight' construction, 'loose' often being used dismissively when the critic has failed to grasp the structure of plays in an unfamiliar idiom. Compressionism, at any rate, is the new drama's opposite pole from the Picaresque. In *A Night Out* Pinter's title seems to announce a change of policy. The hero stays hopelessly shut inside his neurosis; one character actually calls him 'compressed', meaning 'depressed'. But Pinter's hold on the world outside the room is masterly, the office party a tour-de-force. We might have been prepared for this, for Mick in *The Caretaker* remains a visitor from outside the pressure chamber and is as well realized as the victims. It turns out that Pinter's avant-garde route to maturity has done nothing to separate him from the life dealt with by other young dramatists. On the contrary, it has enabled him to combine firm, dramatic structure with a notable command of the English language. If he develops, it could be away from Beckett's defeatism, outwards.

Chapter IX

EXTREMES OF STYLE IN ACTING
From the Method to Comedy of Manners

————————————————— * —————————————————

There cannot be many professions in which to be ten seconds late is unforgivable, or in which the mere sight of a man's place of work may set his nervous system in the turmoil George Arliss endured before he took refuge from live drama in films. We must respect all actors for the discipline they represent. Here, for example, is X. Everyone knows him to be a fool in private life and a bad actor. Nevertheless, he can be relied on to know his lines and not to be late for an entrance. That much he has in common with Olivier, driving from Shakespeare's birth-place to a film location at Morecambe through the night; with Gielgud, lost from the West End afternoon sunshine as the stage door of a Coward farce sucks him in; with Gribov, being made up for Fiers and answering questions about Chebutikin; with the Comédie Française beauty who passed me in a corridor on her way to the stage, tripped, and cried: 'Merde!' X is a part of it all in a way we can never hope to be. Richard Ainley tells a story of two old hams who are trying to hitch a ride on the Great North Road. Having absconded without paying their salary, the manager now drives past them flaunting the leading lady. The two old hams are covered with dust. One of them stands up and threatens the receding car with a gesture he learned from Tree. The other gets up more slowly, full of haughty disdain, taps him on the shoulder and says: 'Never mind, laddie. They can't *act*!'

Actors have a right to their own mystique, but when Clurman writes* that the Method 'does not concern the audience, or, for that matter, the critics' I heartily disagree. The audience is being worked on in a particular way, and sooner or later will recognize the fact when discussing favourite actors unless it is to be undesir-

* *The Fervent Years* (Dobson, London, 1946).

123

ably passive. A critic who chooses to neglect important trends in acting is leaving out something which, as we saw in Chapters II and III, may significantly condition the effect a play has, even to the point of becoming indispensable data in assessment of it as a work of art. To warn him off relevant training methods is like asking an art critic to estimate Seurat without reference to division-ism and the scientific attitude behind it or Cézanne with never a thought for geometry. It is true that the Method is usually debated at the level of a provincial seducer bombarding his victims with ill-digested Freud, but it strongly influences mid-century direction and writing, as well as acting. Here we may define it as an American variation on the Stanislavsky System. In England, where training tends to be empirical, brief and insufficiently subsidized, the Method as popularized by the cinema has raised the status of actors in twentieth-century terms by giving them a small stake in science and convincing the public that acting is work. It has abolished the situation in which a book on acting could tell the beginner that he must learn to stand still, yet not tell him how. The novice, for example, always tends to waggle his hands. What is the cure? Disregarding decades of labour, anyone can learn the answer from a single M.A.T. performance. To avoid waggling your hands, you simply grab hold of the back of a chair.

If we place the Method at one extreme and high comedy or farce, as done by the French, at another, we are in a position to consider aspects of contemporary English acting not covered by the chapters on revivals. Indebted to American drama as they are, the new playwrights reflect its leanings towards sensationalism in varying degrees, and this extends to the young actors who serve them. In terms of the restless-hand problem, where M.A.T. actors would be required to hold casually on to a chairback, the material given Method actors often asks for the equivalent of biting the chair or using it as a weapon. Young English actors now compare well with almost anyone in this kind of thing. It is not to be despised, but it is limited. Gribov, who actually slaps a chair over in *The Three Sisters* as we shall see, is capable also of refined comedy when he turns to the old servant in *The Cherry Orchard*. Tension and violence are only one facet of the Stanis-lavsky tradition. The Method, on the other hand, stems from the Group Theatre of the thirties and inclines to a shaggy proletarian explosiveness, frequently hysterical of late. It puts one in mind of tantrums in which tears increase as the sufferer grows tired of kicking. Recently Paul Newman and Anthony Franciosa, strong men and Method experts, both shed tears in the same film, an adaptation of Faulkner called *The Long Hot Summer*. Such acting brings the same sense of exposure and prurient invasion of privacy you find in Williams and Samuel Richardson. At its best it can offer the moment of revelation Ben Gazzara provides in *End as a Man*, when his career as the military college torturer lies at the mercy of a fawning homosexual. Gazzara at this moment registers the turning point of the entire film by the expression in his eyes.

The late James Dean and his legend suggest how closely this kind of acting corresponded to some widely felt urge for expression. All his words had the privacy of soliloquy. Brooding, restless, slurring his lines in a monotone when not moaning or whispering, he would fall into narcissistic poses, as in *East of Eden* when he leaned his head against a wall. One might call it naturalistic acting with the lid off. Although Clurman and Lee Strasberg, possibly even Elia Kazan, its popularizer in harness with Williams, would wash their hands of the more extreme manifestations, something in the *zeitgeist* has favoured excess. Where this kind of acting is bad, American drama is bad in just the same way. But it can at least be said for the acting that it comes from inside the actor and is not an anthology of other people's mannerisms. As with Stanislavsky, whose teaching should be called the System to avoid confusion with the Method, the basic idea is to find something in your own experience which is consistent with the part. Daily life, for instance, arouses many an aggressive impulse suppressed in the early stages. You may never have actually thrown whisky in the club bore's face, but you may often have wanted to, and, if a part demands it, you try to reconstruct that uncommitted crime from memory. As you are a modern, intellectual actor the whole field of literature can be drawn on for parallels if necessary. The destiny of Julian English in O'Hara's *Appointment in Samarra* hangs on one such indiscretion. For a lower social bracket *Waiting for Lefty* may suggest associational links with James Cagney in a semi-documentary film called *Taxi*. It was coffee he had to throw in his girl friend's face. If we shift the period from the thirties to the fifties and a soft drink is used for the same crude gesture, we may expect a conscientious Method director to explain the different background of social habit involved and decide what is to be done with the straw. In all three cases no amount of preparation could lend the gesture more than a limited theatrical interest, but spread all through a production the expressive results of such care are hypnotic. A critic has to bear in mind that the artistic content of the play may still be negligible. Once, in an underground train, I was rolling my umbrella and became aware of tension among the other passengers. At the moment of truth, when you finally secure the fabric by a twist of elastic at the top, the entire process can come unstuck. My concentration had unintentionally turned a carriage full of commuters into a theatre. 'The creature', wrote Keats of the stoat, 'hath a purpose, and his eyes are bright with it.' Personality forces released by Method training can be fascinating enough to make one overlook a trivial dramatic purpose, almost to accept ensemble achieved by actors and their directors as a super-session of the playwright.

In my view, this tendency of the Method to break clear of its original moorings in well-written drama such as you find in early Odets, to thrash around in what increasingly resembles a creative vacuum and to claim that it is part, even perhaps the leader, of an evolution towards new forms, is highly suspect. In speaking of the autonomous actor in Chapter II, it was not the kind of autonomy which covers a scarcity of playwrights by claiming that play-wrights are not necessary that I had in mind, but the privilege of a great actor now and then to know better than anyone else what a great writer means. New forms in the arts are usually evolved by people who have mastered the old ones, and the Method's record in anything outside an American proletarian context is very thin. Marlon Brando's Antony on the cinema was an anachronism, lacking in the prescribed hedonism, sullen, moody and vocally inferior to versions by Edwardian hams, who did at least recog-nize the existence of a verbal architectonic in the rhetoric. English actors using the Method as a short cut to the classics have fared little better.

Allowing for these defects, which may be overcome when permanent schools and theatres at the New York Lincoln Centre enable American drama to sort out its traditions, it may well be that the Method has influenced English acting favourably: first as the vehicle of plays more stimulating than the routine West End bromide, and secondly as a jazz version of the Stanislavsky System, drawing on its Gorki, *Lower Depths*, element. Many of the fine crop of young English actors are bilinguals on closer terms with American drama than their own classics, and little in the recent history of the English commercial theatre can explain the new seriousness and professionalism of their approach. Michael Bryant seemed equally at home as the Harvard failure in *The Iceman Cometh* and the German tutor in *Five Finger Exercise*. Actors like O'Toole and Alan Dobie, who first came into prominence with Theatre in the Raw, have more in common with American models than with anything in the genteel du Maurier tradition of naturalistic acting. Can one imagine du Maurier spitting on the stage floor as O'Toole was required to do as the gutter rhapsodist in *The Long and the Short and the Tall*? Prole drama thrives on uninhibited acting and has released a flood of talent. On the other hand, it can restrict growth because of the modes of behaviour involved. Albert Finney, for example, has a mercurial sensibility grafted on the stage presence of Tearle. His potential is limitless. To be indisputably great, he only needs an escape from parts which confine him to a narrow and ultimately boring set of responses. It may be the result of the working-class subjects common to both, but aside from all considerations of Method influence, young English actors associated with Theatre in the Raw are often as crude, in a similar way, as Brando was in *Julius Caesar*. During an interval at Stratford-on-Avon, I heard an old man say plaintively to his companion: 'I never knew the ancient Romans spoke Lancashire.'

This type of acting, whether based on the Method or not, is as limited as the du Maurier-Rex Harrison throwaway elegance; how limited was shown when Robert Stephens, adept of the Porteresque hero with one foot in the working class, another in Subtopia and a jaundiced eye on the Establishment, tried to act a Parisian in Feydeau's *Occupe-toi d'Amélie*, as anglicized by Coward. It has, all the same, international authority in so far as it mirrors working-class behaviour. That male tears are recognized in that context as perhaps the only index of superior sensibility is confirmed in Richard Beynon's *The Shifting Heart*, a routine product of Theatre in the Raw in which an Australian truck driver is told by his Italian in-laws that he must learn to cry, and soon after does so, his muscular shoulders turned to the audience as he leans against a fence. The same play exploits facial injuries and a pregnant heroine in such a way as repeatedly to drown its humane purpose in melodrama; yet many enthusiasts forget that acting in primary colours is the easiest part of the job.

It is not reactionary but constructive to point out directions in which the most promising imaginable younger generation of actors needs to extend its range. The new English playwrights have found splendid interpreters of their new requirements, have had not only their mannerisms but their creative successes faithfully reflected in the acting. *A Taste of Honey* is difficult to think of apart from Frances Cuka's wry, disillusioned, invincibly cheerful teenage girl and Murray Melvin's gay and sensitive homosexual. The temporary home they make together is an infinitely touching rehearsal for a better way of life than the surrounding squalor permits, and perhaps the boy represents a feminine delicacy which the girl has had to suppress; she says to her mother's fiancé: 'How did she talk you into it? You must have been out of your mind.' To modulate from this precocious maturity to the vulnerable joy of a slum child in the miniature house at an infant school required acting of some range and sensitivity. The two young players, neither of whom corresponds to a glamour stereotype, made their transitions without a false note; and in *The Hostage* Melvin adapted his sparrowy deftness and resilience equally well to the part of a virile young soldier. When we have subtracted as much as is due to Miss Littlewood's direction of both plays, there remains a style of acting, undeniably English in a new idiom, to set beside the international proletarian bluster encouraged by Theatre in the Raw. Dorothy Tutin and John Neville embody the refined aspect of it.

Central, by the unpredictable workings of a communal art, is Joan Plowright, an actress on whom history has just happened to throw the responsibility for lighting up key sectors of the mid-century battlefield. It would be ungracious, perhaps, to call her a female equivalent of Richardson, although she is the only actress to possess that actor's ripe deliberation. Had she come on the scene a decade or so earlier, Miss Plowright would probably have been type cast as a heroine's younger sister or a comic maid. We shall never know how many similar talents were lost for want of suitable material. Hers is among other things a very mid-century talent for self-education in public. When Miss Plowright is outside her range—in the Wilton Square scenes of *Major Barbara*, for instance, or the murkier depths of *The Lesson*—she seems quite unperturbed and ready to attack her difficulties in connivance with the audience. Her lack of glamour she accepts with the same precocious maturity as leads many of her generation to deride pin-up sex. When Hollywood turned over in 1956 to wholesome heroines like Shirley MacLaine, it looked like a development Miss Plowright had been aware of all along, no more surprising than some future *Hamlet* who should happen to speak with Lincolnshire intonations like hers. As soon as the critic is tempted to write her off as a soubrette, along comes a play like *Roots* in which she can stand on a chair and deliver intellectual tirades in an East Anglian accent. More than once in the past her acting has revealed a gap between the playwright's intention and her powers of expression. Now, not only the audience but the play itself enters into complicity with her; the unseen hero of *Roots* is like a director who must give an actress all the clues to an interpretation and leave the final solution to her. Beatie Bryant in the play and Miss Plowright in the part both succeed. An author of Russo-Hungarian extraction and an actress from Lincolnshire achieve one of the new drama's most illuminating statements in performance. Neither's contribution can be separated from that of the other. There is scarcely a hint of Brecht, the Method or *El Sombrero*, and the final result is as English as the end of Richardson's nose. The drama has caught up with the times again, and it is still ours.

Now, with the first wave of creative energy spent, we may hope for plays increasingly adult and in touch at more points with a society governed, for good or ill, by the intellect. Happiness will have to be conceived as something less rudimentary than *A Taste of Honey*'s dance with a mop and pail or the squirrel fantasy in *Look Back in Anger*. Although nothing so precise as the superannuated forms of tragedy and comedy may ever emerge again, it is impossible to imagine any society which can abolish *l'honnête homme*'s tightrope walk, his balancing act between the extremes of expediency and self-assertion. The new drama, at its least adolescent, has gone a long way beyond the character in *A Hatful of Rain* who remarks: 'There's things I feel I have no words for.' Having let loose a torrent of emotive language, it now has to organize in intellectual depth. So must the actors; and a good way to start would be by cheerful admission that classical comedy of manners, far from being a museum form to be burlesqued or dislocated in the search for a mid-century message, is a discipline second to none for equipping the actor. It can teach him poise, detachment and the finesse which, even if a proletarian drama makes little call on it, is still a property of the human mind. Until evidence accumulated that Gielgud, the master of these three acting weapons, was losing contact with the younger generation of theatre-goers, though still near his prime, it was not necessary to point this out.

Fortunately two things have happened which favour a cure of this blind spot in mid-century English writing and acting. First, John Fernald, as head of the influential Royal Academy of Dramatic Art, instituted a policy of repeated student performances of exacting classics: Brecht, Chekhov, Sheridan and Shaw. It is easier for the beginner to work downwards from the best than, as Stratford-on-Avon and Waterloo Road repeatedly show, for the contemporary professional to achieve a classical style. As Bacon advised, the practice should be harder than the use. Secondly, Benthall loaded the 1959–60 Old Vic programme with comedy of manners, the proper diet for a fine young actor like Alec McCowen. Meanwhile the Comédie Française visit of March 1959 had drawn several ill-informed responses and few of the obvious, painful comparisons with English performance. What the Comédie Française demonstrated, apart from the advantages in polish of a nationally instituted theatre, was a thorough knowledge of what kind of play they were in. Instead of antiquarian reconstructions or crude adaptations, they offer refreshing theatre based on informed appreciation of how much re-thinking a given classic can stand. It follows that they make pretty free with Feydeau and the Molière of *Les Fourberies de Scapin* and *Le Bourgeois Gentilhomme*, less so with the Molière of *Les Femmes savantes*. If we take a closer look at the results, in a survey directed towards English drama, we are indicating the standard our own rising actors may reach when they are provided with suitable conditions of security and cease to be identified exclusively, in three media, with Theatre in the Raw.

Hirsch, as Redillon in Act III of *Le Dindon*, is called on in his apartment by the married woman he has been chasing. She intends to capitulate but expects elaborate preliminaries. The situation is that Redillon is played out, after a night with what boulevard drama calls a demi-mondaine and Delaney in *A Taste of Honey* 'a half-whore'. Both Hirsch and Micheline Boudet are aware that the situation will do much of the work for them. They concentrate on behaving naturally, without the self-conscious posturing with which most English actors vilify farce. Hirsch gives an authentic Method performance of an exhausted man and obeys Stanislavsky's principle of seeming to ignore the audience. No smirks and nothing exhibitionist are permitted. He is hoarse; his back hurts. Trying to meet his partner's demands, he sketches romantic phrases as if struggling to remember a theatrical part. He cannot help yawning and scratching himself. Two levels of consciousness are defined and interwoven. But in the first act we have seen him at his best, a conscious dandy, and the contrast between then and now is funny in itself. A number of English actors could play Act III on these lines, given a director who knew what farce was. Very few of them could get anywhere near the standard of Hirsch and Jacques Charon in Act I.

Why not? Because a sense of period is evolved by constant practice, and, leaving aside the usual ladder of promotion by way of the Conservatoire and the grounding it offers in the grammar of aristocratic behaviour, the continental repertory system calls for intermittent repetition, without continuously flogging the performance as happens in a West End run. You cannot learn overnight to flourish a hat or a cane in public as if it were an action habitual as the lighting of a cigarette. But the essence of comedy of manners cannot be yielded up unless these externals are attended to. Neglected, they leave the play without a necessary framework; overdone, or anxiously improvised, they get in the way. If style, as Gielgud maintains, is knowing what kind of play you're in, it presupposes a knowledge of the play's social context. Often enough one can lay down the principle: no manners, no comedy. Likewise, the quality of burlesque varies in direct proportion to the actor's mastery of the type of behaviour ridiculed. This, apart from the obvious necessity to avoid direct invitations to laugh, is what experts mean when they say that farce should be played seriously. It requires a fine discrimination, and the funniest English performance I ever saw was Denys Blakelock's as the clergyman in Pinero's *Dandy Dick*. One would have suspected type casting, had he not delivered Wilde's epigrams in *Lady Windermere's Fan* as skilfully as the clergyman's innocent fatuities.

The filmed record of *Le Bourgeois Gentilhomme*, with a controversially sympathetic Jourdain by Louis Seigner, makes use of courtiers' arrogance to intimidate the chief character. They have the style which Jourdain aspires to, and not a gesture allows us or him to forget it while the dancing, music and fencing masters put him through his paces and the sponger extracts his money. It resembles the anti-aristocratic social comment Miss Littlewood will draw from a Jacobean play, with the difference that the French actors can interpret courtiers sympathetically, and are here stressing the moral bankruptcy for a special purpose. When the fencing master bellows like a sergeant-major, in a way not demanded by the text, we can be sure that he is doing so under direction, not because it is the only style he knows. Anyone 'committed' to the point of despising finesse should remember the M.A.T.'s practice of it. At Sadler's Wells Massalsky played Gaiev in *The Cherry Orchard* as a fastidious bachelor. Du Maurier himself could not have managed a teacup, or dusted a garden seat with his handkerchief, more impeccably.

Perhaps the generation reared on Theatre in the Raw and Shakespeare without Castiglione have most to learn from Jean Meyer's production of *Les Femmes savantes*, probably the last of Molière's plays they would be likely to want to see. It poses to the author, the actors and the director an overriding problem: how to make a cerebral subject interesting in the theatre. Armande and her friends are, from one point of view, the Joneses, turning from consumer goods to culture in search of status; but everything turns on alexandrines composed by Trissotin, a feeble poet. Can these dry bones live? Yes, if a beauty like Hélène Perdrière can make Armande formidable enough to provide the conflict this play lacks at a reading; if Andrée de Chauveron's farcical enthusiast ridicules anything she approves of in advance, and so on, through a cast which knows its business. As an audience, we must be on the side of the dissenters, of Clitandre and Henriette. They do not ogle us, but behave with relaxed detachment, apart from the others though mannered in the same way. The actors distil an atmosphere in which a hackneyed line—'Mariez-vouz, ma sœur, à la philosophie'—explodes like thunder at a garden fête.

Chapter X

CHEKHOV WITHOUT INHIBITIONS
The Moscow Art Theatre in London, 1958

———————————— * ————————————

'I can hardly form an estimate of a play', wrote Chekhov while at work on *The Cherry Orchard*, 'merely by reading it.' Evaluation of drama on the evidence of the written, or even the broadcast, word is a dishonest critical method, in the sense that it would be dishonest to set oneself up as an expert on Titian, having seen only monochrome reproductions and other people's responses in print. There is no proper substitute for performance, the thing done; and the skilled dramatist is the one who has learned what words and actions will come to life when taken off the page and filtered through an actor. Exactly what sort of life it will be, nobody—not the author himself—can tell. There are too many variable factors. On the Moscow Art Theatre's first night at Sadler's Wells, Fiers made his first entrance and immediate exit in silence; two nights later there was a round of applause as he went out of sight. In between there had been press notices, and Saturday's Chekhov has a different atmosphere from Thursday's. That is the fun of it.

Multiply such trifles and you have the basic appeal of live theatre. It reminds you with a jolt that the Stanislavsky System, as he pointed out time and again, is only a means to an end; that read about in prim translation, or divined from photographs of its inventor (each more like a stern father-image than the last), it had become meaninglessly independent, like Shakespearian variants tossed around from thesis to thesis. Even if you understand only three words of Russian it is now clear that the System is humane enough to produce happy actors, flexible enough to provide entertainment, adaptable enough to assimilate young replacements, tough to the point of surviving purge, revolution, and war, and above all, sufficiently complex to cope with Chekhov. We have seen satisfactory productions of Chekhov before, notably by Komisarjevsky and Saint-Denis. These have been valuable, for any performance tells more than a cloistered reading. But now it seems that even *The Three Sisters* of 1938, in which Saint-Denis directed the finest naturalistic ensemble yet seen in England, was not definitive Chekhov. The Chebutikin was marginal and Redgrave's Baron, played with a skill and sincerity that stole the show, too prominent. Redgrave has a presence and height which rivet the attention, a thing the Baron can rarely do. His opposite number at Sadler's Wells effaced himself, while the Chebutikin was often dominant. The tones vibrated with a different emphasis.

If the M.A.T. compels readjustment of ideas about Chekhov even when considered at the Saint-Denis level of direction, it makes other productions seem to have borne the relationship to these plays of Pater's dreamy Mona Lisa to Leonardo's portrait; the enigmatic sadness of the original caught and the virile statement, along with the earthiness of the subject, left out. Compared with English productions the lighting alone is as brilliant in impact as the primary colours hitting one for the first time from a masterpiece recently cleaned. At the start of *The Three Sisters*, Irina stands radiant at the French window in her white party dress, with sleek birch trees in the background echoing the highlights, while effects range through the amber circle of Andrey's table lamp, subdued and intimate in a darkened room, to Solyony, almost completely blacked out for a moment as he advances towards Irina. In *The Cherry Orchard* the tree tops, loaded with blossom and translucent behind crystalline windows, join with a room very sparingly furnished and a dawn as bracing as the opening act of *Oklahoma!* to weigh the scales heavily on the side of youth. Anya, a coltish schoolgirl with pigtails, is at home in this room, more than anyone else. After all, it is still called the nursery.

This play has been out of the repertoire for eleven years, allegedly awaiting a replacement of Kachalov, the last Gaiev. We know Chekhov wanted the brighter side of it emphasized, but certain aspects of this version are questionable. In flat contradiction to the 'oppressive sense of emptiness' asked for in his stage directions to the last act, the set looks even gayer when its meagre furnishings are covered up; it looks suitable, in fact, for conversion to a recreation room in the most hygienic of youth hostels, and in the only movement undeniably external to Chekhov, Anya and Trofimov strike an attitude reminiscent of propaganda posters as they make their final exit. Still, explicitly in the text, she does say good-bye to the old life and he greets the new. The lines ask for attitudes, though perhaps not that one. Then bronzed work-men are glimpsed outside, closing the shutters and leaving Fiers to die in a room gently dappled with sunbeams through the apertures. It is as benign a stage death as you ever saw, mellow Shakespearian Chekhov.

If there are some brash lighting and scenic effects hardly to be expected from the 'austere' M.A.T., the sound effects are astound-ing. Instead of a few apologetic chirps in *The Cherry Orchard*, there is an all-out dawn chorus and later a solo from a cuckoo. *The Three Sisters* is equally uninhibited. Suppressed a little after the first night—when it seemed nearer to the auditorium than the stage, so that the audience was in league with the absconding soldiers—it is still a loud, swaggering band, with a stake in the future. As for the mysterious sound of a string snapping 'as if out of the sky' in *The Cherry Orchard*, it is deep, plangent, and in context disturbing beyond imagination. Considered side by side with the décor and lighting, this use of sound leads one on to the impression of virile energy—conveyed at times with an almost childish directness as when the clumsy Yepikhodov collides with a door-post—which impregnates the M.A.T.'s acting. Supreme ensemble work was expected of it, but not the rampant individual-ism attainable within the pattern, not the savage power of Gribov in Chebutikin's drunkenness, not this panache and violence, with more than a hint of Tolstoy and Dostoevsky, in Chekhov; and certainly not the revelation of supposedly minor-key naturalistic plays, even when seen from the back row of Sadler's Wells' circle, as broadly theatrical, at times operatic.

The M.A.T. has developed a way of presenting the intimacies of Chekhov in a pattern of external effects which accommodates all the familiar reticences, hesitations, and interruptions of the dialogue without relying on fleeting, inspirational expressions of the eyes and other minutiae that invite camera close-ups. What-ever Stanislavsky may have taught about ignoring the audience, the actors are aligned on it, one often standing behind another when talking to him in a position absolutely meaningless anywhere except on the stage. The relevance of this to drama in general is obvious when you recall the constant attacks on naturalism as something remote, finicky, anti-theatrical, and so forth. As practised by the M.A.T. it is none of these things; they behave as if the so-called fourth wall were a crowded auditorium, as it really is. Hence the slight swagger, the hint of conscious artifice admired in public, which prevents the disciplined actions from appearing mechanical; hence the happy, relaxed faces enjoying applause at the finish.

It was this traditionally theatrical projection of voice and gesture, carried over for very different purposes from the kind of drama Stanislavsky despised, which (along with some unashamedly obvious effects) gave the Sadler's Wells performances their un-expected freshness and punch. In a television programme before the season began, only Saint-Denis emphasized that the ultimate aim of the System is to get across. Guthrie suggested that the M.A.T. might have become a bit old-fashioned, claimed that Ibsen and even Granville Barker had done much of the cleaning up ascribed to them, and said the drama was moving on—in the direction, for instance, of stylization. We now know that the M.A.T. can adopt stylization too, stylized naturalism which throws new light on that old scapegoat of a convention, can allow Astrov to deliver a major speech direct at the audience as if the two other people on stage at the time did not exist. It also accommo-dates extremes of dandyfied bravura (Vershinin, Gaiev, Solyony, Charlotta) and harsh realism (Chebutikin, Lopakhin) beyond the twilit passivity and crude farce we are accustomed to, so that assessment of Chekhov as dramatist aside from this company's interpretation is at present academic, like separations of 'form' and 'content'. No doubt the M.A.T.'s picture of Chekhov is no more definitive than Burbage's was of Hamlet, but it has authority in detail and in total effect.

For violent impact Lopakhin's assumption of ownership in *The Cherry Orchard* is a case in point. Following Chekhov's expectation that Stanislavsky would choose the part for himself, and his re-minder that Varya would not love a boor, Lukyanov plays him for the first two acts in a respectable loose-limbed, restless way, exasperated, kind, and impatient. Getting things done in this environment, he lets us know, is like swimming in treacle, the more frustrating the better your normal rhythm. After the sale he comes in unobtrusively and sits quietly on a settee. What sets him off is Varya's action in throwing the keys on the floor, and to mark this she does not just toss them down, but crashes them down directly in front of her, centre stage, with an overarm movement. Alone with Ranevskaya, he begins his triumphant tirade sitting down, rises after a few lines as if lifted by his own mounting emotion and picks the keys up. He throws them a yard or so in the air and catches them, right-handed in a movement like a punch which carries his whole body up stage towards the ballroom; he storms into it through the first of two arched openings in the wall.

Inside the ballroom he halts, well in view of the audience through the aperture, and orders the band to play. The pause before it obeys is agonizing. When the music starts, Ranevskaya, who until now has held a monumental 'freeze' while seated on the chair she reached out for on hearing the news, and is alone on the main stage, begins to weep. Lopakhin breaks something in the ballroom with a violence in tune with the sacking of the Czar's palace and comes into full view again, a tall man holding high on to both sides of the second aperture. We see him there, a few yards behind Ranevskaya, wild-eyed and panting, bestially dominant though limp from the emotional effort, until the woman's misery seems to restore his humanity as a sense of guilt. He staggers miserably into the room and to the opposite side of the table against which she is sitting, like a child seeking reassurance after doing something outrageous. She does not even look at him.

This episode illustrates, among other things, Chekhov's organic use of the stage, including spatial build-up of dynamic movement and use of props every bit as important as the dialogue, and confirms that if Stanislavsky had not existed it would have been necessary to invent him. By the time he came to write this play, Chekhov knew his interpreters to the extent of making suggestions for its casting within the company. In the scene as now played there are distinct overtones of pillage, arising from director's hind-sight, author's prophetic intuition, or both; and the rhythm of the acting may allude to physical violation, in reinforcement of the spatial penetration required by the author's stage directions and choice of set for the entire act. Add to this the ambivalence, the contrary pulls in Lopakhin of real, if slightly contemptuous, affection for the family and retrospective resentment of serfdom touched off by Varya's insult—which anyway is partly motivated by infatuation—and you have naturalistic modern drama as good as anything in the classical poetic repertoire, without taking account of any additional effect the dialogue has if you understand it. Moreover the preliminary ballroom incidents modify one's response to the climax and deepen its effect, not only by the obvious allusion to fiddling while Rome burns, but by lulling the audience into identification with the family, into their vulnerability. In order to do this, such things as Charlotta's party tricks must be dazzlingly professional and make their own separate effect. We now know why Chekhov made Charlotta a fairground performer in childhood, why he insisted on strong casting for the part. He wanted to draw us into the family circle by direct traditional means.

This seems unwarrantably remote from Lopakhin's big scene, but art on *The Cherry Orchard* level casts wide for its coherence. Lukyanov's acting of the scene has affinities with Stanislavsky's poor relation, the Method, a shaggy quality also present in Trofimov and the Beggar. What we are totally unaccustomed to is the development of a strand in the pattern such as Vershinin's seduction of Masha in *The Three Sisters*. Although it does not obtrude from the general harmony, as happened in an English production with Richardson and Leighton in these parts, the M.A.T.'s version of this episode can be viewed separately at, say, a second visit and found to withstand very close inspection.

Yurieva at Sadler's Wells was playing Masha for the first time, but such is the training and rehearsal that you would not have guessed it. She is what used to be called a fine figure of a woman, solidly sensual, with square shoulders and a rather broad face. Before Vershinin arrives she sits alongside a table, reading her book, very prim and Victorian-looking. One hand steadies the book and another touches, with an elegant upward inclination from the wrist, a chain which hangs from neck to waist and is her anchor throughout, strictly according to Stanislavsky principles of resort to props for the attainment of relaxation. Often her fingering of it is the only indication of the ferment below the disdainful, classically posed exterior. From the word go, this Masha, with nothing to say for some time and marooned in a corner, is indisputably *there*. Vershinin enters at length, as played by Massalsky a dandy of a colonel, done up to the nines, boots and medals aglow. He makes great play with his spotless white gloves, but they do not ask him to sit down until they have found out that he comes from Moscow, and when he does it is Olga, the schoolteacher, eager and looking quite attractive, who monopolizes him. Masha, however, is on her feet now, and although she turns her back on him and on the audience for her quick weep at the memory of those gay military parties, Vershinin is allowed a good view of her most of the time.

Masha's next undertaking is to get out of the corner behind the table and nearer to Vershinin, subtly, as clever women do at a social gathering. The chance comes when Andrey comes in and sits down on a sofa in the centre of the stage. Having shown Vershinin what fun she can be by joining in the teasing of Andrey, Masha sits on the sofa next to her brother. Nothing more natural, and it brings her close to Vershinin. During the set speech about the glorious future he looks more often at her, without neglecting the others, enough to gauge the effect he is making. He is not rude in his casual responses to the Baron's enthusiastic intervention, as might appear from the text, merely absorbed in Masha. She has soon announced she will stay to dinner, walked up stage to the piano, taken off her hat and patted her hair, crisply and without fuss, while Vershinin has manoeuvred so that he can still see her, his audience. Aware of this, she takes a brief interest in Olga's exercise book and is up by the French window when her pedantic husband comes in, so that we can see her disgusted reactions to his chatter, the hypertension when Kulygin and Vershinin shake hands. All this time the other characters are given the focus demanded at any particular moment; during Kulygin's longest speech, for instance, Vershinin is quenched by having his back turned to the audience.

There follows the dinner party, diagonally recessed in deep focus with Vershinin at the extreme end of the table and Masha near the other, closer to the audience but not distracting attention from the forestage, unless you consciously ignore what is going on there from time to time. Basically she gives a display of basking in Vershinin without looking at him, except rarely and covertly. In spite of the tension, happily relieved when the Baron sits down next to her, she has a whale of a time amid the convivial eating and drinking. It is the real beginning of the thaw. The end of it comes in the second act, when she is side by side with Vershinin on a sofa and allows the hand nearest to him to rest invitingly on the fabric. After he takes hold of it there is a demonstration of Stendhal's dictum that it is the first mutual pressure of hands which counts; when he kisses it Masha undergoes a minor convulsion, starting as a tremor of the wrist and transmitted along the arm, visibly, to the shoulder, after which her whole body seems to become limp. Neither seems to resent the Baron's intrusion very much, and Vershinin, the fish now hooked, can afford to give him full attention for the first time, while Masha strokes her fur cape luxuriously. It has temporarily superseded the chain. After Vershinin is called back to his wife, Masha works off her frustration by flirting, with the two young officers, well in the background of the major action.

If one is justified in isolating these elements of the total effect, it is because they show how faithfully the Stanislavsky System operates within it, how economical and theatrical the functioning is, how free from fussy neurotic tension; and how true it is that Chekhov is always inviting one to look between the lines. The present M.A.T. version succeeds, a bit surprisingly in view of those prophetic utterances about the future, in making Vershinin little more than a catalyst and giving Masha the emphasis. It also brings out, so easily that it can hardly be a misinterpretation, a Chekhov more robustly sensual than is generally accepted, as does the Lopakhin scene.

But in that marvellous last act of *The Three Sisters* there emerges an unanswerable vindication of the visual element in drama, to such an extent that the language, it seems, can almost be dispensed with. Television Chekhov has made the point negatively, by showing how much goes to pieces when selective grouping is imposed by the camera. This act, even more than the others, is conceived in plastic terms for a stage, and the M.A.T. actors secure much of their effect, thanks to that austere discipline aimed ultimately at joyful concentration in face of the public, simply by being there, immediate as Franz Hals. We know as much as we are ever going to know about the sisters by now; it is a question of rounding them up and drawing the final conclusions. Masha is centred on a garden seat, with room enough for a man on it, though there is not going to be one. At Irina's age the verandah steps will do. Olga is on the move, placating and protecting as usual.

The surprise, beyond anything possible from a reading, is Chebutikin. Gribov, who has already placed him by one shattering outburst of drunken fury and what can only be called the dynamic reading of newspapers, now sits leaning against the balustrade of the verandah, hunched like a beady-eyed toad, if anything more in relation to the audience than with the characters; something of a vulture, also, ready for a bit of scavenging after the shots have been fired. There is cynical resignation, but there is also an atmosphere of positive, active despair about him, like the blaspheming of an overworked army doctor in an advanced dressing station. Now and then he rubs the back of his hand, deftly, as if applying ointment. At the bottom of his savage mood is a sense of identification, up to a point, with everybody concerned, together with the knowledge that no intervention will make much difference to the course of events. He is a thoroughly Yeatsian angry old man, incurably detached. A likely conclusion from this interpretation is that Chebutikin is Chekhov.

In these regions of final discrimination, it is time to admit, quickly and firmly, the limitations imposed by the language barrier, the danger of being foxed by the brilliance of the acting, the subjective factor. For instance, my wife, who compares the supposedly optimistic endings of these plays to the hope of a cancer patient that science will discover the cure in time, sees this particular Chebutikin as a rough old bear, *au fond* too kindly to hurt a fly. If this is correct, the impression of sinister brooding would have been derived mistakenly from Gribov's rasping diction and the fact that he plays most of the act hunched over the balustrade with his greatcoat draped loosely on the shoulders. Still there is undoubtedly more fibre in the character than we have been able to suspect from English productions, and strength enough to knock over a chair in the drunk scene with one swift slap. The point is that discussion of the essential Chekhov may crystallize here on a single actor's performance. There is no dim subservience to the requirements of ensemble.

Lopakhin, a fanatically hard worker descended from serfs and climbing to equal terms with the landed gentry, seems about as close as a projection can be to the dramatist himself. An extract from the play shown at the National Film Theatre records a Lopakhin coarser and more insensitively rugged than the present one, along with Knipper-Chekhova's Ranevskaya, altogether more perky and resilient than that of Tarasova at Sadler's Wells and with more backbone. It must have been difficult enough to take over a part from the author's widow, who had played it long enough almost to justify a change of name by deed-poll, without being landed as well with a more sympathetic Lopakhin, a livelier Trofimov and what appeared to be an unusually passive place in the action. One was prepared to admit that there had been too

much of Turgeniev, or even Paula Tanqueray, in English interpretations, but scarcely to expect such unwieldy neutrality, such
cosy acquiescence from Ranevskaya. Revolving on this axis,
deliberately no doubt, the production had enough stability under
its glittering surface to show how far *The Cherry Orchard* can be
slanted without collapsing; again a Shakespearian characteristic,
arising here from Chekhov's ambivalent attitude, so faithfully
reflected in Lopakhin, to the feckless and lovable family. If he
rejects anyone it might be Yasha, odious in the text but redeemed
in performance by Leonidov, who does as much for Solyony, so
that both can now be regarded as within the scope of Chekhov's
compassion, though on the hinterland.

This enrichment by humanization runs, with the odd exception
of Ranevskaya, right through the M.A.T. Chekhov and nowhere
more plausibly than in the stranded spinsters, all cast and played
as warm and wholesome, eminently marriageable; it extends to
Uncle Vanya, as recorded by Kenneth Tynan in what reads like
the best dramatic criticism in the English language since the death
of Sir Desmond MacCarthy. All the same, *Uncle Vanya* still
comes across as unsatisfactory compared with the other two masterpieces, too explicit in Astrov-Chekhov and his afforestation
plans, rhetorical in its advocacy of the desperate uncle. Who can
accept a chairborne Don Quixote?

Finally, what about the 'yearning for a better life' aspect of the
plays which the M.A.T. insists on? Do they over-emphasize it?
Kedrov, the very distinguished director of *Uncle Vanya*, has a
theory about the organic construction of the plays according to
which the characters in them are subjected to increasing pressure,
turned inside out and left destitute of everything except hope. The
yearning becomes stronger as the possibilities of attaining happiness decrease, more refined and concentrated until it is expressed
at the close by Olga, Sonya, Anya, or Trofimov. Then, he believes,
'the acting has stopped' and the author is speaking his mind. One
might add that the inflection of Chekhov's voice, the tone of the
message—if it is one—remain as much a matter for debate as ever,
supremely non-committal. When consulted about the décor of
The Seagull, all he would say of the lake was, 'Well . . . it is wet.'

Chapter XI

OLIVIER, 1959

---- * ----

Olivier as Coriolanus again, twenty-one years after he played it at the Old Vic. Casson, the director on that occasion, was now eighty-three years old and the Memorial Theatre production of 1959 was in the hands of Hall, aged twenty-eight. On the afternoon of September 10th I arrived at Stratford-on-Avon to find the riverside lawns flanking the theatre a sapless brown, beaten by the sun and the feet of tourists to the same consistency and colour as the grass of London parks in the most torrid summer within living memory. People sagged in deck-chairs, launches and rowboats moved lazily past the swans; the theatre with its retinue of empty, parked cars had the hushed, barricaded look it wears during a matinée.

Inside it that night Aronson's uncurtained set laid down the rules of the game. This was going to be a vertical production, with coigns of vantage on steps, landings and an isolated projection resembling the Tarpeian rock. The biggest uninterrupted plane, no bigger than a cramped provincial repertory stage, was bounded by the prompt corner, archaic subtarpeian doors and steps leading up to a city gate. There could be no ceremonial entrances between ranked guards of honour, of the kind Groucho Marx discredited in *Duck Soup* by awaiting his own entrance at the extreme end of a file, neither could a dense mob assemble nor a marching column gather impetus. An immediate effect of the arrangement was that Olivier's first appearance, on top of the rock, did none of the usual things to invite applause. There, like the apparition of an eagle, he suddenly was.

His preliminary scorn of the plebeians, which is written in such a way as to accommodate very strong playing, this Marcius flicked casually, like a man so much in the habit of it that no effort is required. 'Go, get you home,' it ended, 'you . . . ', and Olivier

143

paused, searching for a fresh term of abuse, before he came out with: 'fragments'. The passage had drawn on his unrivalled flair for projecting impatience; the next, in which the news of Volscian aggression is given, brought out a grander impatience: to fight and, above all, to fight Aufidius. He seemed to expand with spontaneous joy at the very mention of this man, thus telling us a lot about his own character while accentuating a major issue of the play, which revolves finally on the relationship between Coriolanus and his rival, not on the conflicts with plebeians, senators and his mother. One tragic weakness in Marcius is the chivalrous admiration he has for Aufidius. We are dealing with a Roman seen through Elizabethan eyes, remember, and the conflict is between embodiments of flawed chivalry and ruthless expediency. The Castiglione ideal, which rejects the despotic arrogance of Marcius as excessive, and so ultimately vulgar, would applaud the magnanimity of his attitude to a worthy rival. According to tragic irony, then, it is his redeeming feature which destroys Marcius. He yields to a chivalrous impulse in the age of Machiavelli. ' . . . our virtues', says Aufidius, 'lie in the interpretation of the time', and later: ' . . . a man by his own alms empoison'd and with his charity slain.' It might almost be Iago we are listening to.

The point of this digression from an account of performance is to dispose of the criticism which seeks to convey Olivier's art in terms of his virility, humour and emotional power. Great as these are, they are controlled, as our observations on his Macbeth may have indicated, by interpretative intelligence of a very high order. It operates equally well under the direction of Guthrie, Casson, Saint-Denis, Brook or Hall; and in the Stratford performance it could be seen at work in the immediate glow induced by the mention of Aufidius. A separate style of luminous brushwork, so to speak, identified this relationship throughout. There was no doubt at all where the play's climax comes. It is on the sealing of their pact, or so I shall always believe after Olivier's extraordinary handshake. He had been very quiet during the scene. There was a deathly, premonitory misgiving in the way he eventually shook hands; and his eyes were glazed. Whatever integration the character of Marcius had possessed fell apart at that moment. The rest was crumble, detonation and collapse, with part of him fatalistically detached. Incidentally the transition was as subtle and unmistakable as the one Ben Gazzara brought off under essentially melodramatic conditions in *End as a Man*. In neither case would an emphasis on animal vitality go any distance in conveying the effect.

Another strand firmly interwoven was the relationship of Marcius with Volumnia, his mother. When the action first brings them together, on his triumphant return from the exploits at Corioli, Olivier gave her a long smile with the spoilt son's immodest complacency. Although he greeted his wife with a tender break in his voice, the scene was aligned on Volumnia in a way to prepare us for the capitulation later on. Nobody, I think, lacking knowledge of English public-school *mores* could have hit exactly this note of sulky pride, a result of the man of action's narcissism held back by the necessity to belittle success in the presence of social equals. The modesty of Marcius is false modesty, as had already been obvious when Olivier writhed in discomfort at the praises heaped on him by his fellow generals, only to release a cold smile, unabashed, at the sound of his new title, Coriolanus. But this is no wilful modernizing of a text which asks him to claim in the midst of battle that he has not yet been warmed by his work and to joke about blushing. The play itself draws generously on a rhetoric of understatement which Olivier carried over into the scenes with his family, where it stood revealed, particularly in the nasty reference to widows in Corioli, as a cover for vanity.

Apart from its value in outlining emotional immaturity as a source of weakness, the spoilt-son approach paid off memorably on two occasions. The first was during the rebellion of the plebeians, when Olivier's face registered a few seconds of bewilderment; not fear, but a marked surprise that arrogant statements habitual in the family circle and among patricians could have such an inflammatory effect. Disorientated for a time before drawing his sword, he was briefly in need of reassurance, presumably from his mother. We were not to see him at a loss again until the pact with Aufidius, but something more than the dismay of a cornered animal had been expressed. Then came a playing of the admonition scene, which opens with him unrepentant and ends with a promise to mollify, chiefly for laughs.

Tastes differ about his kind of liberty. At such an extreme it ought to be, though too often it is not, Olivier's exclusive privilege. He listened to his mother's reproofs with infantile sullenness and the tone adopted reduced the whole issue to the scale of some breach of etiquette. An habitual battle of wills, fought out not so long ago about apologizing for rough words or the breaking of a companion's toy, was being reopened. 'Let go,' he interjects to Volumnia, 'Let them hang', and to Menenius, 'What must I do?' Having made the most of lines which well bear a petulant interpretation, Olivier next gave the entire scene a turn on a single one, where Coriolanus is told he must go back to the tribunes and replies: 'Well, what then? what then?' He lent the first 'What then?' his celebrated full brass on a rising inflection, caught Volumnia's eye, paused, deflated and repeated 'what then?' quietly and deferentially. Now he was prepared to listen, as comic, contemptuous *obbligato* to Evans's advice. An unforgettable effect had been reserved, however, for the last word of the last line of the scene. For the third time he is supposed to repeat the word 'mildly', which sums up the advice he has been given as to his conduct in face of the plebeians. On this most reluctant of exits Olivier neither spoke the word nor cut it. Instead, at the moment of shaping it with lips and facial muscles, he convulsively retched.

How far was all this justified? In terms of his performance, all the way. We had been given Coriolanus as a spoilt son and were not invited to sympathize with that aspect of him. If he is not at such moments to be contemptible, he might as well be funny, for little else can be made of him in relation to his mother. Volumnia, the stoical Roman matron, is too interesting a character to function merely as a symbol of antique virtue and yet not be defined as anything else. To adapt Perelman's quip, it is evident that before Shakespeare fashioned her he broke the mould. She is the worst kind of aggressive matriarch, ready to put twentieth-century audiences in mind of ageing Edwardians dispensing white feathers to civilians in 1914; and on her knees she inherits Victorian sentimentality, a wife of Calais posing for some bewhiskered President of the Royal Academy. Dryden would have managed her better. If Paxinou undertook Volumnia she would no doubt find hypnotic splendour in the old harridan, but that could only be at the expense of the title part. The alternative is to give her straight, dignified playing, as Evans did at Stratford, and let the unsympathetic elements take effect, so that she doesn't encroach on the play's main theme. Not being able to take this Volumnia seriously, and not invited to, I found no offence in Olivier's comic approach to the scene. It came as a welcome breather after the fury of the rebellion; it threw light on the immaturity, of which the choleric and impatient tendencies mentioned by Plutarch are symptoms, and it echoed the theatrical imagery. What Coriolanus is asked for by his advisers is, he considers, a performance, but in reality a display of the Machiavellian dissimulation without which he is unfitted to be a statesman:

> *You have put me now to such a part, which never*
> *I shall discharge to th' life.*

Later he says: 'I'll mountebank their loves.' By mountebanking the whole scene, Olivier delighted the Stratford audience, at the same time revealing a fatal frivolity in Coriolanus himself. Although we often see actors unable to compass heroic verse fall back on colloquial humour, his was deliberate and not unjustified by the text. The scene begins in hyperbole not far from comic exaggeration, including the notion of ten hills piled on the Tarpeian rock, and ends in sarcasm. Even the nauseated exit could be justified in so far as the conflict between Marcius and his mother is summed up in the one word 'mildly'. By intuition or an act of selection the crucial word had been picked out, an attitude revealed by vulgar facial spasm. If we add the psychological overtone of a child's rejection of food forced on him and the literary overtone of association with Macbeth's 'Amen stuck in my throat', any lingering suspicion that Olivier was indulging in gimmick can be set aside. This was great acting, to hold a daytripper from Birmingham as tightly as it held American lecturers homesick for the printed page and a bout of close analysis.

All this took place in the tense silence, punctually broken by uninhibited laughter, of an audience piled high to the awkward Memorial Theatre's roof. Any child could have enjoyed it without knowing who Shakespeare was. Olivier, fifty-two years old and already with the afternoon's matinée in the heat-wave behind him, not to mention a day's filming on *The Entertainer* to follow, cleared his throat once or twice between speeches but otherwise exuded the beetle-browed energy further than which so many of his observers fail to see. Subtract him from what was going on, and there would have been much readjustment necessary, no less than a totally different approach to the play. Meanwhile the Apollonian and the Dionysian were at work under the same roof, vested in one person. You could scarcely blame those who were content with the emotive externals and knew nothing of the textual authority for the screamed or vomited word. I only mention it to rebut the fallacy that Olivier is a privileged *id*. The man had brought his intellect to bear on this role; he was not intelligent only in action, from point to point. When he chose to draw a loud laugh from a reference to Hercules in parting with his mother, I did not flinch. Let him enjoy himself; he had earned the right.

Aside from the disintegration before Aufidius and such jewels as the discomfiture of a servant while in disguise, Olivier had three major effects in reserve. Like the others described, they should be read in the familiar context of his martial presence, which had enabled him to beg for his consulate with the tetchy humour of a five-star general trying to unbend in the canteen on Christmas Day. First, the reaction to banishment. Two decades had scarcely dimmed my memory of his 'You common cry of curs!' in Casson's production. Now the delivery was changed. Just before this speech Olivier leaned against the masonry high up on Aronson's set, head rolling from side to side, eyes mad as those of a Sistine Chapel prophetess while he listened to the tribunes. The head movement, I was amused to notice, was one recommended by Elsie Fogerty to her students for relaxing tension in the neck; Olivier was preparing himself. Advancing to the Tarpeian projection on which we had first seen him, he made the speech with less volume than in Casson's production, but with a terrifying concentration of contempt. People who think him a prose actor, because he so often breaks up lines, overlook his sustained power in a passage of invective like this. Only the lyrical escapes him. Here, cursing the plebeians, he gave the phrases such a charge of emotion that he gathered them into a single rhetorical missile, so that the speech had an impact like jagged stones parcelled together and hurled in somebody's face. There was a bizarre impression of one man lynching a crowd.

We had been given the splendours of the verse assigned to this character, the cut-and-thrust of his Elizabethan wit, an appearance fit for some ruggedly aggressive Roman statue, a very few gestures, apt and decisive as Tearle's, to point a climactic phrase like 'mutinous error'. Passages of clowning had all served to emphasize the sometimes inspiring but finally crippling dependence on Volumnia, itself an acted lesson in implied psychology. The boyish eagerness in the chivalrous admiration for Aufidius had its counterpart in an immature spite, equally clearly defined as a motive for his entry into the fatal pact. One of the attractions of such great acting is the confidence you have that the current of expression could be switched off at any moment and the effect just made survive a searching scrutiny. Now, with his subjugation to Aufidius equated with their pact, Olivier's Coriolanus had been fully demonstrated in his extremes of weakness and strength, a tragic figure, doomed long before the alienation effect at the end of the play which turns Aufidius so abruptly from Machiavellian killer to playwright's mouthpiece. Twice before the close, once athletically and once with his voice, Olivier arrested the withering away. He had emphasized the boy in Coriolanus and now must react to Anthony Nicholls, as Aufidius, calling him 'thou boy of tears'. The *fortissimo* he gave to 'Alone I did it, Boy' left one in no state to speculate about the accuracy of the taunt which aroused it. Olivier may have been subjecting Marcius to one of the shocks of recognition he likes to inflict on an audience. But one cannot experience one shock and assess another at the same time. The audience quivered at the sound of Olivier's voice like Avon swans at a sudden crack of thunder. A few seconds later he chose to make the death-fall head downwards from the twelve-foot-high Tarpeian platform, dangling for a time while soldiers, who had caught his ankles, held on. After that, the tragic farewell spoken by Aufidius acted on us like a well-earned tranquillizing drug.

INTERVIEWS

MIKHAIL KEDROV

An important link between the founders of the Moscow Art Theatre and the present company performing at Sadler's Wells is Mr. Mikhail Nikolayevich Kedrov, not only the leading textual authority on Stanislavsky and occupant of the Chair of Acting at the M.A.T. Teaching Studio, but a distinguished performer and director, whose version of *Uncle Vanya* is arousing exceptional interest. Now sixty-five years old, with grey eyes deep set beneath slanting brows, a steeply domed forehead, and hands soft and pliable as those of an orthopaedic surgeon, Mr. Kedrov is stately and composed.

But the preliminaries to an hour's conversation on theatrical ways and means involve a rearrangement of chairs in the hotel lounge, and soon Mr. Kedrov's movements have riveted the attention. Will he make use of the furniture, anchor his hands on chair backs, for example, as freely as the performers at Sadler's Wells? He begins austerely, legs crossed and one thumb hitched in the armhole of his waistcoat, as he points out that, unlike self-sufficient poetry and painting, theatrical art is carried out jointly by actors and audience. As Moscow audiences worked to bring the English visitors' *Hamlet* to life, so London audiences are playing their part now with the M.A.T. in the essential collaboration between actor and spectator which constitutes live theatre. According to the System an actor is 'not only an art-producing machine, but a man, a personality, a creative individual'.

It is enjoined, of course, that something more than mimicry or self-display should occur: the major characters must be not only impersonated but, up to a point, lived on the stage every evening. This requires assent and support from the audience, and when Mr. Kedrov alludes to the pleasure his colleagues are experiencing in acting before English audiences it is rather more than a courteous gesture; he is referring to feelings built up communally in a theatre, to the fact of drama's emotional interaction. From this he goes on to summarize principles of production already well known in England, such as the subordination of effects to the stage director's 'creative idea', the evolution of ensemble acting in the direction of visual emphasis on the listener, the bystander, away from the emphasis, once so dominant, on 'lines' and speech.

Meanwhile Mr. Kedrov's right hand has got free from his waistcoat and joined with the other in expressive arabesques, but he has remained detached and impersonal. A direct invitation to be more specific is met with the first glint of humour in the cool eyes. Mischievously he takes refuge in the actor's traditional secretiveness about his craft: how can you analyse the taste of an orange? He smiles at Mr. Shverubovich, who is interpreting, and asks one next to believe that he can only discuss his art fluently during rehearsal, be eloquent in reproving an actor's mistake. Nevertheless, Mr. Kedrov is now seated in a more relaxed position, his forearms at rest on the back of a chair as he leans forward. To illustrate his concept of Chekhov scenes in terms of music, he straightens up and conducts an invisible orchestra, and as if the rhythmic movement had precipitated it comes the dictum, 'Uncle Vanya is an orchestra and Vanya is the cello.'

This leads Mr. Kedrov, with the important reservation that a performance should speak for itself and not require supplementary explanation, to explain the kind of skeletal basis a director may find at the root of Chekhov's plays and allow for in his approach. There tends, for example, to be an optimism, generally delusive, at the beginning. Hope is then reduced until, in the celebrated early morning episodes of conflagration or storm, the characters are exposed to the core, turned inside out. Less familiar is Mr. Kedrov's opinion that their desire for a better life grows stronger as circumstances deteriorate; it becomes finer and concentrated under pressure: the juice, as he puts it, of an orange after it has been squeezed. In this medium, through some of his characters, Chekhov himself makes a positive, hopeful statement at the end of his plays.

Speaking of *The Three Sisters*, which he directed in Russia with a cast of students, Mr. Kedrov remarks on the vulgarity of Natasha, disguised beneath youth and beauty, just as in *Uncle Vanya* vulgarity of soul underlies age and success in the Professor. As the mesmeric range of gesture accompanying them unconsciously emphasizes, these are the reluctant *obiter dicta* of a practising theatrical artist. But Mr. Kedrov, a pupil of Stanislavsky and Nemirovich-Danchenko, is also the editor of an eight-volume edition, of which the fifth volume is now with the printer, that brings Stanislavsky's writings together; and he is anxious to make it clear that they are not to be allowed to harden into a dogma, for that, according to the author himself, kills growth. Development along the lines laid down by the author, instead of rigid adherence to theories sometimes contradictory, is the aim of his disciples.

The conversation ends with a rare treat: a thumb-nail sketch of Vanya's revolt and its aftermath. With his interpreter as the Professor, Mr. Kedrov, now on his feet, mimes the character's dawning recognition of misplaced loyalty, inflates to the moment of protest, and shrinks. One leaves with the certainty of having scratched, as it were, only the surface of forty years' continuous M.A.T. experience and having left vital questions, about Shakespeare, for example, unasked. But time is limited and Mr. Kedrov's production of *The Winter's Tale*, three years in rehearsal and more than a decade in contemplation, is scarcely a subject to be introduced in the closing minutes. In contrast to the hypersensitive tabloid performance of Vanya, his final handshake exerts the sustained pressure of a nicely adjusted vice.

[4 *June* 1958]

RUDOLPH CARTIER

———————————— ★ ————————————

Dominated at the moment by a tall crane and calling to mind the Colosseum or Shakespeare's Globe Theatre, if these had been adapted to the uses of contemporary showmanship according to the fantasy of H. G. Wells or of Mr. Fritz Lang in the mood of *Metropolis*, the B.B.C. Television Centre seems to have the scale of a mountain already. Can it really justify the little mouse of an artistic end-product it exhibits on millions of screens? How, if at all, does that differ in the end from a film, made in confinement under exaggerated pressure and viewed in miniature?

One puts this question to Mr. Rudolph Cartier because he is one of the few producers in the medium to have evolved a personal style. Fifty years old, a Viennese who came to England in 1935, Mr. Cartier is neatly and informally dressed. A slight flourish of the hair at the nape of his neck might suggest the musician. 'How does television differ from films?' he begins. 'Let us assume sufficient time and resources to make it as close as possible to the image we carry in our heart of a subject. The television end-product is different from a film or stage one because it is destined for a very small audience, sitting secluded in a semi-darkened room and trying to look through a small sheet of glass, a window, into the world of realism, fantasy, and so on we are trying to create.

'The film audience sits in a mass of perhaps two thousand people who share the emotions, the laughter, tears, or suspense. When a Danny Kaye film is shown, for example, if three people start laughing the rest join in, whereas at home the comedian has to work very hard to make a group of four people laugh. The viewer at home is annoyed by the studio audience when he does not feel their group reaction, is not infected by the presence of those others. Studio audiences are an encouragement for the comedian. Actors should be able to do without them.'

After the success of *Quatermass Experiment*, Mr. Cecil McGivern gave Mr. Cartier an assignment which made television history. 'In *1984*', says Mr. Cartier, continuing his account of audience response, 'I could create suspense and fear among millions of people sitting at home and watching the terrifying image of Big Brother glaring at them. They were unable to find comfort and help, as they could have done from other people sitting in a cinema striking matches and rustling chocolate boxes. The emotional impact of the film of *1984*, which was most expertly made, could not reach the same level of fear as the television production. After half an hour of that, and before the torture scenes, the switchboards at Lime Grove were flooded by callers trying to release their pent-up anxieties in protests.'

Mr. Cartier recalls this without apparent smugness, as a part of the distinction he is demonstrating between the two media. Talking in an ante-room away from telephones and floor plans, he remains stiffly seated and hard to associate with the lavishness of *Salome* and *A Tale of Two Cities*. 'The main weapon of the television producer', he goes on, 'is the close-up, because it gives the viewer a chance to watch the emotion as portrayed from a distance of less than a foot. Because it is the main weapon it must be used sparingly. Music at a continuous *fortissimo* would make dull listening. The television producer cannot afford to let the visual impact of the close-up be blunted by frequent use. He has no other resource to increase the dramatic power of a scene, once a close-up has reached the maximum size the frame permits.

'My practice is to save it until the final dramatic scene, so that the viewer can see the agony of decision, twitching in the hero's cheek muscles from as close as possible during the crisis of the play. When Eli Wallach came to do *Counsellor-at-Law* I had great difficulty in preventing myself from using big close-ups of his wonderfully mobile face. I knew I had to save it for the moment when he is alone at the switchboard of his office and is told on the telephone that his wife has left him to go on a cruise with what he had thought was his best friend. Before that I had to keep saying to the cameramen: "Go back! Go back!" In that play I used the largest studio available, aligning the sets diagonally to make the distances walked from office to office even greater and so encourage the speed inherent to the scenes. I saved up the longest tracking shot for the hero's secretary (Barbara Chilcott) whom I sent to fetch his hat from the farthest corner of the set. The effect aimed at was a joyous run.'

Mr. Cartier winces at the suggestion that floor plans 'made' his cast do this or that. In recalling an effect he scrupulously names the actor concerned, as in speaking of 'the two-shot, which not only shows the face of the speaker but also his listener's reaction without cutting from one to the other. During the cross-examination of the Winslow Boy the camera was firmly fixed on the face of Sir Robert Morton (Peter Cushing), who had to react in a very subtle way to the lengthy story of theft as it built up to a salient question.' As a producer his range extends from nuances of facial expression to seething crowds. 'Yes, that needs money and facilities, but also', he adds with almost impenetrably dead-pan irony, 'a certain amount of thought as to the focal points. I think we have exploded the myth that crowd scenes cannot be done on television.

'Yes, I was trained as an architect, have been a pupil of Reinhardt and worked with UFA. In concentrating on television I decided to rid my mind of the past and start thinking in a new medium. I studied it in America before starting work for the B.B.C. in 1952 under favourable conditions at Lime Grove. We used to think the small screen did not permit extended long shots, but I claim to have developed deep focus shots by opening up the sets in depth and to have introduced many people to opera who knew nothing of it before, in *The Saint of Bleecker Street*, *Salome*, and *A Tale of Two Cities*. The approach has been to treat it foremost as drama, with music as an additional dimension and narrative device. The singers must be taught to avert their faces slightly from the camera so as to avoid the "dentist's close up".

'The essence of television', sums up Mr. Cartier, 'is that you can control the viewer's response to a much greater extent than other media permit. The B.B.C. is producing producers as well as plays. They are feeling their way towards what television drama one day will be, and we are trying to create a generation of writers who study the medium.'

[1 *December* 1958]

PETER HALL

'Speaking has lagged behind other aspects of present-day production', admits Mr. Hall. At twenty-seven his face is still boyishly rounded, enlivened by what one cannot avoid calling merry brown eyes, and unlined as yet by any of the stern sculpture conferred by executive power. 'Shakespearian actors need a great deal of practice', he goes on. 'They do not get it. Those who can act Shakespeare have been doing so on and off for twenty years. More often than not the director is in the position of a choreographer asked to stage a ballet with people who haven't had a lesson. A girl may have acted successfully in television and realistic drama. How can she trip gaily into a Shakespearian part and bring it off? It is as if you were to call on a singer with a natural aptitude for folk-song to undertake Isolde. Given a month to stage a Shakespeare play you cannot also teach your cast to speak him.'

With that sudden swoop the wan realism of the professional pins down Mr. Hall, the artist who has just referred to five different forms of the drama. 'Consider', he says, in what is now very much the voice of experience, 'the case history of a young actor. He is singled out at drama school and does a term in repertory, during which he will play one or two Shakespearian parts if he is lucky. This leads to some success in London, usually in a realistic modern play. Then, quite rightly on the strength of his talent, he is invited to the Old Vic or to Stratford, where he is faced with playing a part for which all his past training is largely superfluous.

'Now Shakespeare is not a dramatist of understatement. What he says, what he literally means and what he emotionally means, is fully expressed in his writing as if it were a piece of music. A Shakespeare play, like an operatic score, gives one the end-product, a complex image. You must work from that back to the actor, and from that the actor finds the realistic human motives which make him able to sing or say the poetic impression. In a realistic prose play the dialogue is a raw material tending to become a realistic or poetic product which the actor has a greater hand in. He can phrase a line in an infinite variety of ways and still create the same effect. He may be forgiven for saying: "I can't speak this line. I don't feel it." But a Shakespearian actor who did that would be like a violinist in an orchestra who got up and said: "I can't play A. I don't feel it."

'And so the critics often say of a newcomer that he is a good actor but cannot play Shakespeare, that his voice is too modern and his personality, too; that he cannot play heroic drama. It was said of Sir Laurence Olivier and of Dame Edith Evans and of Mr. Richard Burton and recently of Miss Dorothy Tutin. So the actor leaves Shakespeare sore. But he may sooner or later come back, and if he's got guts and keeps on shooting he'll get it in the end. By and large, training consists in doing it. The verse imposes itself on them at last, and after struggling to turn Shakespeare into modern prose, and suffering agonies, the actor sooner or later finds it plays itself.'

After the lack of practice, Mr. Hall cites two other reasons for unsatisfactory diction. 'Both the Old Vic and the Stratford Memorial Theatre are unsuitable for speaking Shakespeare. You have to have more spectacle than the words can allow, because these are still picture-frame stages. Moreover, ours is a visual society in which, other than to music, people are not trained to listen. You've got to parade a bit. There is the lady who said: "It's so beautiful. The dresses are so pretty. It's charming. I'd never have known I was at a Shakespeare play." '

In the tradition of our post-war University Wits, children of the black-out, the formative influences on Mr. Hall range from panto-mime to the disciplines of literary discrimination, from Kirby's Flying Ballet to the lectures of Dr. F. R. Leavis. 'The Old Vic seasons at the New Theatre made me want to be a director. They were of a blazing and total theatrical quality which is unforget-table.' Whenever one hears this, one blesses the wisdom of those who released Sir Laurence Olivier and Sir Ralph Richardson from the Fleet Air Arm and made artistic continuity possible. Mr. Hall pays tribute to the Gielgud seasons at the Haymarket almost as much. As the son of a stationmaster in East Anglia, poor at that time in theatres, he had the benefit of cheap railway travel. His father's transfer to Cambridge was a decisive stroke of luck.

'Music was my first love', Mr. Hall says. 'For some time I wanted to be a pianist, having some aptitude, then a conductor. The Sadler's Wells Opera was evacuated to Cambridge, where they gave *Figaro* and *The Magic Flute*. I saw Sir John Gielgud's *Hamlet*, Sir Donald Wolfit's company, the Marlowe Society's Shakespeare productions. Cambridge from 1942 onwards was full of good work.' In other words Cambridge had become an artistic capital, and Mr. Hall, starting as a primary schoolboy, took his place in it. 'I won a scholarship to the Perse School, where a former master had founded a tradition of acting. In a tiny theatre, the Mummery, we improvised scenes from the *Odyssey* and Shakespeare. When I was fourteen Shakespeare came into the classroom as an object of footnotes and elucidation. So I went to the theatre in London as often as I could, thanks to my parents and a kind aunt in Lewisham who put me up.'

Having played Hamlet at the Perse School ten years before the announcement of his Stratford appointment, Mr. Hall can fairly be called a veteran in Shakespeare, for a scholarship then took him inside the University, within, for example, the sphere of Mr. George Rylands, that recurrent influence on contemporary heroic drama. Under the director of a Gielgud Hamlet Mr. Hall went from small parts to directing Shakespeare for the Marlowe Society himself, then to the direction of one-night stands under the auspices of the Arts Council. The progression by State aid, determination and individual talent to early achievement and recognition is as typical of our time as disgruntled Jimmy Porterism, the precocity in part a fruit of war-time disruption, like penicillin.

'The ideal solution', concludes Mr. Hall, 'is a corps of actors based on Shakespeare, a permanent company. In reality as soon as you say: "We'll do that", in drama, compromise begins. The rhythm of *Waiting for Godot* is organized to such a point that you can't take a line out without altering the balance. But Beckett kept saying to me: "Play it slower", and if you slow down beyond a certain point you cannot hold the attention. As director you've got to come down on one side or the other. Inevitably in the theatre you're going to be right for some and not for others. The greatest art, even Olivier's Macbeth, is alway controversial. I am resentful if criticism is uninformed or dismissive. After all, it is the only record of our work.'

On his tenth birthday Mr. Hall heard Mozart's Requiem in King's College Chapel. When one remarked that this impact of perpendicular Gothic might excuse his long gallery and bay-window in *Twelfth Night*, he laughed with no rancour at all. Tall and placid, he wandered out through the crowd assembling in the Memorial Theatre foyer before a matinée, more like a successful athlete than the youngest theatre tycoon.

[22 *December* 1958]

MICHAEL BENTHALL

During a brief return to London from his duties in the United States, for which he leaves again by air today, Mr. Michael Benthall, Director of the Old Vic, found time to discuss the company's experiences on tour and his own evolution, notable in a stage director often taken to task for elaboration, towards greater simplicity. As befits the dual capacity of artist and administrator, he has two distinct manners. Behind a desk, with his short, powerful neck and eyes narrowed almost to a cutting edge, he could still be the artillery major demobilized in 1946. The kind of man who relaxes by standing up, he is then a casual Old Etonian, at home in West End theatrical circles, who will say: 'I played Hamlet at school when I was sixteen. It must have been horrible.'

Executives are more and more concerned with 'personalization', with avoiding human brakes on efficiency. 'It may sound a commonplace thing to say', Mr. Benthall began, 'that if the company is happy the work is good. And the more happily they play together the better the work. Our touring company in North America is headed by some very interesting personalities, and there is always harmony. The selection of such a group, along with planning for the smooth working back-stage, takes six to nine months. This time we have Mr. John Neville, Miss Barbara Jefford, and Mr. Laurence Harvey, backed by a solid body of good heavyweight actors.

'On the West Coast we were breaking new ground. We were quite unknown to San Francisco and frequently being asked: "What, or who, is Old Vic?" The exciting part of the whole venture was that audiences came not expecting to be entertained and then found the plays were alive. They are "taught" Shakespeare at school and have had visiting stars, but had never seen a major Shakespearian group playing together. So the plays themselves came as an absolute revelation. At the start of the first week, in spite of Mr. Sol Hurok's efforts, San Francisco was not interested; by the end of it we were sold out.'

Was spectacular staging the cause of this conversion? Mr. Benthall thinks not. 'What surprised them was the rather colloquial —is that the right word?—method we're developing in England of speaking the lines. We try very hard to speak them as if they are realistic, and at the same time keep the rhythm of the verse. One got the impression that in San Francisco and other places they were used to hearing people intone the lines. They look upon verse acting in the United States as something different because the lines are so beautiful. Now verse speaking you can do on a concert platform and catch a mood by adding slightly false music to the lines. But verse *acting* is a question of expressing your words, thoughts and emotions through the rhythm of poetry. American actors naturally accent individual words in a way we do not. In fact, Shakespeare composed his phrases so carefully that if you phrase them truly and pay attention to the stops the rhythm will take care of itself.'

This theory, based on more than ten years of continuous experience, was put forward as briskly as an estimate of logistics at a Staff conference. 'Having accomplished correct thought and feeling', Mr. Benthall went on, 'you must also get the emotion behind the lines which is going to touch the heart of an audience. Because', he added with a sudden flicker of well-bred embarrassment, 'only the heart touches the heart in the theatre. . . . Very often when audiences say they cannot hear, what they mean is they cannot understand. The actor is not *thinking* what he's saying. If you intone Shakespeare it may sound lovely, but it's meaningless.

'Sir John Gielgud has been touring America solo and his delivery of the lines has been a revelation to everybody. He is, if I may make so bold, the greatest English-speaking verse actor in the world today. Sir Laurence Olivier is perhaps the greatest actor and his delivery of Shakespeare's lines is very realistic, truly phrased and acted. I think that as a result of their leadership we, all of us, directors included, find ourselves striking a mean, somewhere in between their styles.'

This led to the problems of forming a company. 'I feel very strongly about this. Nobody realizes the enormous care that goes into it. Every season there is fifty per cent new blood. Each newcomer has a different kind of music in speech. It takes two to three months of working together to catch a consistent delivery. There should be two basses at least, a lot of baritones, some tenors, and of the girls quite a lot of sopranos and at least two contraltos. You cannot have a baritone actor playing Romeo, it must be a tenor.' Could this, one thought, be the man who began his directing with Mr. Tyrone Guthrie, who has often been held to neglect the verse?

'We disciples of Mr. Guthrie', said Mr. Benthall, 'took over his exuberance, which gave the plays new life in a pre-war time of light comedies and so on, when they badly needed it. He has prepared the ground for us to simplify the productions now and aim for the heart of the play itself. A year or two ago I produced *Cymbeline* with no scenery at all, so that the accent should be entirely on the play and the players. It was not a great success, partly, I think, because the play was too much of a rarity to be experimented with like that. As a result I planned *Hamlet*, a play so great that it can stand on its own, with similar simplicity. This time it was an acknowledged success. The more you do the plays, the more clearly and simply one wants to see the production. I think Mr. Glen Byam Shaw, who is probably our best Shakespeare director today, has arrived at the same conclusions.

'The Old Vic seats 1,000 and the Curran Theatre, San Francisco, 1,700', Mr. Benthall resumed, as if his position at thirty-nine as artistic mediator between two generations of directors had been another item disposed of, 'There were at first a few complaints from the Curran audience that we couldn't always be heard. As we were going to play in theatres seating as many as 5,000 and didn't want to be reduced to using microphones, which take all the heart out of performance, we had to find a way of delivering loud, clear and yet fast enough for the purpose. At Los Angeles in a masonic temple (capacity 3,000) with a font beneath the stage, and where normally only very big musicals play, we had not one single complaint. But on rejoining the company later in Montreal I found that the variety and quality of the voices had disintegrated, after difficult acoustic conditions in a 3,000-seat cinema. For Broadway I re-rehearsed each play in detail to restore quality suitable for a 1,900-capacity theatre. There *Henry V* opened on Christmas night during the newspaper strike with the house only two-thirds full. Chiefly by word-of-mouth recommendation, all subsequent performances were sold out.'

[7 *January* 1959]

SHELAGH DELANEY

***

The wildest of fiction could offer few parallels to the success of Miss Shelagh Delaney whose play *A Taste of Honey* (nursed by Miss Joan Littlewood) will be transferred to Wyndham's Theatre on February 10 after its second run at Theatre Workshop. In the eyes of the law this author is an infant too young to enter into valid contracts, other than for necessaries, or to marry without parental consent. Yet her play has already aroused serious critical attention, brought her a small fortune in film rights and put her name at the head of the list of contemporary dramatists in a new series of paper-backed plays. A conversation with Miss Delaney last week left one convinced that here is a case of logical precocity more relevant to the arts than that of the Regency 'Infant Roscius', William Betty.

Without any retinue of chaperons or advisers Miss Delaney came into the deserted coffee-room of Theatre Workshop and introduced herself. She is six feet tall, with the poised, rangy figure of a dancer or Californian tennis player, has hazel eyes and dark hair, worn in a style she cannot classify, though it could be Italian. Consoled by a cigarette and her raincoat for the desolation to be felt in all theatres outside performance hours, she patiently tried to isolate events and people one takes for granted at twenty with eyes on the road ahead.

'My grandparents were Irish', said Miss Delaney, 'and my father half Irish. He was a bus inspector and a very great reader and story teller. Yes, true stories about his war experiences in the Lancashire Fusiliers—North Africa, Monte Cassino. He was badly wounded at Medjez el Bab and two Germans helped him. An officer handed his gun over to them and they let him be taken back to hospital. They said something which meant, "War is no good". He used to tell me it in German, but I can't remember the words.' There seems to be no rhetoric or sentimentality in Miss Delaney's nature, and none in her distinct but not in the least broad Lancashire intonation. The relationship with her father, who died last July, leads back to a Socialist grandfather of the Keir Hardie tradition and forward to the welfare state, which provided her education, in a uniquely British social pattern. In Salford, where she was born, there were many slum houses with outside lavatories and no bathroom, in fact the detritus of the Industrial Revolution; there was also a radical solution for it. Thirdly there was a tradition of popular culture: the music-hall and the 'penny crush', a ritual Saturday cinema show.

'That's what it used to be called', said Miss Delaney. 'It was the week's climax for us, too, and we had a roaring time. We used to take part in it, laugh and shout. I remember in the Kit Carson serial there were masked men, dressed in black. We used to sort of traipse round the streets singing their song. Of course, there was pantomime. The first I saw was *Goldilocks and the Three Bears*. It was a habit to go to the Salford Hippodrome and the cinema, often three times a week.

'I was at three different primary schools—confusing? No, I enjoyed the change. My father rang them up after I took the eleven-plus, but they said there were not enough places in the high school. At fifteen I was transferred there and got five passes in G.C.E. I left at seventeen and, instead of training to be a teacher, I took jobs as a shop assistant, a clerk in a milk depot, usherette, and in the research photography department of Metro-Vickers, who employ 23,000 people. That was my longest job. There was a great variety of people to get to know. All the time I intended to write. I knew I could, by comparing my essays with the ones the other girls wrote.

'Straight plays? They took us to see Sir Laurence Olivier in *Caesar and Cleopatra* when we were doing Egypt at school.' Suddenly Miss Delaney remembered the first play she had ever seen. 'I'd been kept in after school at Broughton Secondary. I had done something. I was in the headmistress's study and had just finished some lines. Miss Leek said to me:" I'm going upstairs to watch a performance of *Othello*. Do you want to see it?" '

It was by some school amateur group. 'I said to myself: "Anything for a laugh",' Miss Delaney remembers. 'But I enjoyed *Othello*. It made a great impression on me. I was twelve at the time. I already realized I could write and I am grateful to Miss Leek. What I wrote she understood, and she didn't harp so much as others on rigid English. I write as people talk.

'I began *A Taste of Honey* as a novel, but I was too busy enjoying myself, going out dancing. I wasn't getting very far with the novel and I suddenly realized I could do a play better. I had strong ideas about what I wanted to see in the theatre. We used to object to plays where factory workers come cap in hand and call the boss "Sir". Usually North Country people are shown as gormless, whereas in actual fact they are very alive and cynical.

'Then I saw *Variations on a Theme*. It seemed a sort of parade ground for the star to traipse about in Mr. Norman Hartnell's creations. The thing that did get me was this: I think Miss Margaret Leighton is a great actress and I felt she was wasting her time. I just went home and started work.'

'In the evenings ?'

'No', said Miss Delaney, obstinately evasive as if still under the scrutiny of a Salford schoolteacher or employer, 'I was "off" for a fortnight.'

Soon afterwards a newspaper report of conflict between the Lord Chamberlain and Theatre Workshop caught her eye. Miss Delaney sent off her manuscript to Stratford, E., and had a favourable reply within a week. A promising dramatist and an organization ready to help her development, by admitting her into its artistic routine, had made contact. Miss Delaney's inflexible sense of vocation has taken her from Salford to London, but without too marked a change of environment. Theatre Workshop began as the idea of a group of radicals in Manchester.

[2 *February* 1959]

SIR DONALD WOLFIT

---------------------------------- ★ ----------------------------------

Always a wanderer, ready to give of his best in Camden Town, Bath, or in the West End when bombs were falling, Sir Donald Wolfit came back a week ago from acting Shakespeare with Lady Wolfit (Miss Rosalind Iden) in Nairobi (twenty-one performances), Addis Ababa (two), Rome and Milan (one each). As this actor's Tamburlaine bestrode even one of Mr. Tyrone Guthrie's most elaborate productions, the audience granted him by the Emperor Haile Selassie of Ethiopia must have been something for every onlooker to remember. The Emperor gave Lady Wolfit a bangle of gold and silver, remarking: 'Pas pour valeur.'

'First', said Sir Donald, recalling the tour and still aglow with Marlovian delight at having crossed the Equator by air three times in six weeks, 'first, the object of the exercise. A large company travelling abroad was out of the question, so we planned recitals based on plays from which you can take the whole body, or at least a whole aspect, and give a composite picture. Costume was restricted to one medieval, one Elizabethan outfit and an all-purpose gown. To these we added veils and the like, always giving a change of appearance. It was a slight elaboration of Ruth Draper's technique. We had records of Elizabethan music to link the scenes.

'We also experimented with recorded off-stage voices. For the lead-in to "How all occasions . . . " Hamlet asks: "Whose powers are these?" He had his reply—"They are of Norway"—from the loud-speaker. In general the longer items were the more successful. We did the whole opening scene of *Richard III*. I spoke to Clarence, I spoke to Hastings.' Here Sir Donald paused and, contrary to popular fallacy, made his point on a falling inflexion, at slower tempo: 'There *was* no Clarence. There *was* no Hastings.'

Cabined in a small office like a lion in a telephone booth, Sir

Donald was by this time living his recitals again and 'talking shop', a privilege to hear. He spoke of lighting as 'the new magician', but also of human elements often forgotten. 'We began each recital with the Prologue to *Henry V*, an appeal to the imagination of the audience. We have been experimenting with speech and imagination, going back to the troubadour, the jongleur, the story-teller. In *Richard III*, Rosalind as the Lady Anne entered with an imaginary *cortège*. In *The Shrew* we played the dining scene alone. No servants.' His hands spread downwards and outwards, dismissing. 'We selected the whole core of the play, without the sub-plot.' At the memory of discarding it Sir Donald smiled gleefully, and clasped his hands together.

Then he described selections from *Macbeth*, based on 'the relationship between the two, progressing towards evil. We tried to avoid sound-effects—even the knocking. . . . No, there were no murderers and no particular difficulty in Macbeth's briefing of them. I brought them on and I took them off, with my hands. You have to work on the audience for the first fifteen minutes or so. But they're digging in that stage music which is part of their inheritance. It slowly grows on them.'

Whatever one may think of tabloid Shakespeare, this attitude is clean contrary to the present habit of overloading heroic drama with balletic spectacle. Issues wider than the scope of one tour had been raised; but Sir Donald, no theoretician beyond his respect for Poel, was soon deep in *Othello*. 'There was *no* Iago. We selected the relationship of Desdemona and Othello. By dint of just a tiny bit of stage carpentry we left Venice for Cyprus. Jealousy has to come in, of course. We did a very cunning little thing: a black-out during which a voice alone said: "Look to your wife. Observe her well with Cassio." This was enough to lead on to the handkerchief scene and the murderer. If we had a double-draw curtain the bed was already set.'

The tour began at the new Donovan Maule Theatre Club in Nairobi. With a capacity of 220, it is Mr. Maule's reward for pioneering the drama in the first place to maximum audiences of eighty, accommodated over a shop. When he returns to Kenya Sir Donald's preference must be to act in the National Theatre of Kenya, seating 400, in order to reach a wider audience, including students who cannot afford a club subscription. At Addis Ababa the theatre holds 1,300 and is 9,000 feet up. 'You had to re-breathe Shakespeare's lines', he recalled. 'As for the audiences, *Cymbeline*'s comedy is not easy, but they took every laugh. The portfolio of education is in the hands of the Emperor himself, seventy per cent of the University College staff is English and ours is the main language of the country. I think we were the first British dramatic artists to visit Ethiopia.'

None of our great actors conforms, perhaps, so well to the popular idea of one as Sir Donald Wolfit. His expansiveness, his slightly Bohemian haircut, are grandly Dickensian; he is from Nottinghamshire, with the ruddy complexion typical of the rural Midlands. Having heard him speak so realistically of dispensing with Iago, a part he plays second to none, one thought of other titled stars educating, improvising, travelling abroad when many of the new generation of theatre-goers here have seen little of them. Was there some danger of a great tradition growing weak at the centre, of his own alliance of drama and poetry, rhetoric and simplicity, being lost to the British drama in transit?

'We are growing older', Sir Donald said. 'If we had a National Theatre properly based and founded, all of us could be Sociétaires as in the Comédie Française and be called upon when required. The Comédie Française, giving thirty classics every year, is still the bloodstream of French drama. Here, I would favour directors of plays at a National Theatre being given a permanent place on the board automatically; productions, instead of being hastily put on and soon taken off, would remain in the repertory three years. I have just seen a wonderful Danish play, but you could not act it seven times a week.

'There has got to be a National Theatre building. You can't have the Commons without the House of Commons; they only used the Church House temporarily. Meanwhile, every other country is building itself theatres and we are discarding them. I say, dig the hole and lay the foundations.'

[23 *February* 1959]

LOUIS SEIGNER

*

'*Je suis Molièriste.*' Thus M. Louis Seigner, having come off stage after the second act of *Le Dindon* last Thursday afternoon, insisted on giving his interviewer the only comfortable chair in a dressing-room small enough to make one blush for the status of English drama, and shed all the fatuity of Feydeau's Major. ('He is an old cavalry officer who has been on active service', M. Seigner explained. 'Therefore he is bent forwards at the hips, but his back is straight. Also, he has rheumatism.')

What it is to be a sociétaire of the Comédie Française emerged during an hour's talk, to a distant accompaniment of lines and laughs over the loudspeaker system. It is to be so secure in the rhythm of repertory as not to know what part you will be acting in Paris next week; M. Seigner said he had not yet seen the programme. It offers such a continuous high quality of work that you can take part in an historic production like that of *Le Soulier de satin* but not recall which roles you played. In M. Seigner's case membership of the Comédie Française, which he joined in 1939, co-exists with a temperament able at once to despise the intellect where he considers it misused and to worship it, almost, where it builds on common sense. At sixty-five he seems an incarnation of *l'honnête homme*.

If this implies limitations of sensibility, the same could be said of Molière. Limitations of sociable interest, of adaptability, there were none to be found in M. Seigner's views, although it was amusing to note the great names he did not mention. Bourdet, for instance, is the modern French dramatist he most admires, and he added the names of Anouilh, Achard, and Roussin. At the idea of Copeau having sparked any radical change of methods in the Comédie Française he rounded his lips delicately and puffed away invisible thistledown. It was not a dismissal of Copeau, mentioned by M. Seigner without a prompt, but contempt for the idea that any director can add more than nuances to the basic laws of the drama. Had there been no marked differences of approach in M. Seigner's time, then? In answer to that he expanded from head to foot in one vast shrug and said: 'All directors feel the same things. Everything else is theory.'

Then he spoke of people in the contemporary French theatre *'pourris de culture,* so cerebral that the public can't follow them. A minority does, while the others go to the cinema instead.' He has played in ninety-nine films himself and was a Chaplin fan before he went on the stage. His favourite actor in any medium was Raimu: *'humanité, vérité, puissance, comique ou dramatique, faisait rire ou pleurer',* and to sum up *'instinctif'.* As M. Seigner's phrases built up, like mounds of smooth pebbles, the ebb and flow of theatrical fashions was tidily charted. The Russians were marvellous actors, halted at Stanislavsky, realism perfected; the Americans were not impressive, except in their average comedy; the Comédie Française *'époque des diseurs, du chant'* was ended by Bourdet in 1936, changed under the cinema's influence towards a more realistic delivery. He himself would like to have played Alceste and Harpagon, but he was too old for the first and too big for the miser.

A curious impression of wisdom, neither academic nor Parisian but rootedly French, came through M. Seigner's disdain of theory and praise of energy. When, out of all his film parts, he said he had most enjoyed that of Grillo in *La Chartreuse de Parme* the first clue appeared. It seemed to fit in with his opinion that higher education was not essential for theatrical artists. That made sense only when he grudgingly admitted that he had always been a great reader. In the small town in Dauphinyé where he was born he used to read by candlelight far into the night. The authors were Balzac, Stendhal and Maupassant, the great provincials, all of them, as M. Seigner said of the plays he likes best, 'solid and well made' in effect. Analogous qualities, tempered for flexibility by the conservatoires of Lyons and Paris, took him by way of Grand Guignol and the Odéon to his present spokesmanship of Molière, who was, wrote Lytton Strachey, 'the most unromantic of writers—a realist to the core.'

Certainly, to be Molièriste on M. Seigner's terms is the reverse of skulking in the past. He is the current Comédie Française

Tartuffe, in his own production. 'It can be done', he said, 'as farce, drama or detective story. In my opinion it is the best constructed, the most perfect play. It deals with an unusual problem, yet it could be acted in modern dress. In my production it is transposed to a comedy of our time and played very straight. There is no longer any question of adopting a classical tone.

'Orgon is often treated as grotesque, a stage cuckold. Nothing points to that at all. In fact he is stubborn, and so is the whole family. He is a man of good breeding. He is cheated, but in a manner which is dramatic and not grotesque. He is *so very stubborn*!'

Down came M. Seigner's left hand as if hammering Orgon's obstinacy through the dressing-room floor. The matinée was over, the theatre quiet. M. Seigner, still in the Major's uniform, stood up automatically as he spoke of what is, to him, the actor's motive power: a curtain going up in a room of which the fourth wall is a live audience. This strength and simplicity then let in a mood of baffled introspection. But for a chance move to Lyons, part of the national touring circuit, in 1916, he could think of no choice or crisis leading him to the stage. On the contrary, as a young man he wanted to be a mechanic.

[26 *March* 1959]

LINDSAY ANDERSON

———————————— * ————————————

Thirty-six years of age next Friday, radical in outlook, and the son of a major-general, Mr. Lindsay Anderson is an influential spokesman of young people in search of valid artistic expression among the bewildering social changes of the past decade. In the essay contributed to *Declaration* (1957) he emphasized the problem of adjustment to a changing society; he has proved his own adaptability by achieving success as critic, director of documentary films, of episodes in the *Robin Hood* television series, and now of Mr. Willis Hall's *The Long and the Short and the Tall*. Mr. Anderson has been on the Royal Court strength since January, a valuable recruit to live theatre from the mass media.

As this is the reverse of the usual process and would benefit the drama if others of like talent followed, one was curious to know how it came about.

Poised, characteristically of the all-rounders more plentiful in the arts than in cricket, between a West End first night and a television relay, Mr. Anderson said he now felt there had been some 'unrealistic liberal aspiration' in his *Declaration* statement. 'I now feel that in fact the artist is pretty well alone in Britain at the moment, by which I don't mean that the artist shouldn't have a sense of social responsibility but that he will probably find himself fighting a lonely battle to exercise his sense of social responsibility. Yet I think the social position in Britain today does present a wonderful opportunity and a challenge to artists.'

Earnestly radical, with a Shelleyan impatience towards compromise, he thinks of the *status quo* in terms of an Establishment, as Voltaire would speak of 'l'infâme' or Cobbett of 'The Wen'; and it would be based, not on the Tories and All Souls—Mr. Anderson was at Wadham—but on the three main political parties. A number of trends in recent drama would be meaningless unless

175

this hypothesis were taken into account. Mr. Anderson's view of entrenched conformity is that it is, first, irresponsible, and, secondly, philistine.

'We have', he said, 'a vast new potential audience for the communal arts of the cinema and the theatre. (If one analyses it aesthetically television, I think, has no qualities not possessed by the other two.) But the audience is not being given opportunity to develop, because of the economic organization of these arts. In a modern industrialized, centralized society, media like the cinema and the theatre can only be exploited with the help of the community. But ours is a philistine society which does not value the arts sufficiently to nourish them. You can take twopence off the price of beer in a budget, over two hundred million pounds off income tax, in a country whose Governments of Left and Right refuse to honour a grant of one million pounds which has actually been voted by the Commons for a National Theatre. It's a fantastic state of affairs, and even more fantastic that nobody seems to protest against it. If you do protest you are dismissed, whatever your age, as an angry young man.'

Mr. Anderson thinks that the theatre now enjoys more freedom than the cinema, thanks to a sounder tradition of artistry and responsibility, to the lower overheads, and the absence of obstructive distributors. He agrees with Mr. John Osborne that what they regard as a revolution in the drama is likely to run up against 'the grim fact of the economic organization of the theatre in Britain' and favours a larger Government subsidy to the Arts Council, so as to increase the small percentage available to the drama without loss to opera and the ballet.

'It is very undesirable', he went on, 'that the function of supporting the living theatre should go increasingly to commercial television, as in the hook-up between Southern Television and the Old Vic. If you accept the *status quo* this may seem to be a neat solution, but basically it is an instance of the community shrugging off its responsibilities. The moment we get the theatre geared to an advertiser's conception of the needs and capacities of a popular audience, there is a danger that standards will be debased and experiments discouraged. In fact I'm certain that the popular capacity for enjoyment is far higher than is admitted by journalists and programme planners who make it a rule to appeal to the lowest common denominator. They want their returns to be too quick and too safe.'

But what of the tendency to primitivism in Royal Court plays, not least in *The Long and the Short and the Tall*, with its emphasized bayonet and threatened victim? Did it have to be so close to the l.c.d. of viewing and the urban gangs? Mr. Anderson was indignant at the suggestion and his answer came without hesitation: 'One should evaluate the motive behind such scenes and the comment of the artist. So I don't feel that at any point do we have violence for the sake of sensationalism, I think violence is shown for what it is, in its ugliness and its stupidity, and the comment of the play is a moral and humane one.

'Some critics', he added, 'are not prepared to accept the stage of experiment that must be gone through if a real change is to be effected. They will moan about the implacable upper-middle-class policy of the West End theatre, and when they get something else which breaks new ground, promisingly but perhaps not with complete success, they seem to panic. Maturity would be easier for us to arrive at in an atmosphere of greater economic security. All this criticism is going on on a bridgehead where we're under fire from the Philistines.'

[15 *April* 1959]

SIR TYRONE GUTHRIE

—————————— ★ ——————————

For many who saw it, Olivier's Henry V at the Old Vic in 1937 marks the start of an approach to Shakespearian acting which persists today, usually without the vocal splendour needed to digest twentieth-century habits of thought and feeling into the bloodstream of heroic drama. The young king endured a lengthy recital of genealogies by his prelates as impatiently as any modern audience, drummed a tattoo with his foot and finally asked, 'May I with right and conscience make this claim?' in the tone of one irked by tedious protocol. Whose idea was it? Last week Dr. Tyrone Guthrie, the director on that occasion, replied: 'I haven't the slightest recollection. Probably Sir Laurence's. He was always a great comedian.'

This mentality, running to epigram as inevitably as water to its own level, is one of many things which render interview with Dr. Guthrie a continuation of rehearsal by other means. Through a fusillade of assertive evasion, 'off the record' quips, after-thoughts, deletions, scrupulous definitions, and stage grouping of the tea things in a Stratford-on-Avon café, he let it be known that he blames proscenium theatres for many deficiencies in current Shakespearian production; that in Canada he has had promising results from an open stage, nearer to the requirements of the plays, and that he is soon to direct Mr. Paddy Chayefsky's *The Dybbuk of Woodhaven* in New York.

'For the Shakespearian festival at Stratford, Ontario', he said, 'they were willing to try placing the stage in relation to the audience as Miss Tanya Moiseiwitsch and I believe the Elizabethans did it. They scooped a big cement arena from the side of a hill, put a stage in the middle and a tent on top. In this way a great many things which are problems in the proscenium theatre solve themselves at once. I do not think we have found the complete solution. I think the principle is right and that details of what we have done will be refined and improved on, that we were practising something which all the practitioners felt had to be done. We just happened to be fortunate and a little persistent in getting the opportunity.

'First, you get more people closer to the stage. Row M, which would normally be only half-way back in the stalls of a theatre approaching two thousand capacity, is the farthest one from the stage at Stratford, Ontario. Therefore the plays can be done as they are written, as intimate and not bombastic, and the speaking does not demand the extraordinary virtuosity which is required to make Shakespeare come to life in a great operatic house. Secondly, there is no possibility of scenery at all. Any scenery is created in the imagination of the audience by the words. And that is the right way.'

If Joyce had declared his intention of rewriting *Ulysses* in Basic English one could scarcely have been more taken aback. It is of the first importance that Dr. Guthrie, the undisputed master of pageantry, now gives priority to the verse he has never handled with equal success. But he is a pioneer of radio drama and the director of *Peter Grimes*. His own speech crackles and soars.

'This is impossible to achieve', he went on, 'either at Stratford-on-Avon or the Old Vic, because of the architecture of the buildings. The audience is placed all on one side of the actual or, still more, symbolical barrier of the orchestra pit—or the half-hearted compromise that has replaced the orchestra pit. They are looking at a picture frame, conditioned by the shape of the auditorium and ten generations of play-going to expect a picture. Whatever you put in there becomes an illusionary picture, paradoxically more emphatic the simpler it is, nothing more so than a black velvet curtain.

'If you are going to play fair with the audience under such conditions the only grouping is the way Gilbert arranged the D'Oyly Carte company.' Dr. Guthrie leered wickedly. 'Consider Henry V, plumb centre. If he addresses his peers he will have his back to the audience; if he addresses the audience he must turn his back on the court. It will be lined up like the policemen and brides in *The Pirates of Penzance*. Yet grouping has a meaning. We couldn't be having this conversation for instance, back to back on the Albert Memorial.'

He grinned. 'I'm not for *The School for Scandal* in the round of course.' But for plays up to 1660 he advocates the open stage, led up to by steps which reduce masking by allowing groups to form at different levels; and he claims that soliloquies can be spoken with turns of the head enough to protect everyone from a frustrating back view of Hamlet. Usually either speaker or interlocutor is always in sight.

At fifty-eight, more than twice the age of Mr. Peter Hall, Dr. Guthrie is indulgent towards younger directors and sees them as handicapped by the theatres available, as presented with 'mechanism for creating a picture, and a budget.' He also points out that much weakness in speaking comes from the shortage of actors around forty-five with 'education, weight and experience', who prefer minor parts in the classics to lucrative television. After launching the present *All's Well That Ends Well* at the Memorial Theatre he is to discuss New York plans for Mr. Chayefsky's play and for a Solomon and Sheba musical, with libretto by Mr Robert Graves. He is to direct *The Thrie Estaitis* again at Edinburgh.

Dr. Guthrie, who was at Wellington and St. John's College, Oxford, first appeared as an actor at the Oxford Playhouse in 1924 and directed *The Anatomist* in 1931. From 1939 to 1945 he was administrator of the Old Vic and Sadler's Wells. A random dip into his achievements might recall *Measure for Measure* (1933), *Peer Gynt* (1944), *Tamburlaine the Great* (1951), and an illuminating *Hamlet* in modern dress (1938). He is the first *régisseur* to have established himself as such in the main stream of English drama; and the book he has just finished about his life in the theatre might well be of permanent value.

[20 *April* 1959]

INGMAR BERGMAN

———————————— * ————————————

Mr. Ingmar Bergman, director of *Urfaust*, which opens at the
Princes Theatre tonight, and creator of many films now showing
in the National Film Theatre's tribute to the Swedish cinema, is
already something of a legend, though scarcely past forty. Even
the official publicity connected with this his first visit to England
tends to dwell on *farouche* aspects of his personality and to brand
him as one who puts his art before public relations. Cornered for
interview as he was last Saturday, however, he is so polite, relaxed
and gay that one suspects the legend is fostered to guard his
privacy. How could he otherwise sustain a prodigious output of
work?

Looking, while shaking hands, at features which would not seem
out of place on a Gothic cathedral, the writer told Mr. Bergman
that he had resembled an inquisitor in session during his Press
conference on Friday. This brought a full-throated laugh. Indeed
the only discomfort of a two-hour luncheon with Mr. Laestadius,
of the Malmö City Theatre, and a charming Swedish couple,
making five in all, was the interviewer's nagging duty to record.
That, too, was lightened when Mr. Bergman himself wrote down
with a touching humility the names of four masters to whom he
feels indebted: Viktor Sjöström, Torsten Hammarèn, Martin
Lamm, and Olof Molander, 'the greatest of all Swedish directors,
a specialist in Strindberg'.

'The time came', said Mr. Bergman, 'when I wanted to break
off my literary studies at Stockholm University. I said to Professor
Lamm: "I want to go into the theatre." He said: "Yes, but finish
your studies first." He gave conferences—lectures?—on Strindberg. His points of view, angles, had their influence on me in late
theatrical work. . . . No, I do not agree that Strindberg plays on
the nerves without catharsis. That is only true of his earlier work.

The later plays such as *The Spook Sonata* are very important. I think he is a writer's writer—O'Neill always admired Strindberg.' A lithe, youthful figure in light grey suit, cream shirt, brown tie and brown suede shoes, Mr. Bergman was talking with an impersonal, eager conviction. This took the sting away when he said of a Theatre Workshop performance in Stockholm: "I think it was terrible."

'I think you always have to start with a human being', he explained in reference to the applied stylization which he had disliked in the production, 'with a soul. I think in their experiments with form they lose the individual human being. If they make formal experiments they should know the soul of the human being. *After*, they can start to simplify. Picasso, for example, will first draw his bull realistically. Afterwards it is simplified. Theatre Workshop go into formal generalization first, as young people do. I have made the same mistake myself. It is a tendency in all expressionists. But Strindberg began as naturalistic.'

So did Mr. Sean O'Casey, I suggested. 'I don't dare say anything about him', Mr. Bergman said, 'with Mr. Laestadius here.' And Mr. Laestadius called Mr. O'Casey expressionist 'not always in form but in feeling.' Although that may well be true, one said his argument was Jesuitical, and the room vibrated again with Scandinavian laughter. The mood led on to what the British Board of Film Censors thought of a scene from *Smiles of a Summer Night* in which Miss Eva Dahlbeck has a bath behind a screen while talking to her lover. Mr. Bergman's wide, arched eyes, which resemble steady flames, flickered in glee. 'An edict was given: "The nipple of Miss Dahlbeck must be cut." It was the first I knew of its being seen in the film at all. I ran the film through, very slowly; and there, for perhaps half a second, it was. I had not seen it, but the English censor had seen it. In Chaucer's own country the public can't be trusted to see Miss Dahlbeck's nipple.'

Criticism of Strindberg, sacrosanct one assumes, had roused a gentle malice in return. One hastily changed the subject to Emily Brontë, our nearest equivalent to the Bergman world. He remembered his mother reading *Wuthering Heights* among other classics, in the family circle on Sunday afternoons, but the parallel is in the religious environment and he has not read it since. 'The theatre is my profession', he now said. 'I can live without making film, but not live without making theatre. I have been working together with that man [Mr. Laestadius] for seven years, the best years of my professional life. Ever since I had a home projector as a child, the cinema has been a fascination. But the theatre is basic.

'I have one principle: what is in the text.' After a digression Mr. Bergman returned to this, tapping me on the shoulder. 'The text! To make clear to the audience what the writer has meant. To lose the text in spectacle? I think that is terrible. The principle is the same for *The Merry Widow* or *Macbeth*. I have produced *Macbeth* three times.' He smiled and shrugged. 'The fourth time I think I will make it. The difficulties are, first, the witches. Second, to let the audience feel sympathetic to the hero to the bitter end. You have to have an actor who in spite of all that he does is sympathetic. Third, you must have a young couple and you have to feel the sexual passion and Macbeth's dependence on his lady. You have to feel it in your stomach, from the very first time they meet. So!' And Mr. Bergman's right fist hit the palm of his other hand with a crack.

He has produced *Le Misanthrope*, with Mr. Max von Sydow as Alceste, and sums up the creative impulse of the play as pithily as any Latin thinker. 'Molière is Philinte, Molière is Alceste.' His roots are firmly in Sweden, but one may think he has the capacity to enrich a national tradition of turbulent drama by classical control such as *Wild Strawberries* benefits from. Moreover, *The Seventh Seal* marks an increase in range. Mr. Bergman did not deny that its demagogic priest and realistic crusaders are a comment on problems of today beyond the traditional concerns of any one country. They seem reported from a forward observation post, rather than from the shelter of his medievalism or Sweden's supposed 'neutrality complex'.

On Saturday the conversation ended as it had begun, in holiday mood. Mr. Bergman, admirer of Mr. David Lean's Dickens films, had convinced himself the previous day that at least the London of Mr. P. G. Wodehouse still exists. With delight he had seen for himself our umbrellas and bowler hats. In the Cup Final, even when offered the preliminary hymn singing as bait, he showed no interest at all. His first objective as a sightseer seemed inevitable, once made known. 'Madame Tussaud's', he cried. 'That I must see.'

[4 *May* 1959]

KATINA PAXINOU

———————————————— ⋆ ————————————————

Her performance as the mother in Lorca's *Blood Wedding*, which will be given on B.B.C. television tomorrow night, was already possessing Mme. Katina Paxinou a week ago. 'Naturally', she said, 'television doesn't excite me as much as the stage, but this gives me an opportunity to express myself in a new play I have never done, though I have played Lorca's Bernarda on Broadway and in Greece. To this offer I said: "Ho, yes! At once!"'

After a sleepless night and a day given over to rehearsal and costume fittings she was lying down, fortified by her Press cuttings and photographs against the danger of belittling in talk an art so mysterious, so intertwined with the personality, as that of acting. Luckily there was a way through this barrier, for one of the pictures was of Epidaurus during a tragedy. 'What is it like to play to twenty thousand people?' she was asked. 'Frightening!' said Mme. Paxinou, unexpectedly. 'The acoustics are marvellous. You can whisper and be heard by everyone. But you can hear the audience too. Rustle of a programme, friction of a sleeve.' 'You can hear *that* at Epidaurus?' 'Hear it!' said Mme. Paxinou, who loads monosyllables with dynamite. 'Before I played Hecuba there I wished let there be an earthquake.'

For the next hour her temperament played like a strong and variable force of nature on the themes of Greek tragedy, Eugene O'Neill and the search for perfection by repeated attacks, such as she has made over the years with Mrs. Alving, on the same part. 'The cothurnus, the masks', she began. 'Dead and past! We can't any more start copying, working from learned books. There is the drama and its lyrical expression, the chorus. As for recitation, who cares? It is even boring for the pupils of the schools. Bring it down to the audience. It is nowadays drama. Never mind if it involves the gods. They still come down to humans and speak.

'I don't know any play like *Oedipus Rex*. It has suspense like a murder story of today, the peak of suspense. It is the most modern thing in the world, while the other is already *passé*. Sophocles is so modern. We have the Freud coming out. Jocasta says: "So many sons have slept with their mothers in a dream". I'm asking you, what is more modern than that? Yet there are recent authors trying to take over these myths and making poor adaptations. They didn't have to choose such immortal things.'

Mildly one asked whether O'Neill had not erred in this way. 'O'Neill! Ha, ha!' cried Mme. Paxinou, like an eagle in the triumph of its lethal swoop. 'He brings it in a modern family. We have Atrides in any family. That happens every day. What else do I like in O'Neill? His force, dear. For me, O'Neill and Shaw are the only two dramatists of this century. Many good authors are already dead and they don't know it.' The noble scorn in her face and tone was melting to a softer mood, soothed by the name of O'Neill.

'Let us not kid ourselves. He is a great figure. My husband and I were the only living persons to have heard *Long Day's Journey Into Night* before he died. "It is a confession", he said. "I do not want it known until twenty-five years after my death. I will hate anyone who knows it, but you two are not so young." He read it till 2 a.m. crying. "You may hate *us* tomorrow", we said. "I may", said O'Neill, "but I have to read it."

'The first time we met him was before the film of *Mourning Becomes Electra*. It was 8 p.m. and the doctor allowed not more than twenty minutes. We left at two in the morning. O'Neill met us at the lift. He had big, huge, burning eyes like red coals. So elegant, tall, lean, with beautiful hands. After midnight he invited me to act poetry in Greek. For the part in the film he insisted: "She or nobody." I had to go back to California by train instead of by air, for safety.'

Long before, as far back as 1930, Mme. Paxinou had been inspired by reading O'Neill's plays. With her husband M. Alexis Minotis, most revered of her colleagues and producer of the forthcoming *Medea* at Covent Garden, she staged some of the plays in Athens. 'Abbie in *Desire Under the Elms* was my first real part. I thought: "My God! This is something extraordinary, and I have to play it." Ephraim is a tragic figure, of ancient tragedy.

'Mrs. Alving? I am always finding new things. The great parts

must be played with humility.' Mme. Paxinou brought a hush to
the hotel room. 'You have to be very humble when you approach
authors like Ibsen. The part lives with you for years. You find
new things in it as you become more ripe—you understand? In
a taxi, perhaps, suddenly a line will come back. I think. "My God!
I could have said it this way." It suddenly dawns, "I could have
done it better, I have to say it again." Then my sole interest is
when I am going to revive the play. Meanwhile it will haunt me.'

On the subject of Gertrude in *Hamlet*, this great tragic actress
became worldly and sly, the picture of cynical acquiescence. 'Did
she know about her husband's murder, dear? . . . I don't think
she knew. But sex is stronger. She didn't *want* to know. A kind
of . . . complicity. You understand?" It was in a spontaneous
miming, however, that her power and tender simplicity were
transcended in a way never to be forgotten. Mme. Paxinou ran
out of words in an attempt to convey what the creative writers
mean to her. She rounded her lips, breathed through them and
sifted invisible earth through her fingers.

The unconscious reference to Michelangelo was too obvious
to be ignored. 'Yes', admitted Mme. Paxinou, 'he is The One!'
As well as some affinity of temperament, they share in art, one
may think, a monumentality poised on the verge of collapse, a
tragic tension. But now, for a time, Mme. Paxinou had laid aside
her *terribilità*. She was settling down to some embroidery, in red
and green, to a pattern traditional in the smaller Greek islands.

[1 *June* 1959]

MARIA CALLAS

★

'It's the Greek in me that speaks', said Mme. Callas last week. 'Nothing to do with tragedy. My only background is what I have done in opera. Before I sing I know nothing, don't remember the part, don't know where I start. It is panic, not knowing one thing before you go on stage. When I'm there I don't know what gestures to do, until they come pouring out. Each gesture goes with the word. I did not learn them anywhere. I am not a tragedienne, like Paxinou or Judith Anderson. I have to calculate in the dark and go by instinct. Yet I have noticed that the formal Greek dances of the chorus at the beginning of *Medea* have the same poses that I take in classical works like *Iphigenia* and *Alceste*.'

Instinct, calculation, stagefright were among the aspects of acting in opera she discussed. Like her gentle transatlantic intonation, the hotel suite overlooking the Thames, vivid with roses and beset by telephone calls, seemed far away from emotions that can struggle forth to luminous expression and take audiences by the throat. Lithe, tall, and cool, tailored with a prim Jamesian elegance, Mme. Callas concentrates tremulous beauty in her great anxious eyes. Reinforced by a generous mouth, she has the magnetism of the ancient world, at once enigmatic and blatant, as caught by Botticelli in *Primavera*. Her interviewer is soon in the grip of an Orpheus complex, racked by the contradictory urges to work and to look.

'The greater I grow', she went on, 'the more doubts I have, the less I feel sure. Each time there are new gestures. Years of love go into the search for perfection. Someone may write: "Callas sang well." But millions of details are ignored. You feel as if you have worked for nothing because it isn't noticed. . . . On stage I don't joke. For those hours we must be serious and we don't find seriousness today, especially in opera. Let's face it, we

187

are used to hammy, stuck-together productions. People would love opera if given a chance, but there are singers who don't act, who sing the notes and don't bother about the sense. They think that singing notes well is enough, but it is just the beginning. There are the mechanisms, such as phrasing, and on to *fioriture*, *legato*, *portamento*, scales, trills. Then recitative, speaking in music, which is difficult because there is no exact indication, and the values are approximate. Still it is only a beginning. Some critics, even, don't understand, are content with sound. It is not your own personal sound. You serve the composer, the period, the kind of music. The sound I make in *I Puritani* is not the same sound as in *Norma* though both are by the same composer. The characters are different in age, circumstances, class. It's being able to sing everything with a different personality. I cannot, for example, act sweet if I use a big solemn voice.'

This attitude, consistently firm and logical, persisted through all the shimmer and flux of Mme. Callas's conversation. She arrived at it, she said, ten years ago. 'My duty is to bring some new thing to opera—or rather, it's not new, it's old. Art is very old. When a person like me comes along they think I'm capricious and temperamental, and if I change sounds according to the meaning they will not accept it. Singing is the placement of the voice as in drama. Then you put it to the service of interpretation.'

Thinking of Ebert, not to mention Stanislavsky, it seemed strange that Mme. Callas made these statements with an air of protest, as if unlikely to be understood or approved. She was unaware that Mr. Ernest Newman, two decades ago, held up Chaliapin as a model precisely because he gave the dying Don Quixote a feeble voice. Her own experience with *La Traviata* has often been discouraging. 'I break normality', she said. 'Often normality is just notes poured out. As Violetta I was accused of sounding sick and tired, short of breath, which', she added, with a faint, rare glint of humour, 'I think is characteristic of her illness. That is the sort of risk I run, to be accused of not feeling well, vocally and physically.' But she treasures a letter from an English nurse who heard this performance and was amazed by its realism, as of an actual sufferer or one who had studied tuberculosis in the wards.

If this insistence on *verismo* is, as the devil's advocate might suggest, a rationalization to cover any possible loss of sheer vocal splendour, one can but admire the result in terms of new dramatic force released. She works, it seems, in a fanatical search for compromise between the needs of dramatic truth and loyalty to the composer, reliving thus, in one hypersensitive personality, the crucial paradox at the heart of opera itself. Hence, perhaps, the violent opinions roused by her work, based as it is on powerful instinct and ruthless discipline stripped of the charm or artifice which seals many a truce between artist and critic. Hence, too, a febrile sincerity, a total lack of complacency and affectation in discussion.

'I am shy', said Mme. Callas, 'in rehearsal. Sometimes I stand still and sing words and wander with the mind. At such times I only use my body to pace up and down. I may be angry, not with others but with myself because I didn't do things as I should. I get terribly cranky.' Her touchiness about the effect on others, her eagerness to be understood, are typically American. She was born and brought up in New York, where she saw her first opera, *Aïda*, at the Hippodrome when ten years old. Again: 'In certain operas, *Medea* for example, I am not sure I am good enough for it. Until I'm there.'

Is Violetta a weak person, incapable, according to La Rochefoucauld's maxim, of sincerity? 'No', said Mme. Callas, confident and lucid immediately. 'That was her way of life, listening to the senses. But if she was weak she could not have recognized Alfredo's deeper feelings as shown by his concern for her illness.' She illustrated this by close reference to the Dumas original; then: 'What bothers me is the aria "E strano . . . " in the first act. She says good-bye to her guests, and as soon as they go out she has this aria. But she hasn't had time to ponder. The timing is wrong. If you hold a pause, the audience is uncomfortable.'

There are two preliminary phases, comparable to the rhythm of literary creation, in Mme. Callas's study of a part. 'First, cold calculation. How would this person react? Social class, nationality, period, individual. Then blend this with the libretto and the music in an approximate. . . . ' She mimed a sculptor modelling. 'Later, start putting in the eyes, the nose.' She mimed this, too. 'When I learn the part musically and rhythmically, I close myself in a room, with little light, no noise and the score at hand. I try to discover. You must hear the whole thing put together in your own head.'

Mme. Callas's face had taken on a frail, hunted expression as she spoke of this. She had already compared certain opera houses to the bull-ring, and one marvelled at the discipline which regulates her volatile nature in the age of speed, anxiety and publicity. Then a noise tinkled suddenly. 'Prosaic reality!' said Mme. Callas, ice-cool again. 'Who invented the telephone?'

[22 *June* 1959]

SIR JOHN GIELGUD

————————————— ★ —————————————

'Critics, like clergymen', wrote Sir John Gielgud in his auto-
biography, 'are out of place behind the scenes.' Nevertheless, he
had much to say the other day, talking at high speed in his dressing-
room at the rebuilt Queen's Theatre. Affable and aloof, the apo-
theosis of the traditional English actor with a public school
education, Sir John avoids both the rigidity of prepared statements and the outbreaks of improvised acting which great
Continental performers are given to. Not without an undercurrent of professional impatience, he displays his deep wisdom
in terse, colloquial phrases. For instance, he said of a Shakespeare
play which first came to his notice in an experimental modern-
dress version: 'It had me foxed.'

So bland a manner and ready, staccato thinking take their own
route to essentials. Remarks about the 85-degree weather led to
Sir John admitting he was glad not to be wearing the costume of
Noah or Lear. From there it was a short step to his present
recitals, with for him a sense of freedom and for the audience a
chance to listen. 'They can attend to the words', Sir John said,
'without any distraction. There is no distraction of colour or
movement, both of which the public attends to more readily.'
He followed this up with a sentence full of relevance to contemporary entertainment. 'It is easier to look than to hear.'

Asked whether verse is generally well spoken now, he said:
'Actors of each decade sort of smell the feeling of modernity and
have a modern comment on the traditional way of speaking which
makes it new. Progress should be towards a more and more
faithful expression of the text. When I was young I enjoyed
colouring the words. I tried to deliver them in an emotional and
colourful way. Now I try to shut the phrases, so to speak, in rat-
traps. I try not to sing (*smiling at his chronic mannerism*), not

to elongate the a—o syllables and vowels. As in a musical phrase, you should try to do no more than exactly what the text demands. I am in favour of the permanent set. Once that is accepted the words do double office, one of which is to supply scenery and colour as Shakespeare intended. It would be helpful if one company under the same director were to do four productions in succession at Stratford-on-Avon, trying to do the thing as simply as possible. Not seducing the audience by scenery and movement, but straight and classic. Variety would be in the costumes.

'So many directors and actors go to extremes without fully baring the meaning of the text. In a modern-dress version it is difficult for the cast to behave like, say, Georgian ladies and gentlemen and still convey Shakespeare. . . . I found our Haymarket season with Rylands and Coghill invaluable with the text. But they were not interested in motive and character and were appalled by the insubordination of the actors. I had to be a kind of liaison officer. Yet Rylands's productions at Cambridge are well spoken, perhaps because students are more obedient.

'As well as the meaning', Sir John continued, 'there is the musical context and rhythm. So many actors are devoid of musical sense. I never cease to be thankful that Father forced me to listen to concerts, on very hard seats, when I was young. There are passages—"the soldier's pole", "cloud-capped towers"—in which meaning is not the important thing. The sense will be different for different members of the audience, like when a great piece of music is played correctly. Toscanini.'

Theatrical perfection, for Sir John, lies in the Saint-Denis production of Obey's *Le Viol de Lucrèce*. Unable to select an ideal Shakespeare production, he spoke highly of *Titus Andronicus* and *Measure for Measure*, both directed by Mr. Peter Brook. Hoping to disturb the somewhat frustrating objectivity, I asked him to define his style in relation to Sir Laurence Olivier's. 'Olivier is a great impersonator', said Sir John placidly. 'I am always myself.' At which I reminded him that his *Hamlet* is more often thought of as classical, impersonal almost, in its fidelity to the part; and, for the only time, a crease of satisfaction, soon smoothed out, appeared in the texture of his eloquent reticence.

Sir John's acting has had three periods: of youthful rhetoric touched with hysteria; of rich prime, within the limitations of a physique incapable of martial glamour, a voice unable to trumpet or thunder; thirdly, of an inward poise emerging as Virgilian sunlight and shadow, humanely classical. The rest of what he had to say should be read in that context.

'At last I've learnt that when I'm bored I must study to do a little less rather than a little more. In the old days I was always forcing. Now, when a thing is set I never change. To be in a part you must not allow personal emotion to disturb the execution. For example, I go back to the punctuation of Shakespeare's text in different editions, with varied spacing and type. Then I see them in front of my eyes while I'm speaking it, in actual letters while acting. . . . Dame Edith Evans refines by cutting away the dead wood until she has chosen the relevant emotion, cadence or nuance. Then it is played so that no one can miss it, like the right place for a vase of flowers in a room. Style—Congreve, Wilde, Chekhov, Hunter. It is to know what sort of play you're in.

'I try now to exert a rigid discipline, above all not to indulge. Tears, for example. As Leontes or Wolsey I cry on the same words for the same amount of time each night, and no longer. When I hold any tone or mood too long, I recognize it. Poetry has a beginning, middle, and end, held in a kind of arc which must not be broken, although inside it there are variations. Like a Gothic arch. Within it there can be elaborations, but the arch remains intact.

'The most successful part of my recital has been a hotch-potch of the last scene of *King Lear*. In 1941 I rehearsed the part with Granville Barker for an hour and a half, day after day. Everything he said seared into my brain and I follow that interpretation still. When I was monotonous he would say: "You've *done* that!" Again, of tone and inflexion, "The scaffolding must be firm. That will always hold you up if the pinnacles are wobbly." '

[31 *July* 1959]

ARNOLD WESKER

———————————— * ————————————

On the way through Hackney to interview Mr. Arnold Wesker, author of *Roots*, *Chicken Soup with Barley* and *The Kitchen*, a working-class world largely excluded from the theatre before 1956, and since then more and more influential, caught one's eye on every side. Youth employment bureaux, therapeutic baths and technical colleges were more prominent than street markets surviving from Gissing's East End; multiple stores, second-hand cars' and housewives with loaded shopping baskets testified to busy prosperity. The political fervour of *Chicken Soup with Barley*, Act I, seemed to have dwindled to the slogan 'Ban the Bomb', daubed in white on the brickwork of a railway bridge and sabotaged by 'Don't' prefixed in black.

Mr. Wesker's basement flat is in a trim suburban avenue adjoining blocks of flats which line the main road. His living room, with television set, record player, contemporary standard lamp, abstract paintings by his wife alongside a photograph of young men playing football in the street, a bookcase devoted to good books bound in boards and a long shelf of excellent paperbacks resembles those of many mid-century lovers of the cultured way of life. Dressed in an open-necked green shirt, narrow buff trousers and suede shoes, he himself spoke softly and readily in a standard English one might hear in any quadrangle or West End art gallery. After spells of employment as carpenter's mate, apprentice to a furnisher, bookseller's assistant, kitchen porter, plumber's mate, beet picker, seed sorter, and pastrycook, why?

'A fair question', said Mr. Wesker. 'I think I got it from my sister.' And he named her school in Spitalfields, as if that explained everything. His own formal education, begun in Hackney at the Jewish infants' school, continued in three elementary schools in Stepney and Hackney, rose to a climax with a course in book-keeping, shorthand and typing at Upton House Central School, was interrupted by wartime evacuations to Ely, Buckingham, Barnstaple, and South Wales, and came to an end when he was sixteen years old. Two years later National Service in the R.A.F. led to a brief experience of educational duties after several transfers and much time spent on dustbins and salvage. 'I suspect', said Mr. Wesker, 'that I was a suspicious character because I had left-wing associations. Soon afterwards I wrote a bad novel, unpublished, about my experience in the service. I was under the influence of D. H. Lawrence at the time and able to talk about the "oneness" of everybody at square-bashing.' A Socialist, of Communist East End parentage and Russo-Hungarian ancestry, Mr. Wesker must, one feels, have been as much of a problem to his commanding officers as Aircraftman Shaw.

Although he took part in plays as an amateur and saw himself as Marchbanks in *Candida*, for which his slight figure and luminous brown eyes well suit him, it is by way of an interest in films that Mr. Wesker has become perhaps the most promising and mature of playwrights under thirty. After an Orwellian period of kitchen work in Paris, during which he saw no plays because he couldn't afford it, just as at Buckingham he never saw Stowe or in any case doesn't remember it, he went to the London School of Film Technique and became a convert to Free Cinema.

'I owe a particular debt to Lindsay Anderson, the inspiration behind that movement. I recognized in his writings something which I was trying to do, to affirm something I felt which was in contradiction to the mood of the time, its cynicism, despair, and disillusion. For example, the poems I was writing were simple and ballad-like. The one poet who meant anything to me was Dylan Thomas. Sometimes he might seem muddled and obscure if closely analysed, but there was an unashamedness, an expression of the love of words and the love of living.' In addition, Mr. Wesker admits debts to Mr. Sean O'Casey and Mr. Arthur Miller. Like Brecht, whom he did not mention, he responded across the fences of political commitment to *Waiting for Godot*: 'Beckett seemed to be saying in an odd sort of way the kind of thing I try to stress in *Roots* about the terrible lack of communication that reduces us to the rumblings of Lucky, the man in chains. One way across that gulf is indicated by Harry Kahn in *Chicken Soup with Barley*, when he says: "You can't alter people.... You can only give them some love and hope they'll take it." You can't change them, but you can marry them.'

This humane warmth and tolerance shone, quite without affectation, in Mr. Wesker's face as he summarized the story which first drew Mr. Anderson's attention to his talent. 'It's about an old East End woman whose family has disintegrated. Her husband was killed in the war. He had always done the football pools. Then her son had done them. When her son married and her daughter moved away, the old woman had been left alone with only the pools to do. If she were to win £75,000 she would be able to get the family together again, pay off debts, buy her son a house. She became convinced that she will win. Meanwhile the neighbours collect money to send her on a holiday in the country. She goes.

'The old woman has been very meticulous. Every Wednesday she has done her pools, every Thursday she has posted them. She has checked them in the Sunday paper, thinking there might be a mistake in the classified results on a Saturday evening. But on holiday she is staying with a couple who take no Sunday paper. The old woman goes to the village, where the shops are sold out. At length she gets her paper from a delivery boy, only to find that she has left her coupon at the house. Her habits have been disturbed and the writing sort of builds up to a state of panic. She returns, but leaves her paper on the bus. That afternoon she goes back to London, to security, and by the time she arrives is convinced, not that she ought to win the money, but that she has. It is then too late to buy a newspaper and she sends a telegram to the promoters, claiming her winnings. On the way out of the telephone box, she sees a newspaper on the floor. Shyly watching to see that nobody is looking, she picks it up, and when she finds out she has not won, accepts the situation: "Silly Mrs. Levi . . . who are you, anyway?" This woman represents millions in England.'

Mr. Wesker was at his happiest in telling this story, and only slightly less so in admitting he had had no worries about spacing the three acts of *Chicken Soup with Barley* at intervals of ten years. 'It was one advantage of being theatrically uneducated. I was not frightened of anything.'

[21 *September* 1959]

ALEC McCOWEN

———————————— ⋆ ————————————

Mr. Alec McCowen's flat overlooks King's Road, Chelsea. The living room, furnished with a few objects of high quality, all placed in such a way as to combine tidiness and comfort, gives no hint of its occupant's profession. Not a script, a photograph or a mask is to be seen. Although even the television set has a glossy austerity, the cool efficiency of the room is softened by the presence of an upright piano and a homely landscape painting. On the table lies a paperbacked copy of a novel by Miss Ivy Compton-Burnett.

Mr. McCowen himself, aged thirty-four, and now appearing in Wilde, Congreve and Shakespeare at the Old Vic after six years of repertory, followed by steady progress in the West End, on Broadway, in films and television, has a neat, narrow head, with only the nose as prominent as one might expect in an actor. His eyes, however, are so humorous that they might be leading an independent existence, and he has big hands, expressive in repose as the roots of a beech. A black pullover adds a touch of solemnity to his informal dress. During the following conversation, aside from a moment of annoyance and another of deep thought, he is consistently relaxed.

INTERVIEWER: For the past two years you have been very much in demand on television.

MR. McCOWEN: I have had parts in eighteen television plays during that time.

INTERVIEWER: Then, why have you now gone to the Old Vic?

MR. McCOWEN: I've always wanted to work there and I've always felt I should do classical work, I think most actors feel that if they're serious about it.

INTERVIEWER: What do you think is the reason?

MR. McCOWEN: Actors, I think, are finally judged on their performance in classical roles. Perhaps they are more of a challenge.

INTERVIEWER: Finally judged. . . . That suggests high standards. Whom do you most admire among contemporaries?

MR. McCOWEN: Sir Laurence Olivier, Sir Michael Redgrave, and Sir Alec Guinness in particular. I was in the Cleopatra plays with Olivier in New York.

INTERVIEWER: Can you specify anything to be learned from him?

MR. McCOWEN: It is . . . an . . . an intensity of concentration that differentiates an actor like that. There is a magnetism. It can't be defined, but is something to do with concentration. (*He spreads both hands, palm downwards, and tightens them powerfully.*)

INTERVIEWER: And Sir John Gielgud?

MR. McCOWEN: He is an actor I admire enormously, yet feel I am seeing an actor who is slightly remote from me, whereas Olivier, Redgrave, and Guinness seem to me contemporaries. I have been greatly influenced by acting in New York and observing the American approach. Marlon Brando's acting in *A Streetcar Named Desire*, which I saw on holiday from repertory in Newfoundland in 1948, was a revelation. Many English actors have as assured a technique, which he seemed to combine with a far greater reality.

INTERVIEWER: Is Brando, uttering Stanley Kowalski's mating call, more real than Gielgud in the pathos of King Lear?

MR. McCOWEN (*smiling*): Yes, he is to me.

INTERVIEWER: Is Brando's animal energy in the part of a low-grade character, really so difficult to project?

MR. McCOWEN: I think you're assuming he's a low-grade person. He did Marchbanks in *Candida* before he played Stanley, and his Antony on the screen was very imperfect but not a disgrace. One believed in the passion of the man.

INTERVIEWER: On the contrary, isn't rhetoric and cold calculation the basis of Antony in *Julius Caesar*?

MR. McCOWEN: That is an argument which gets me very much on the raw, because of the assumption about how classical parts should be played. People have told me that Touchstone is an old man, or that he is embittered, or that he is a pathetic clown. And (*with a forceful gesture*) none of this seems to me in the script whatsoever. He seems to me a very happy clown.

INTERVIEWER: Is that your director's, Miss Wendy Toye's, interpretation?

MR. McCOWEN: Not necessarily. She let me work on it myself.

. . . It's also been remarked on that I play Algernon Moncrieff much younger than he should be, and this again is an assumption. From the script he seems extremely young.

INTERVIEWER: Do not new interpretations of the classics sometimes cover limitations of acting style?

MR. McCOWEN: I have no idea what the word 'style' means, and when I listen to critics I don't think they do, either. I think performances are either good or bad.

INTERVIEWER: Would you agree that classics may be distorted and emphasis made to suit particular actors? Do not some classics require training in the manners of their period?

MR. McCOWEN: If you are working, as I think you must, from the script, then the manners are dictated by the script. The only external thing is the costume of the period, which dictates deportment.

INTERVIEWER: Can that be learned overnight? The Comédie Française . . .

MR. McCOWEN (*in explanation of a secretive grin*): Some years ago I went to a matinée of theirs in London. I wasn't too sure what I thought about it. Two schoolboys were talking it over on the way out. The athletic one said: 'I say, wasn't it marvellous?' The other, a scholarly type, said: 'If you really understood French you wouldn't think it was so marvellous.' . . . To talk seriously, I'm assuming that actors in the classics can (*a*) speak and (*b*) move.

INTERVIEWER: But can the Method compass the classics, other than by cutting them down to its limitations?

MR McCOWEN: Yes! Julie Harris in Anouilh's *The Lark*.

INTERVIEWER: You admire both Olivier and Brando. Have they anything in common as actors?

MR. McCOWEN (*eyes glinting*): There is an edge of humour in the approach of both, in Olivier's contempt and Brando's savagery. As Stanley on the stage Brando was sometimes intensely funny.

INTERVIEWER: More so than on the screen, perhaps?

MR. McCOWEN: Film does deaden a performance slightly. The microphone causes the voice to lose colour.

INTERVIEWER: What a pity so many actors discuss these technicalities only among themselves.

MR. McCOWEN: For the past two years I have talked a great deal with Vivian Matalon, the actor, who is a teacher at L.A.M.D.A. and a pupil of Sanford Meisner. The Meisner creed is, very simply, that acting is doing. It applies equally to comedy and tragedy. The actor is concerned not at all with his feeling or characterization, only with what he is doing in the play. This is my approach. I have learned it and it seems to work. You are making me articulate.

INTERVIEWER: Then, could you give an example of this approach?

MR. MCCOWEN (*after moulding his hands, hitherto emphatic or relaxed, against his chin in sculptured gestures of contemplation*): The moment when I lose my temper with my father in *The Elder Statesman*, and ask: 'What is my inheritance?' (*He stands up.*) This is a line on which one had to be angry. (*He clenches a fist.*) If I just felt angry, the line would be phoney, self-indulgent, wrong. What I am actually doing is challenging my father, and from the challenge comes the anger.

[9 *November* 1959]

DAME PEGGY ASHCROFT

*

The least flamboyant of distinguished actresses, Dame Peggy Ashcroft at the Comedy Theatre is now excelling a strong cast in an unusually good production of *Rosmersholm*. Yet nothing in her rendering of Rebecca West, not a tone or a gesture, exploits her star quality or stands irrelevant to Ibsen's grand design. With two arduous performances ahead of her the same day, she talked about Ibsen and Chekhov last week as objectively as a research chemist comparing specimens. The insights offered by Continental actresses, less averse to revelation, were not forthcoming; neither were generalizations which might be thought arrogant. But within five minutes the structural methods of the two playwrights were being tidily laid out for inspection, using *Rosmersholm* and *The Three Sisters* as examples.

'Chekhov's work,' said Dame Peggy, 'is totally based on ensemble, completely orchestrated. Duologues, the rule in Ibsen, are rarer in Chekhov. *Rosmersholm*, aside from the first act, is a series of wonderful, contrasted duologues in which different sides of a character come out according to the changing partners involved. The fascination, to me, is in the gradual uncovering of the characters. Always the action is on two levels. We say something, and it always implies something underneath.'

Then what is implied by the sudden spasm she is seized by, as Rebecca, when Kroll cross-examines her about her foster father, Dr. West? Although she would be reproducing this unforgettable effect on the stage in a few hours' time, Dame Peggy replied at once, and matter-of-factly: 'Incest. To my mind Ibsen lays the clues quite clearly and there is no doubt about it. The affair she confesses to in Act IV was with Dr. West. Then there is the line in Act I, "When we were up north in Finmark . . ." The second time I read *Rosmersholm* I realized that she had been Dr. West's mistress. When you examine the text it appears that Rebecca's sense of guilt springs from the fact that she knows Dr. West had an affair with her mother, whom she supplanted, though not until Act III does she realize he is her father.' Dame Peggy referred to an essay by Freud in confirmation and added: 'Too much attention cannot be paid to analysis and trying to find the intention of the playwright. The living author can tell us at rehearsal. Not so with the classics. What was the intention? It is a challenge.

'The mind can never let up in *Rosmersholm*,' she continued, 'because Ibsen has constructed it like an architect. He has decided on his premise, his theme. He reveals it through a story which he unfolds by beginning, as it were, at the end. Because of their situation, his characters tend to be on the defensive. They have something to hide, which he exposes. Chekhov's, on the other hand, have few secrets. They are trying to find out what they feel about life and are eager to express it—the three sisters are continually preoccupied by what they feel, why, and what they want. Through them and the other equally important characters Chekhov paints his subtle picture of life. An Impressionist?'

Unwilling or unable to recall a precise example of personal experience made use of in performance, she said: 'One also learns *from* the characters one plays. They are an experience in themselves,' and one thought of the richness of the material at her disposal, from the early Old Vic lyrical heroines, a definitive Juliet, Komisarjevsky's *The Seagull* and Saint-Denis's *Three Sisters*, Gielgud's *Much Ado*, to her present mid-century pictures of *la femme fatale* in a modern idiom. She found Hedda Gabler bizarre until a clue to something more familiar was offered by a critic stressing Hedda's type and confirmed by Ibsen's words, reported by his grandson: 'I write about ordinary men and women.'

'And yet they are *extraordinary*,' said Dame Peggy, much as she emphasizes the adjective when describing Brendel at the Comedy Theatre. 'A remote country parsonage, a country clergyman, his schoolmaster friend and his companion-housekeeper—out of this he creates an extraordinary, tragic world. His form is still conventional but the characters are so complex, so modern, one is almost surprised when he uses the dramatic curtain line. But the whole construction of Chekhov's plays was an innovation—the audience is eliminated, we are almost surprised to find there is a curtain! One can imagine a group of actors familiar with one another coming near to a satisfactory production of Ibsen by working things out for themselves, but a Chekhov play is so much a director's creation; he has to bring to life on the stage not only the characters, but time and the seasons. In the first act of *The Three Sisters*, the spring, the morning, and the birthday atmosphere pervades everything. In the second, it is winter and fatigue as people come back from work. Then comes the fire on a hot summer night in the third act. All this makes a part of his writing, something Chekhov has used and the director must use—and, through him, the actors.

'If you have seven weeks' rehearsal you can spend an entire rehearsal on what it is like to be at 2 a.m. with a fire going on outside. That is what we did for the Saint-Denis production at the Queen's. He said: "To-day let us think only about how tired these people feel." Adequate rehearsal time is one of the most important things in the theatre. For that production we had seven weeks. I've never had it before or since.'

Dame Peggy's last remark, made without rancour, says little for a system which hustles even the best interpreters. She now set off for her afternoon's work, agile and balletically Russian-looking in a Cossack hat, but a solemn responsibility to escort through West End traffic if one remembered her place in the history of European drama. With little or no resort to shock tactics she has come near to identifying herself with large areas of the most exacting texts from Shakespeare to Brecht for three decades. An afterthought, recalling veiled mockery in her eyes during pauses in her disquisition, hardened into certainty that the interview just over had been subtly histrionic, a minute, pedantic curtain-raiser before two performances of *Rosmersholm*. She had, after all, been invited to talk about Chekhov and Ibsen, not about herself.

[1 *February* 1960]

THE LUNTS

---- ★ ----

Having by-passed social realism and the more exacting classics in favour of Giraudoux, Molnar, Coward and Rattigan, the Lunts are now in London rehearsing Dürrenmatt's *The Visit*. Their acting, according to the *Oxford Companion to the Theatre*, 'rises to great heights when they approach material worthy of their exceptional talents'. It has, in fact, the durability conferred in the theatre by teamwork and impeccable comic style. Hence they successfully toured remote parts of the United States with a repertoire of Chekhov, Giraudoux and Sherwood at a time when progressive American drama was geared to proletarian subjects. Now, when social changes threaten to leave proletarian drama as dated as inter-war comedy, the Lunts remain to embody an elegance, a glossy frivolity of mind and heart, without which the art of the theatre in any society is felt to be drably incomplete.

That they can do this is in the long run a matter of personality and technique. The other day Mr. Alfred Lunt found a quiet corner in the lounge of the hotel and made the star actor's customary pretence of ignorance, not wholly insincere where the data are so elusive. 'I ran some courses after the war', he said, 'and the G.I.s asked me what technique was. I told them I didn't know, would have to go home and ask my wife. Her definition was: "Saying things with truth a little louder than in a room and not bumping into people".'

This gambit increased Mr. Lunt's likeness to some N.A.T.O. general fretting to be back in uniform. His grim mouth and steep forehead, offset by brown eyes and a gently nasal intonation, make him seem less of an actor than an ideal American statesman, absorbed, under a courteous manner, in responsibility. However, he loosened up at the mention of the Moscow Art Theatre, having seen it in America and Russia between the wars; and into the room now came Miss Lynn Fontanne, cool and radiant. From this point onwards, the interviewer was in the predicament of an actor improvising on the fringe of a polished duologue.

MR. LUNT: Moskvin ... Kachalov. The most beautiful actor....

MISS FONTANNE: Terrific style. You might compare him. ...

LUNT: Nobility. ...

FONTANNE: ... with Charles Wyndham or George Arliss.

LUNT: No, Arliss was smaller. I saw Kachalov in Moscow in 1932.

FONTANNE: Moskvin. Wonderfully versatile. He had tremendous *sweep*, comic sweep. He would blow up a situation, blow up the bubble until it burst. Like Charles Hawtrey.

INTERVIEWER: On a film I saw, Moskvin came near hamming.

LUNT: Oh, he could be awful. As Fiers in *The Cherry Orchard* ...

FONTANNE: Nails in a packing-case. His idea of something extremely funny was to miss the packing case with the hammer.

LUNT: In *Dead Souls* he was superb.

FONTANNE (*defining with white-gloved hands*): There was a beautiful, virginal young girl, here, in a white crinoline. Moskvin walked round like this. He worked it up (*arms wide apart*) until he was embracing the entire stage. Then he lifted her, kissed her, threw her down on the chair and exited.

LUNT: Moskvin was earthy, Kachalov more cultured. But he could be brutal. In *Ivanov*, for example, when he had to say 'Jewess!'

INTERVIEWER: Talking of Chekhov, how did you enjoy doing *The Seagull*?

FONTANNE (*cunningly*): We got better as we went along. (*Proudly*) It was such a success on the road, it paid for production before it opened on Broadway.

The Lunts then said they had not considered acting together until offers from five managements left them no choice. A respected adviser thought it unwise 'because we were both so eccentric. He didn't think the marriage would be a success, either'. Molnar's *The Guardsman*, in which they gave an incomparable display of *panache* later to be filmed in 21 days, was entrusted to them with reluctance by Molnar's agent. Since they persisted in recalling business matters when not praising other actors, a trite technical question was put. Had they ever had difficulty in deciding who was to be, at a given moment, upstage of whom?

FONTANNE: That's a fallacy. Positions, in general, are done by the director. Otherwise it doesn't matter where you are. You can project yourself just as well if you have your back to the audience.

LUNT: We played *Love in Idleness* more than 200 times in London. In New York we tried reading the lines in ways you'd not advocate—your face in a pillow, in your hands, between your legs. . . .

FONTANNE: Don't take that literally.

LUNT: . . . back to the audience. We tried them all. It didn't make any difference.

FONTANNE: If the line was funny enough, it got its laugh. And we have made a discovery. If you have a very funny line it is much funnier if you let the audience just overhear it. If you place it squarely in the audience's lap, it's less funny than it will be if you whisper it and the audience inadvertently overhear. . . . Only once or twice have I taken anything from an actor in another play. I like to go to life. Some of the most effective things Alfred does on the stage, he has seen done in a room. There was a moment in *The Visit* when he laid his hands on a table, looked down at them and said: 'I see'. I once saw a woman hear the news that her son was missing in action. When Alfred did that, I was reminded that she had done the same thing. Both actions had a sort of modesty in grief.

LUNT: I altered it.

FONTANNE: He changed it! And I was on his back like a tigress.

LUNT: There's another gesture I have noticed: Hands pressing on the back of one's own neck. (*Illustrating it, withdrawn.*) And on the stage there's something that doesn't happy often. I can't explain it. You suddenly find yourselves really talking to each other. There's no self-consciousness. You're limp, relaxed. (*His left hand stretches out, palm downwards, enforcing attention.*) It's very thrilling. Both people feel it, then keep it up awhile. Then it's dissolved.

They both remember vividly a performance of *There Shall Be No Night* given during the war for the Dean of Windsor, privately to an audience of about 25 persons in a drawing room. The audience was so absorbed that the legs of those in front gradually stretched forward on to the acting space. The Lunts walked across their feet, rather than break the spell, and did not raise their voices until some were crying loudly enough to make that necessary. When they got back to their hotel, it was to find the windows of their room wrecked by a bomb. They had escaped death and experienced the maximum power of their art in the space of one night. All this they now recalled in the humid weather, until Mr. Lunt became restive, for he was due back at rehearsal. As the final questions were asked, one pictured him already hurrying down the Strand among lounging holidaymakers, a handsome, grey-suited American, sternly preoccupied. The unlikeliest of their guesses would be that a New York theatre had been named after him and his wife.

INTERVIEWER: Has there been an American dramatist better than O'Neill?

LUNT: Sherwood was a better writer. But O'Neill was a wonderful *playwright*. Powerful stories, powerfully told.

FONTANNE: I played in *Strange Interlude*. The writing is common.

LUNT: Not so in *Mourning Becomes Electra*.

FONTANNE: He had enormous practice. There are nine acts in *Strange Interlude*. By the time he finished that he was writing fine.

LUNT: And think of his titles. *Desire under the Elms*! For God's sake, what a wonderful title! It's all there. . . . As for Giraudoux, we loved him as a man.

FONTANNE: If you read him, it sounds coldly intellectual, not good theatre. But it plays like a dream.

LUNT: *Ondine* would do well, even now, when there's so much spit-and-sawdust.

INTERVIEWER: Why have you never done Molière?

LUNT (*with deliberation*): I don't like Molière in English. (*Meaningful pause.*) Do you?

[20 *June* 1960]

PETER HOLMES

---*---

'Having a day off from the pick?' asked a man in the pub while Mr. Peter Holmes was explaining his double life as navvy and as leading actor with the O.U.D.S. Not every graduate with a head full of Marlowe, Tourneur, and Schiller would be of any use in building a by-pass, but there is more than this contrast to justify some attention being given to Mr. Holmes; for he embodies the drama's current urge towards proletarian vigour, its cult of athletics and its flight from genteel preciosity. When not sporting a high-necked pullover and gym shoes without socks, he can be the gilded graduate to perfection, executive type. Not much of a scholar ('In English I took a Third, which is usually called an actor's degree') he actually is a gypsy, by extraction on his father's side.

Now 23, he has already played Angelo in *Measure for Measure* at Versailles, as well as an admired Escalus in the same play at Oxford, and at this year's Edinburgh Festival he will have the title part in Schiller's *Wallenstein*. But as a performance only nominally to be classed as amateur Mr. Holmes's handling of Tamburlaine in St. John's College garden this summer is the high water mark so far. By the last performance his voice, which normally spans three octaves, had become displeasingly harsh, yet he held the attention for 332 lines of monologue and action for some 25 minutes in competition with recorded organ music from four loudspeakers and with dance music from the Commemoration ball at neighbouring Wadham. Since academic audiences are not uncritical, this argues an outsize, compelling presence of the kind which may produce great acting when discipline and experience are added. Even a passable 'get-through' rendering of more than a thousand lines of heroic verse is beyond the scope of most actors, amateur or professional.

'I read *Tamburlaine* at school, at Liverpool College', said Mr. Holmes, 'and thought it a tremendous part.' While one noted the significance of his seeing it as a part, not a play, he went on: 'We gave seven performances of it this summer and two dress rehearsals, one of which was seen by the press. One matinée had to be cancelled because of my voice. On the Thursday the middle register went, on Friday the top register. But at the third performance I regained for a time an ability of my voice lost since school, where I sang bass in the choir. . . . The main difficulty was having to speak immediately after a 30–40 yard sprint. Our producer, Mr. John Duncan, had decided that Tamburlaine's god was Energy. Instead of stately processions he wanted us to *sweep* across the stage. For the last two weeks of rehearsal I gave up smoking, cut down on beer and did morning runs, the round of Christ Church Meadow. After that, fitness improved and running about Oxford to and from rehearsal was enough.'

Although he had acted Faustus and Oedipus at school and went to Oxford only on his father's advice, he was kept off the stage throughout his undergraduate years by a tutor aware, not without justification, that St. Peter's Hall is not the R.A.D.A., or even a satellite of the O.U.D.S. Instead, Mr. Holmes's irrepressible talent found devious outlets—cabaret ('I like to see separate faces in the audience and talk to them as individuals') and cricket: 'I was captain in my last year of The Harvesters. I wore a top hat, choker, velvet waistcoat, high-winged collar, and my grandfather's wedding trousers. Once took three for 26 against the Senior Common Room, bowling underarm.' His intention, in May, 1959, by which time he thinks he had given up all hope of acting, was to go to work on the roads and to find out whether he was fit for manual labour. The sight of many of his contemporaries 'rushing around from firm to firm in search of a secure position' repelled him. However, his repressed acting had emerged in 'one or two readings', including Enobarbus, and Mr. Kenneth Loach, O.U.D.S. president, called him into the E.T.C. production of *Bartholomew Fair*. That summer he played Justice Overdo at the Stratford-on-Avon open air festival.

Nevertheless, in the autumn, he was at work on the Southern and Western by-pass in a gang which is one of the first to arrive on the site of a fly-over or bridge. They bore the shafts to about 60 feet to be filled with reinforced concrete. 'My job was to follow the instructions of the winch driver and service the rig.' At up to £15 a week, including with overtime hours of from 7.30 a.m. till

9 p.m. when daylight was good, the shovelling and carting brought him by Christmas almost enough money to go abroad. But the University lured him again, and this see-saw existence swung him from the company of the Irish labourers he speaks so well of to the Théâtre Montpensier. After that he was back on the roads, this time digging trenches. 'It is a very good firm', said Mr. Holmes, relaxing between Tamburlaine, trench digging, and Wallenstein. 'I know the foreman well. He says I can come back and I probably will, next week.'

His infectious vitality, and a curious air of calm independence, almost of isolation, gives Mr. Holmes's conversation an authority like that of his stage presence. The theatre's glamour seems to mean nothing to him aside from the process of acting his own parts. He has never seen Olivier or Gielgud in the flesh, never seen *Look Back in Anger* or any play by Chekhov, never seen Mr. Peter O'Toole or Mr. Albert Finney, the actors whose style most resembles his. He has seen *Ghosts* only, of Ibsen, and no Brecht. Pressed to recall an inspiring performance, he can remember Wolfit in, of all things, *King John* on television 10 years ago. Yet he preferred Gielgud to Brando in the film of *Julius Caesar*. Both for guidance in acting and for the teaching of critical appreciation he acknowledges a debt to Mr. L. G. Fluke, the senior English master at Liverpool College, who 'taught me anything I know about acting'.

It is reported of Mr. Hoimes that during a party in his rooms after the last night of *Tamburlaine* he was found playing cards alone on the stairs, that two hours later he was projecting courteously florid speeches from an upper window to couples strolling home from a ball and later still identifying himself with the glimmer of fish below Godstow Bridge. That may be written off, perhaps, as routine youthful extravagance. But a young man who sees and describes the prison scene in *Measure for Measure* in terms of Goya has an imagination of his own, a lurid flamboyance useful in the classics. 'I see things pictorially,' he says of *The Revenger's Tragedy*. 'It begins with this black figure. I see him down right, and over the back goes this green and gilded procession.' Characteristically he has never seen grand opera. 'But in Liverpool I heard that they wanted soldiers when an Italian company came. I was a Swiss Guard in *Tosca* and a militiaman in *La Bohème*.' It sounds like the basic, indestructible egoism of the born actor.

[11 *July* 1960]

TIMOTHY O'BRIEN

'There was a wonderful Brechtian moment when we crept in on him with the camera and after the line, "You sells me" he spoke the next—"You buys me"—to the audience.' Thus Mr. Timothy O'Brien, recalling a production of *The Emperor Jones*, illustrated the way in which creative thinking disregards the boundaries between stage and screen as casually as interpreters now move back and forth from one medium to another. Head of Design for ABC television, Mr. O'Brien has also provided décor for straight plays (*The Bald Prima Donna, The New Tenant, Hunter's Moon, Five Finger Exercise, Dreaming Bandsmen*) and for grand opera (*The Flying Dutchman*, Sadler's Wells, 1958).

At 31 he has grown 'shyer of people than of subjects' and frequently during our conversation referred to the key relationship of designer and director, one, incidentally, which poses many problems to the critical playgoer, too. 'With a good director I would even attempt a drawing room set for a country house week-end before the war and with a bad director I would be nervous of Verdi's *Otello. The Flying Dutchman*, for example, under Mr. Dennis Arundell's direction, was a cordial compromise between our individual views of the design.

'Let me run a string of words across that. . . . He made a definite effort not to reject the things I brought to the production and I in turn thought a good deal about what he said and acknowledged the greater value of much of it. In Act II I wanted to give the interior of Daland's house a scrubbed, light look and he wanted to give the same structure human warmth, touches of ochre light, stretches of peasant decoration and an overall warm reality to constrast with the icy sprays and phantom ships outside. He pulled me, protesting, towards his view and got about 60 per cent of what he wanted. At the same time the structure of the scenery was unaffected and the surface texture could not destroy its general shape. I remember with some satisfaction the onrush of the Flying Dutchman in Act I when he was brought out of the swirling projected mists and dashing seas by a series of overlaid projections of increasing size till the moment when a great maroon and 10 seconds of darkness covered the setting of two great skeletal silhouettes that formed the black halyards and rigging.'

'You design for movement, then?'

'Heavens, yes! Highly individual light and fluent scenery afford the perfect ball-bearings on which to run the action of a play. There Brecht is my patron saint, and the Saturday in 1956 on which I saw *Trumpets and Drums* and *Mother Courage* the memorable day. A play going on and scenery resting quietly behind it—many directors feel that a perfectly satisfactory state of affairs and in some forms of theatre it is, but scenery may draw attention to itself without damage to the play if it makes an apt and parallel comment of its own.

'Ted Kotcheff and I were once discussing the production of *Julius Caesar* and he had the notion of reinforcing the mob audience for Antony's speech with a drawn audience to give overtones of propaganda, viewing figures and so on—an audience thin as paper. Somehow it made them more frightening. They were immovable. They were *there*. Who could sway a mob with painted faces? As for *The Emperor Jones*, it's a motorway of a play. It has a projectile quality. Once the hero is out of his palace he never stops running. For television we saw the palace as stone galleries and halls cut out of the summit of a mountain. Here was a natural citadel of power, with long passages and doors 24 ft. high. We struck it all during the first commercial'.

Light lancing in, the hero launched off an inclined ramp—in a stream of such pungent phrases Mr. O'Brien spoke of Jones 'reliving in reverse the history of his race', on television, fluently mobile. In keeping with this he imagines a stage set for the prison scene in *Measure for Measure* consisting of a series of cages in basement twilight with, characteristically, 'wind sweeping through them.' But he has an equally strong feeling for the elegantly static and said that Klee's 'emphasis on filigree bones of design, his airy style, has tempted me towards structure.'

How far does the theatre lag behind other arts in the visual sense, at a time when people queue up to see Picassos? 'You need', said

Mr. O'Brien, 'a man of stature to involve artists of stature, artists capable of a more distinguished statement even when they are not aware of the technical tricks of a medium. Diaghilev called on Picasso, Derain and Tchelitchew. For the picture-frame stage of the time, that was a good idea. I believe there is a breed of artists so secure in their manner that they can invest a stage with their work and give it an ineradicable personality of its own. Hence the objections when a notable artist is invited to design a play. He has inevitably a great chance of satisfying the needs of his own personality in advance of the needs of the script. Working in the theatre one recognizes the primacy of the script, but the more visually educated one is the more one regrets the undesirability of the expert hold which an artist of stature can have over his material. The Noguchi Lear. What a marvellous thing to have done, but it didn't succeed'.

After leaving Wellington, Mr. O'Brien read History at Cambridge, designed a number of productions for the Marlowe Society and was awarded a Henry Fellowship to the Yale drama school, where he studied under Mr. Donald Oenslager. At present he is planning the set for a fashion show.

[21 *September* 1960]

FRANCO ZEFFIRELLI

————————————— ⋆ —————————————

Mr. Franco Zeffirelli, over here to direct *Romeo and Juliet* for the Old Vic, has already given a stimulating shot in the arm to the Covent Garden repertoire with his productions of *Lucia de Lammermoor* and *Cav.* and *Pag.* He is a compact, wiry, clean-shaven Florentine of 36, astute, humorous and tidily articulate as Florentines are generally supposed to be. When asked a short while ago to picture in conversation a director at work, he obliged for 90 minutes in fluent English and aptly dynamic gestures, the most striking of which summed up his approach to a script. 'You do not', he said, raising his arms, 'catch a falling stone like this, but like this', and he made a basket of drooped shoulders and incurved arms, riding down a little with the imagined trajectory.

'I once saw a production', he went on, 'of *La Forza del Destino* with tanks and gas-masks. That kind of thing is betraying the nature of a former creation. Direction is not pure creation. You take somebody else's conception and have to respect it. Your work is going to pass, their work is remaining. You can't take the Fifth Symphony and play it as jazz.' This statement of principle, which many a spectacular director of stage classics has disregarded, accords well with Mr. Zeffirelli's physical presence. One is scarcely aware of his personality in the flow of discussion, so complete is his absorption in sharing an experience, so precise and effortless the concentration of energy. His objectivity extends to quoting the chief critical lines of attack on his work: 'My stage design for the last act of Visconti's *The Three Sisters* production in 1952 was thought by most of the Russians who saw it to convey the wrong atmosphere, too idealized.' How? 'The garden was described by the lower part of tremendous trees, a cathedral of trees. Golden amber air and white trees. And a carpet of autumn leaves.'

Asked about the limits of realism, with reference to *Cav.* and whether it can stunt an audience's response by leaving nothing to the imagination, Mr. Zeffirelli had three lines of defence: (1) A high estimate of *Verismo*, as practised by Verga and Zola, (2) The use of real ingredients for imaginative purposes in surrealism, and (3) That *Cav.* is the most realistic opera ever written ('Why should I do anything else?'). Perhaps only a Florentine could have so subtly spiced his defence with a suspicion of counter-attack on his English inquisitor, for it included high praise of Salvador Dali's black limousine, exhibited in a vast, empty room with effigies of an English king and his queen as passengers, and artificial rain inside the car, not, as Mr. Zeffirelli scrupulously pointed out, 'not raining on the car from outside, as it usually is in London'.

The essence of his interpretations is a controlling image, a core. 'In *Cavalleria* I have always seen the core as a wide, white street, going uphill in a Sicilian village, that and the sky. At night the wind blows and a tiny figure with a black shawl comes down running, closing under her shawl her pain and sorrow. It is the destiny of some Sicilian women. I built the set that way. The stage hands at Covent Garden can tell how fussy I was about the platform. The curtain goes up on the prelude. After that it's easy. You are on your path and you follow the consequence. What happens at dawn in Sicily? All the old women come to church. And so on.' What happens in Sicily he knows not only from Verga but from eight months in a village there, working with Visconti on *La Terra Trema*.

'You don't need many ideas, you need one. On that you work and the idea carries you if it's right. For *Lucia*, mine was the image of a woman shouting in a tremendous room, a castle hall, with her wedding veil covered with blood, crying and chasing her cries. How would that woman arrive at that point? How? I couldn't bear a kind of mechanical bird performance in the mad scene. It's a great tragic scene. Covent Garden wanted me to do new sets and costumes and wanted to know whether I could make of Miss Sutherland a great dramatic singer. She lacked confidence and dramatic experience. I knew I must first establish a human friendship and get her trust. In this case I also demonstrated the acting effects myself.

'With Mme. Callas the director's problem was different, to find new solutions and put her in the right frame. She is a creature who absorbs what is around and becomes the centre of attention. The first time I directed her was in *Il Turco in Italia* at La Scala. I was much younger and less confident than now. I would come to her with a series of ideas. She would listen to me and suddenly swoop on one of them, develop it until it had become something of her own. She can grab the essential thing from your head, the thing you keep secret and to yourself even cannot express. The work of development I usually do, she did it herself.

'She can do 10 different *Traviatas*, yet when I directed it she would say, "Tell me how to do it," would question me, "She feels what?". The creative idea I worked on is that Violetta loves Alfredo because he is the only one who cares for her health, puts kindness before love. Not love but sympathy wins her. She is accustomed to pretty boys who want to go to bed with her, but Alfredo is the one who follows her to her room and begs her to take care of herself. It is already *there*, when you analyse the score. . . Mme. Callas works by instinct, in her mind. Things go around in it and the process can be prompted by simple images. One day I held in front of her a contemporary print and said "This is Violetta." Some time afterwards she was sitting before an enormous make-up case and staring fixedly at something held in her hand. For ages I thought it was a mirror, but it was not. It was the print.'

Although the boudoir languors of Dumas Fils and fighting with the partisans against the Wehrmacht belong to different worlds of experience, Mr. Zeffirelli's delight in drama easily bridges the gap. Heading southwards to link with the Allied forces advancing from Rome, he was first halted in a valley while armoured battles raged across it. Then, mounting an apparently deserted hillside he stumbled alone into a patrol and put up his hands. 'Are you English?' he asked, trying to identify the helmets. 'No!' said a contemptuous voice. After the most sustained dramatic pause he can remember, it added, 'We are Scots.' Put into the uniform of The Scots Guards, he later interrogated partisan comrades, including his best friend who didn't see through the disguise as Mr. Zeffirelli, in his best British manner, said: 'We don't need this kind of help' and much else in character. 'When he recognized me, he had almost a stroke.'

Demobilized at 22, Mr. Zeffirelli joined the Moretti Stoppa company as an actor under Visconti's direction and later designed the sets and costumes for *A Streetcar Named Desire*. As a film technician he worked also with de Sica and Rossellini in the full flush of Italy's cinema revival, of neo-realism's most creative phase, still his most exhilarating working period. It has left him with a respect for improvisation and a deep concern for the human relationship with his cast, so that he accepted the direction of *Romeo and Juliet*, which opens on October 4, as collaboration with an established Shakespearian company.

Squeeze Shakespeare's characters to the utmost, he thinks, and you still find poetry. It is on this poetry of the human relationships that he will concentrate: and on the twin themes of love and the total breakdown of understanding between two generations. 'Forgetting décor cleverness', the stage design will be spare, the actors as young as possible. Reminded that this company has neither the security of tenure nor the established disciplines of others in Berlin, Moscow and Paris, he rubbed his hands together and said: 'So much the better!'

[19 *September* 1960]

ROGER PLANCHON

———————————— ★ ————————————

Although recent visits by the Berliner Ensemble, the Moscow Art Theatre, and the Comédie Française have accustomed Londoners to theatrical teamwork of a very high order, it has been left to M. Roger Planchon to prove that comparable, though obviously less mature, results can be achieved by a young man in less than 10 years, starting from scratch. His satirical commentary on *Les Trois Mousquetaires*, now on at the Piccadilly Theatre, sprang from answers to a questionnaire issued to potential theatregoers in Villeurbanne. But several aspects of the burlesque indicate something more than a determination to cater for popular taste; and the other day M. Planchon amiably submitted to answering a questionnaire himself. The hope was to absolve this crew-cut D'Artagnan from artistic misdemeanours of the kind which stage pioneers in search of a public are often guilty of.

QUESTION: Thinking of accepted masterpieces, what is the director's duty to his public?

M. PLANCHON: Theatre is the only art involving the paradox of two simultaneous modes of composition, textual writing and scenic writing. First there is the type of author such as Molière in whom both go on in the same mind. But what about textual writing like Joyce's or Thomas Hardy's? Briefly, in cases of that kind, the text remains constant and the scenic writing can continue to progress, to evolve. Do Molière according to his own method ('exact') today and it would be a parody, like records of Bernhardt in a manner which once pleased millions and now seem entirely ridiculous. Not that she was. Simply the fashion has changed. When Olivier wanted to show Elizabethan acting in *Henry V* he made it absurd before going on to a modern style. It was not in itself absurd, but the conventions had changed. . . . To answer your question, one must not reproduce scenic writing in a revival.

218

The director's duty is to pass the text through a new scenic writing.

Q.: What is the director's duty to the masterpieces, the plays?

A.: They change, evolve even, with the passage of time. Greek temples, for example, were polychromatic. Yet they have become symbolic of purity, whiteness and clarity. In the eighteenth century, Gothic was a joke. There is a dialectic in the process. The more one progresses, the more one finds out.

Q. (supplementary): Isn't there a danger of directors losing what's valuable in the plays, while we progress?

A.: Yes.

Q.: Marivaux. Has he an atmosphere of his own?

A.: Normally he is staged in a neutral setting, a sort of laboratory of the emotions. We have tried to enlarge that, drawing on the flavour of his novels, which are rated higher than his plays in France. We try to show how the emotional pattern arose, by showing the soil, as well as the flower. In the English climate you couldn't grow olives. In Marivaux the characters deal in refined sentiment because they've nothing else to do. For his contemporaries, of course, that climate would be actually in existence. There would be no need to define it on the stage.

Q.: Did Marivaux, in *La Seconde Surprise de l'amour*, require a bed on the stage?

A.: No, he left no stage directions. There are five sets in our production, not counting corridors, and in only one of them did we have the bed. After refusing the Chevalier, the Marquise has to say '*et je suis prête à épouser le Comte*'. It was essential to indicate that she's prepared to go to extremes.

Q.: In your production of *Henry IV*, Hotspur is liquidated by a group of Prince Hal's bodyguard?

A.: First, let me point out that in French you can't convey Shakespeare's language, so we occupied ourselves with the content. The idea was to show that Hal beats Hotspur not because he's a better man but because he's learnt to fight.

Q.: To bring superior numbers to bear at the right moment?

A.: Precisely.

Q.: Isn't it the intention of these plays to present Prince Hal as a hero?

A.: We make the point that absolute monarchy is superior to feudalism. *Le roi a raison, même quand il fait des saloperies*. Why does he win? Because he's more expert. Hotspur, weighed down with armour, is an anachronism. But any divinity in the King is left in parenthesis. The plays have an ambiguity and we haven't suppressed it. Our Hal is devoid of nobility but not squalid.

Q.: Producing Shakespeare at Villeurbanne, how do you handle passages meant for the equivalent of Sir Philip Sidney?

A.: We try to interpret at all possible levels. In Paris and Villeurbanne the laughs at *Les Trois Mousquetaires* came in different places.

Q.: Are you aware of an international style—emphasizing visual effects and action—in which the text has small place?

A.: For me, the theatre is one big text.

Q.: Will you produce Racine?

A.: We are not competent to do so. We haven't done verse plays yet, but we are working towards Racine. We don't want to act Racine slapdash.

Q.: In *Les Trois Mousquetaires*, was some of your satire aimed at debased romanticism on television?

A.: Very much of it.

Q.: Even your company cannot make the theatre pay its way without heavy subsidy. Most of the public prefer television and sport. . . . Are not many directors becoming anxious and making experiments to cheer themselves up?

M. PLANCHON: We must wait for another great dramatist to appear. Companies must be ready for him.

[23 *September* 1960]

PETER O'TOOLE

★

Late, for the disarming reason that he had been left in sole charge of his baby daughter and then had to drive through Midlands traffic on the wettest of November nights, Mr. Peter O'Toole swept in to an office at the Shakespeare Memorial Theatre at 6.15, whisked his interviewer to the cocktail bar of an hotel, stationed his wife, Miss Siân Phillips, just out of earshot, with a book to read, ordered two stouts, said it would not take him long to make up for the last night of *Troilus and Cressida* and waited for the first question to be put.

He had begun the play scene of *Hamlet* (at the Bristol Old Vic) in a strikingly original attitude, head between knees. Was it premeditated? For about five seconds Mr. O'Toole considered his answer: 'Everything keyed up to that, almost like a fencing or a boxing match. It was a thing I used to do before exams or interviews, when I felt tension in the stomach. I crouch. They—the Elizabethans—very rarely mention the heart. They thought the stomach was the root of feeling. The episode of Claudius praying, did I plan my approach to that? Perhaps a fusion of thought and feeling. It's pretty difficult to apply logic to Hamlet. It's in the script that I don't kill him then.'

Of his last three remarks, the first was hesitant, an unconscious quotation from one of his press notices; the second slyly triumphant and the last secretively professional as well as brash. What up till then could have been an earnest undergraduate had tightened into the strange, moody integrity of Mr. O'Toole's stage personality, which is like no other in the contemporary theatre. 'I did less intellectual work on *Hamlet* than I've done at Stratford this season', he went on. 'There was no time. I had three weeks' rehearsal while playing the Dame in pantomime at night and thinking of *Man and Superman* to follow. As Hamlet, though, I felt, not consciously, in rebellion against the Victorian head prefect. For me, *Hamlet* is an essay in the passions, in the Elizabethan sense. I was anxious to make the play work and not use it as a platform for head-back and sonority of utterance, what I call the sonneteer school of acting, which I can't bear. . . . Catapulted as one is through repertory, there isn't much time for deliberation. One relies on tested technical allies in what is a terrifying battle to establish contact with an audience. The most one can hope for in repertory is to give a pretty fair shadow of what would be the substance of the part given more time.

'In any case I hadn't got the vocal control to get within 100 yards of the part, which makes great demands not only on the intelligence but on the voice. You get as far as the 'How all occasions' soliloquy and then have 20 minutes in the dressing room to change your shirt. You come back to the gravedigger scene as a totally new Hamlet, quiet, reflective in a different sense from the others. Life and death viewed objectively, all of a sudden. Next he's down in Ophelia's grave and that's where the voice is taxed to the absolute. Then there are the exchanges with Rosencrantz and Guildenstern. Then the duel. By the end of four weeks I'd learnt a great deal about when to soft-pedal and when to save. Hamlet is saving, saving, saving. Like crossing the Swiss Alps.' He gestured a series of peaks and valleys.

'The sonneteers? Their technical ally was to stand perfectly still and utter. I didn't believe they were human beings involved in an action. At least I tried to bring excitement back to *Hamlet*. By developing "inner feeling"? Truthfully, no. Perhaps by relying on instinct. I had to pick up *Hamlet* as if it were an acting edition of *Rookery Nook* and simply get on with it.'

Mr. O'Toole's progress at Stratford-on-Avon in a single season seems to vindicate the attempts there to establish a régime taken for granted by Continental actors. He testifies to the benefit he has had from Miss Warren's coaching in diction, which can be put to the test on stage an hour after, and to the sense of relaxation given by repeating performances at intervals. The result is a margin for refining and experimenting. He thinks he is ridding himself of a tendency to break up lines, learning 'to sustain the thought to the end of the sentence. Easier. If you think right, the sound is right'.

Some think his Shylock already great. He prepared five weeks and rehearsed for nine. 'My wife and I spent a week discussing it with Dr. Moelwyn Merchant, a lecturer in English at Cardiff. Then we went up a mountain in Wales to learn the part. That is the easiest and dreariest bit of an actor's job. I see Shylock as a man of enormous substance, who loves making intellectual points, as in the distinction between business and usury, the parable of Laban's sheep. I spoke some Yiddish as a boy. My father was a bookmaker and his clerk was Jewish. We lived in Leeds, where there is a large Jewish population. Experience can subconsciously ring bells when you come to act a part. And what isn't experience you *make up*!

'For instance, I have no actual experience of what a Jew feels like with his patriarchal responsibilities, so I found out one or two of his rites for cursing and the Prayer for the Dead, and the Rending of the Garment. I was assisted by a Jewish Tubal and we composed our own little ceremony. I'm in the very happy position of never having seen Shylock before. I gather he has often been played as a grubby pawnbroker from the Ghetto. Yet the Jewish father has the power to say the Prayer for the Dead which I mutter to myself after Jessica's flight. There are rivers of irony in the part and at the end he is deprived of his three main supports: family, religion, and business.'

'My failure!' said Mr. O'Toole when asked about Thersites. 'I couldn't make the words flesh. The idea was to be both part of the action and a commentator. I couldn't do it. Even in soliloquy, nothing is revealed and there is no development. But I am the better for having played it.' At the mention of Macbeth, a part he fancies, he at once touched the wooden panel of the cocktail bar's wall, a superstitious ritual older than the music-halls he frequented in Leeds, where he saw *Rose Marie* at the Grand when six years old and 'fell in love with Hard-boiled Herman'. G. H. Elliott, Buster Keaton and Hetty King enchanted him on the halls, Sir Donald Wolfit in Shakespeare. He was then working for the *Yorkshire Evening News*, having left school at 14.

The dominant influence he pays tribute to is that of Mr. Wilfrid Lawson, both as a teacher and as an actor to be marvelled at. But Mr. O'Toole is himself the idol of younger audiences. Restless, emotional and intellectually tough, he is a mediator between them and the great drama of the past. That is to be a myth at the age of 27, and two of the ingredients are significant. Alongside the objective humility about his own achievements there goes an arrogant contempt, for acting which seems to lag behind the rhythm of youth, for the Dutch company acting Molière who 'trod three inches into the stage' and for a Schiller trilogy at Zürich, 'endless and noisy, very hefty and porky'.

[8 *December* 1960]

STELLA ADLER

---------------------------- ★ ----------------------------

When the name of Miss Stella Adler appeared on the cast list of
Oh, Dad, Poor Dad, which comes to the Lyric, Hammersmith, on
July 5, many a student of drama was put on the alert. She was a
leading light of the Group Theatre, which in 10 years—from 1931
to 1941—defied current fashions on Broadway and ended by
imposing the strenuous realism which still reigns over stage and
screen, effectively countered only by the influence of Brecht. Add
to this Miss Adler's function as pipeline between the Method and
Stanislavsky himself and she may count as the most significant
American theatre personality to have visited London since the war.

When I called on her the other day to hear her views on contemporary acting in the United States, she turned out to be a cool
American lady with a dancer's figure and large, watchful brown
eyes, a born survivor of revolutions as was soon revealed. She had
been trained by her father, Jacob Adler, then by Boleslavsky and
Ouspenskaya, both formerly of the Moscow Art Theatre. In Paris,
Chekhov's widow insisted that she meet Stanislavsky. 'Clurman
and I went to meet him. I held back.' They walked side by side for
a time without speaking. 'Then Mr. Stanislavsky asked me, kindly:
"Do you want to say something?" So I answered, "Yes. It's this.
I loved the theatre until you came along, and now I hate it".'

For several weeks after that they met daily to work on specific
problems which Miss Adler felt were getting in the way of her
acting. 'Mr Stanislavsky explained that the source of acting is
imagination and that the key to its problems is truth, truth *in the
circumstances of the play.* . . . Once, during a revolution in Buenos
Aires I was on stage when people broke into the theatre with guns.
Everyone left, the leading man turned white. It just didn't trouble
me. I don't feel terribly frightened of police or military people.
I didn't give a goddam. Well, I asked Mr. Stanislavsky how I could

learn to react to such a situation in a play. "Tell me", he asked, "what would you worry about if everything was threatened?" "My children." "Then, if the play demanded you run for your life and your own life didn't interest you, you would run to save the children".'

'But', said Miss Adler, 'he didn't mean you can always use your local self. The circumstances of Hamlet are in Elsinore, in the fact that he is a Renaissance man who is not modern man. Not modern psychology and modern attitudes. It wouldn't help him at all. Renaissance man is looking for the truth, but a different truth from the man who's looking for truth in a Marxist society. It can mean he's afraid of dishonour and not of death. No style is as simple as the actor wants to make it if he lacks education and humility. You have to go to the style. You must not pull the style down to you. If you cannot expand you are not an actor. And you can't depend on domestic aids to relaxation in Shakespeare. No cigarettes! A throne is a throne.

'Interpretation in America has been in many ways successful. There's the fact of a school running from naturalism to realism taken for granted—until you come against a play which demands really powerful realistic acting. What we all accept will inevitably fall to pieces against a playwright as profound as Ibsen, Chekhov, or Strindberg. Odets came close to his period through identification with his own problem, but if you want to take it back to Chekhov, we don't have that in our environment. Nobody is Hamlet, nobody is Hedda. The largeness of the drawing of Hedda and *Ghosts* needs size. We don't have O'Neill's size any more, and he's our biggest writer. . . . I built my own theatre in 1948. I had capacities developed over the years that seemed to need growth. I had to know the difference between Ibsen and Strindberg. And I don't want to depend on the director. The actor has to take his place again. He had it and he lost it. He's now the tool of the director, often of the director-writer pair.'

'Ought he not to be the tool of the writer?'

'No! The actor should come knowing the key to the interpretation. If the key is not known he is not an actor and has lost his right. He can collaborate, but he cannot be governed. For example, if Hedda reveals openly to the audience or to the others on stage that she dislikes her husband, there's no play. She cannot reveal this because the whole point in Ibsen is that the society concerned does not reveal its deepest torments. It has to dissimulate. The audience will understand and fall in. If they, too, are lying, the thing has an Ibsen value. A tough school to act.

'In Strindberg they don't conceal. You say: "Please take care of me!" and you slap the man the next moment. Miss Julie. Everyone knows there's a psychological illness. In Ibsen, the social lie, in Strindberg, insoluble conflict. Now there's a big difference. It's much better if the actor knows. He doesn't want to have some master come and tell him. . . . In Tennessee Williams, you have the heroine surviving madly through a lowest common denominator of circumstance to cling to a dream. In his early plays he found the key to something deeply felt by audiences. He revealed an intrinsic need of living in a world you could survive in, by stubborn withdrawal. Later, as the vulgarity and materialism of society got bigger, he showed the need to escape through drinking and whoring in *Streetcar*. Yes, I know Miss Mary McCarthy has a low estimate of his plays. She is a very brilliant literary woman. She sees the theatre from her own viewpoint and doesn't bother to understand its development from Aeschylus onwards.

'As for the Method', said Miss Adler, 'it's like Christianity, started with one idea and now there are how many denominations? It's so creative it can never really be taken back. It's anybody's secret. But actors must know what they want to accomplish, like other creators, and never let success interfere. A limited aim, such as television or money, interferes with why he became an actor. You can't start art with millons. I don't believe in that. . . . But I'm a nut.'

[24 *June* 1961]

INDEX